Origen of Alexandria

MAPPING THE TRADITION SERIES

Paul Rorem, series advisor

Mapping the Tradition is a series of brief, compact guides to pivotal thinkers in Christian history. Each volume in this series focuses on a particular figure, providing a concise but lucid introduction to the central features of each thinker's work and sketching the lasting significance of that thinker for the history of Christian theology.

As well, the series utilizes primary source works from each figure as an entry point for exposition and exploration. Guided by leading scholars in history and theology, primary source texts are reproduced with explanatory commentary, and are accompanied by orientating essays on the context, contours, and historical and conceptual legacy of the corpus.

The series is designed for beginning and intermediate students, as well as interested general readers, who will benefit from clear, helpful surveys of thinkers, texts, and theologies from throughout Christian history and from introductions to major issues and key historical and intellectual points of development.

Volumes in the series:

Published by Fortress Press:
Paul Rorem, *The Dionysian Mystical Theology* (2015)
Gillian T. W. Ahlgren, *Enkindling Love: The Legacy of Teresa of Avila and John of the Cross* (2016)
Romanus Cessario, OP, and Cajetan Cuddy, OP, *Thomas and the Thomists: The Achievements of Thomas Aquinas and His Interpreters* (2017)
Paul R. Sponheim, *Existing Before God: Søren Kierkegaard and the Human Venture* (2017)
Thomas G. Weinandy and Daniel A. Keating, *Athanasius and His Legacy: Trinitarian-Incarnational Soteriology and Its Reception* (2017)

Published by Lexington Books/Fortress Academic:
Terrence N. Tice, *Schleiermacher: The Psychology of Christian Faith and Life* (2018)
John T. Slotemaker, *Anselm of Canterbury and the Search for God* (2018)
Paul Rorem, *St. Augustine, His Confessions, and His Influence* (2019)
Robert Kolb, *Luther's Treatise* On Christian Freedom *and Its Legacy* (2019)
Beverly Mayne Kienzle, *Hildegard of Bingen: Gospel Interpreter* (2020)

John Anthony McGuckin, *Origen of Alexandria: Master Theologian of the Early Church* (2022)

Expected from Lexington Books/Fortress Academic:
Khaled Anatolios, *Irenaeus of Lyons: The Making of the Great Tradition*
Andrew Louth, *John of Damascus*
John Slotemaker and Jeffrey Witt, *Peter Lombard and the Origins of Systematic Theology*
Karen Scott, *Catherine of Siena*

Origen of Alexandria

Master Theologian of the Early Church

John Anthony McGuckin

LEXINGTON BOOKS/FORTRESS ACADEMIC
Lanham • Boulder • New York • London

Published by Lexington Books/Fortress Academic

Lexington Books is an imprint of The Rowman & Littlefield Publishing Group, Inc.
4501 Forbes Boulevard, Suite 200, Lanham, Maryland 20706
www.rowman.com
86-90 Paul Street, London EC2A 4NE, United Kingdom

Copyright © 2022 by The Rowman & Littlefield Publishing Group, Inc.

All rights reserved. No part of this book may be reproduced in any form or by any electronic or mechanical means, including information storage and retrieval systems, without written permission from the publisher, except by a reviewer who may quote passages in a review.

British Library Cataloguing in Publication Information Available

Library of Congress Cataloging-in-Publication Data
Name: McGuckin, John Anthony, author.
Title: Origen of Alexandria : master theologian of the early church / John Anthony McGuckin.
Description: Lanham : Lexington Books/Fortress Academic, [2022] | Series: Mapping the tradition | Includes bibliographical references and index. | Summary: "In this book, John A. McGuckin reviews and assesses the monumental influence that Origen of Alexandria has exercised over the shape and content of the Christian tradition over seventeen hundred years"—Provided by publisher.
Identifiers: LCCN 2021062038 (print) | LCCN 2021062039 (ebook) | ISBN 9781978708433 (cloth) | ISBN 9781978708440 (epub)
Subjects: LCSH: Origen.
Classification: LCC B686.O84 M39 2022 (print) | LCC B686.O84 (ebook) | DDC 270.1092—dc23/eng/20220203
LC record available at https://lccn.loc.gov/2021062038
LC ebook record available at https://lccn.loc.gov/2021062039

"For so many years was Origen a Master of the Church and grew old in the Church catholic."

—St. Pamphilus, *Apology for Origen* 16

On the cover of this book: *Origen Teaching the Saints*, icon by Eileen McGuckin, Icon Studio, St. Anne's on Sea, UK; (69) FY8 1PG. The icon shows Origen standing in the classical rhetorician's "throne" or teaching podium, in front of a symbolic church in Byzantine style. He is dressed in priestly robes (he served as a presbyter in the ancient Palestinian church based at Caesarea Maritima), and he holds in his hands a scroll that is meant to synopsize his teaching, or offer the viewer a quintessential quotation from his works. In his case it is a reference to his lifelong focus on the primacy of the Christian scriptures, and the eminence he attained as perhaps the church's greatest ever exegete of the Bible, reading, "Attend above all else to the teaching of the Scriptures." Beneath the throne—at his feet, as it were—are a massive number of the great saints of the church's tradition, both from the East and the West, stretching off into the distance (as the book demonstrates, Origen's influence is as much alive today as it was in the third century). Some are in the forefront and named: the greatest of them are the Cappadocian Fathers, Gregory Nazianzen, Gregory of Nyssa, and St. Basil the Great. There is also St. Maximus the Confessor and notable martyrs (several of them his own students). Some are in the background, with a title in the halo but no features—notably St. Jerome, who at first lauded Origen as the greatest theologian since the apostles, and then turned against him and denounced him posthumously, though still using his works, albeit surreptitiously. Ironically, in all this sea of saints who made up the backbone of the Christian tradition, Origen alone stands without the halo around his head, designating how his reputation was assaulted posthumously by those who (incorrectly and anachronistically) accused him of aiding and abetting the Arian movement. His teachings were censured at the court of Justinian the Great in the sixth century, and after that point, although his exegetical work was still read, a cloud fell over his name. Despite so much censure (often by those who had never read him rightly, or at all), many of the church's greatest saints and intellectuals, such as the Cappadocians or St. Athanasius the Great, defended him vigorously and argued that his work was essential reading for Christian theologians. In its vivid and lively colors, this modern Byzantine icon by a renowned professional icon painter sums up Origen's importance in the history of doctrine and celebrates his stature as master theologian of the early church.

Contents

PART ONE: ORIGEN'S LIFE AND THOUGHT—A BRIEF INTRODUCTION 1

Chapter 1: A Short Biography 3

Chapter 2: Aspects of Origen's Thought World 19

PART TWO: ORIGEN'S CONTESTED LEGACY 41

Chapter 3: Prolegomena 43

Chapter 4: The Ancient Origenist Crises 79

Chapter 5: Origen in Medieval Times and in the Age of Reformation 105

Chapter 6: Modern Rediscoveries of Origen 135

Chapter 7: Epilogue 147

Appendix 1: The Origen Volumes in the Sources Chrétiennes Series (SC) 149

Appendix 2: The Origeniana Series of Studies on Origen 151

Select Bibliography 153

Index 167

About the Author 171

PART ONE

Origen's Life and Thought—a Brief Introduction

Chapter 1

A Short Biography

Origen (c. 186–255), renowned in his own third century as the world's leading Christian theologian, was born and had his first successes in Egypt's great city of Alexandria, before moving on to found a higher educational establishment, one that became his final base, in Palestinian Caesarea. He was the first truly international philosopher the Christian church had ever produced. His combination of profound spiritual energy, mental acuity, biblical sophistication, and reverence for intellectual culture made him a figure of such significance in the classical architecture of the ancient Christian religion that he is arguably the most important Christian in the history of the church after the evangelists and St. Paul; he was intellectually far more impressive and influential than the great Augustine, though the latter is much better known in Western church history and, of course, held his larger sway there with unbroken centuries of papal approval.

That Origen is not even remotely as well known, and certainly not much read, in the church today probably comes down to the very heavily contested legacy his life's work left behind it. But as we shall see, his influence, though often not recognized or admitted, is massive in its quiet pervasiveness. Whether in following his suggestions or even in reacting against them explicitly, most of Christianity's classical doctrinal structure, practices of biblical exegesis, and history of spirituality have been deeply shaped by his scholarly agenda. Those theologians (many of them great saints of the church) who followed him quietly corrected the disputed peripherals and popularized the main thrust of his great and overarching vision of salvation, and even those who publicly censured him (such as Jerome or Theophilus of Alexandria) often kept on using his writings, just pretending now that they were their own thoughts. In antiquity plagiarism was rarely called out.

There were three major periods in ancient times when Origen's writings were ordered to be set aside, even burned, by church and state authorities. We shall look at them in more detail shortly. In these crises popes, councils, or emperors anathematized him long after he was dead. This was even though he had died in a martyr's glory (if not in a martyr's blood) and had spent his life solemnly declaring that, as a faithful churchman, he would only advocate and stand by the church's assured tradition taken from the apostles (the *regula fidei*). He did think, however, that there were many things in his contemporary Christianity that needed an answer the apostolic writings (meaning the scriptures) had not clearly provided. These were the points, Origen argued, where believers were called on to exercise their spiritual intelligence (*nous*) according to their level of inspiration and wisdom by the divine Logos.

But it was precisely on this point, even in his own lifetime, that he ran up against more anxious and conservative Christian teachers. Even so, despite levels of hostility such as led one great monastic leader in Egypt to throw his books into the Nile, only very few were ever ready to burn or drown his writings, and an exceptionally large amount of his texts has survived regardless (a major achievement when one considers how ancient books were customarily republished across the generations). This was how Origen established a veritable school of important followers that ran on through all the centuries of the church's history. In the hefty folio-sized tomes of Abbé Migne's collection of ancient Christian writings, known as the *Patrologiae Graecae Cursus Completus*, Origen has volumes 11 through 17 to himself, an unrivalled achievement in the history of antique Christian literature.

His enemies were often those who did not like intellectual change (or perhaps just did not much trust scholarship) and certainly did not like people thinking about the faith or studying the sacred texts with an open intelligence. His friends tended to be those who were not afraid of the life of the mind. One of his (many) adages was *Hopou Logos Agei*: "Let us go wherever the Divine Logos takes us." The force of the witticism being that, in Greek, the terms for "Divine Logos" (the Eternal Son of God) and "wisdom" (either human or divine) were synonymous. So here, Origen was advocating that where intelligence took Christians was where the Divine Word was leading them anyway; in other words, a person of faith had nothing to fear from true wisdom and knowledge, ever. Many of the greatest and wisest saints of the church, especially the Greek Fathers of the Church, used and developed on his writings. St. Gregory the Theologian, arguably the greatest of them, called Origen "the sharpening stone for each one of us."[1]

In his body of work Origen set the foundations and terms for the Christian disciplines of systematic theology, scriptural commentary, mystical theology, cosmology, and Christological soteriology. His personal foundation of the first significant Christian university school at Caesarea[2] marked a major turning point for the worldwide church in its approach to classical culture, and he spent much of his life's labor after that point trying to make his campus library internationally significant, in which task he more than succeeded. Caesarea became a great Christian theological center and renowned scriptorium for many centuries afterward. When Constantine the Great ordered fifty pandects (complete versions of the Old and New Testaments) to be made for the great new churches of his Christian empire, it was the scriptorium of Caesarea that got most of the commissions. Two of these are still surviving as mute testaments to the Origenian tradition of biblical scholarship: the beautiful *Codex Sinaiticus* in the British Library and the *Codex Vaticanus* in Rome.

In short, it is a sad loss that Origen is not much better known in the standard courses of the history of Christian theology and philosophy, as his system of thought is both rich and intriguing. Over many generations, this dismissal of him and his achievement has led to somewhat narrow and even naïve accounts of his work being given in older standard textbooks. Since the latter part of the twentieth century, this lack of accurate editions and informed scholarly analyses has been increasingly repaired as a new wave of scholarship has accessed his texts directly and begun again to appreciate his real achievements. This new interest in the work of Origen has been part of a wider rethinking of the ways and processes of early Christian thought that has taken place over the last sixty years, and has offered a rich new understanding of the ways the foundational Christian tradition was mapped out across the early and creative centuries of the first half millennium. This present book tries, in an introductory and synoptic way, to give an account of that sea change in the scholarly (and theological) approach to Origen, and also to give a relatively simple account of why he still matters.

His very name is redolent of that early period of church history before the use of "Christian" names became common. Origen ('Ωριγένης) is the Greek term for "Born of Horus." And the latter was an Egyptian god in the trinity of the Isis religion, a very extensive and popular religious faith in the period of Roman Egypt. The fourth-century historian Eusebius of Caesarea (c. 260–340) inherited the leadership of Origen's school and library several generations after him, and in his *Ecclesiastical History* he dedicates a whole book (number six) to the life story of his hero, where he tells us a lot about Origen's life.[3] It is one of the very first examples of deliberate hagiography—writing up the life of a Christian hero saint who was not a martyr.[4] Markus Vinzent has recently set the context for this in the following way:

> As a dependent, student, *famulus*, librarian and successor of Pamphilus (he calls Pamphilus "my lord"[5]) Eusebius organized and managed the literary heritage of Origen, at a time when Origen became *the* "father"; and with him the beginnings of fatherly[6] authority in Christianity began, or more precisely, when the signet "Fathers of the Church" was formed by Eusebius,[7] using it for the first time in his claim for tradition and authority derived from his school background.[8] Eusebius counted himself among this class of church "fathers" to equip himself, on the one hand, with the authority of the forefathers, on the other hand,

however, to distance himself from his contemporary critics and to immunize himself against them.[9]

Eusebius thus characterized Origen as a model for all (not simply Christians) who value the intellectual life, and also as the greatest intellect of his time, as well as being (although he actually predates the movement) a prototype of the celibate ascetic that was then becoming very popular in early monasticism.

Origen was certainly an ascetic: but more of the type that was then familiar among sophists of the Greek tradition—advancing the adage of the philosophers and turning it to Christian usage, Μόνος πρὸς Μόνον: literally, "The Single person [oriented] toward the Single." It can also be translated: "Alone with the Alone." It means, basically, that the person who is serious about wishing to find the absolute cause of all things (God, or the One, or the Alone in ancient terms) has to devote so much of his intellectual and psychic and moral energy to that task that he will be required to live singly (μόνος) and ascetically (single-mindedly) in order to do so. In book six of his *Church History*, Eusebius holds up Origen as an example of an intellectual who devoted himself so much to the task that he stands (now in Eusebius's day when monasticism is becoming more popular) as an example to all Christian ascetics and scholars.

From Eusebius we learn that Origen's father, Leonides, was a Christian and a *grammaticus*, that is, a teacher of literature to young upper-class Roman citizens in Alexandria, which was one of the leading university towns of the empire. His father would become a martyr, executed for his faith during the later persecution under Emperor Septimius Severus in 202, when Origen was turning seventeen years of age. His mother was either Jewish or Christian, for Jerome tells us that she used to read the Psalms to her young child.[10] Eusebius also tells us that when Leonides saw the infant in his cradle, he used to come and kiss him gently on the heart.[11] He adds his opinion that this was not just a father's tender fondness, more a martyr's prophetic sense that this child would be a vessel of the Holy Spirit.

Leonides was his son's first teacher and centered the curriculum on the classics of Greek literature and philosophy and the biblical basis of Christian religion.[12] He made the child (as was the custom of the day) recite large sections of the scriptures by heart. But it was a habit Origen continued to develop throughout his life, and he was obviously possessed of a very sharp memory for detail, so that later when he started to make comments about one passage of scripture in a commentary, his mind naturally and creatively associates related passages from all over the biblical canon. His awareness of scriptural texts is encyclopedic, more so than any other Christian writer of antiquity, and has only come to be matched in modernity after the invention of biblical concordances. Eusebius tells his readers that soon the child was asking his father questions about the Bible that he was unable to answer.[13]

When his father was decapitated, Origen himself wished to run forward and proclaim himself a Christian, but his mother hid his clothes and would not let him out of the house. In later life, when he was very famous in the city as a leading Christian intellectual, another Roman persecution came along, once more specifically targeting the upper-class intelligentsia who had adopted Christian faith. Origen then accompanied several of his students to their executions, giving them words of comfort and encouragement on the way.[14] The crowds jeered at him for "leading astray" the young (a motif we also find in Plato's account of Socrates's death). It is a curious incident, for one wonders why he was not arrested himself and put to death as a Christian teacher? The answer is surely given in the fact that this Severan-era persecution was only directed at the political upper classes who had publicly declared themselves for the Christian religion.[15] His indemnity at this time suggests very strongly that Origen was not "qualified for execution" because he and his mother were not of the upper class. The Romans were very bureaucratic, and if a member of the citizen class (*honestiores*) married a noncitizen (*humiliores*), none of his civic privileges[16] passed on to the children. But Origen would suffer later in life, when his prominence as one of the world's leading Christian philosophers made him a key target in the persecution of 250, started by the emperor Decius.

After his father's execution, Origen, the eldest in a large family, had to become the breadwinner. He set up himself as an independent teacher, a *didaskalos*, and started to attract pupils, probably along the line of his father's trade of grammarian, consisting of early stage literary interpretation of the classics. The following year, Bishop Demetrios of Alexandria also gave him some duties to prepare catechumens in the faith, possibly as a way of supplementing the income of the orphaned family of a martyr.[17] As a catechist, Origen was a minor cleric under the direct authority of the bishop—and in Demetrios's case we find one of the most imperious bishops of Egyptian church history, bent as he was on making all the Christian officials of the entire country subordinate to his own authority, which included even making other Egyptian bishops into his suffragans rather than freestanding agents in their own dioceses.

However, as a *didaskalos*, a private teacher-lecturer (whose tasks then included a wide range of subjects, not least religious philosophy), Origen was a free agent. He ran his own school, which like many of them in this period covered religious metaphysics as well as literature. Bishop Demetrios, like several of his predecessors, was highly suspicious of these private schools in the city, perhaps especially of the ones who claimed to be "Christian independent," for at that time several of them were, in fact, Valentinian gnostic in character. It was this double identity of Origen's, servant of the bishop and independent scholar, that would soon cause friction between him and the powerful Demetrios. It was a clash that has, perhaps, been repeated many times since across the academic and clerical divides of the church.

It did not help matters that Origen shortly afterward moved into a lodging house provided by a rich patroness where another Christian *didaskalos*, from Antioch, was also holding shop as a fellow client.[18] This teacher, Paul, however, was well known to be a gnostic under the ban of the bishop, and Origen was soon forced to defend himself, protesting that he "never once prayed" with the man. He leaves unsaid whether he ever exchanged views or students. Mere association was enough to disturb the vigilant bishop, who had no intention of allowing the Valentinians to assume the mantle of Christian teachers uncontested.

Some time in his early twenties Origen, who had studiously scrutinized a raft of Hellenistic learning and so far had taught grammar to students for his income, decided to sell his father's library.[19] This marks his definitive turning away from a grammarian's life for that of the more sophistic *didaskalos* (Σόφος)—a turn more to the higher study of philosophy and religion. Many modern commentators (and some ancients) have criticized Origen the theologian for being "too symbolic" a reader of texts. If one pays close attention, however, it is abundantly clear he never lost his grammarian's skills. Unlike many others, then and since, he never once moves from a scriptural text to the symbolic reading without careful note of the immediate syntax and the literal sense. The price he received for the library (probably from his rich patroness or from another rich patron he attracted soon after, called Ambrose) was in the form of a subsistence lifetime pension that freed him from the need to teach large classes and allowed him to devote himself to philosophy.

After that point his school of students was more handpicked and advanced. One of his executed students, Plutarch, had a younger brother Heraclas, whom Origen now inducted as his assistant. Even when the latter became the successor to Bishop Demetrios, he still chose to wear the philosopher's cloak. His disciple Ambrose, who was a very wealthy convert of Origen's from Valentinianism, also paid for twenty young women stenographers to attend Origen's lectures and take down the text as he spoke.

At this time Origen was himself studying advanced philosophy with Ammonius Saccas in Alexandria.[20] The latter would shortly afterward be the teacher also of the great neo-Platonist Plotinus. Origen's philosophical tradition is more eclectic than can be summarized by any school allegiance. He is generally classed as a Christian Middle Platonist in many respects, though he is certainly not averse to many severe criticisms of Plato, which he makes from a biblical basis. But he appreciates several aspects of Pythagoras and Aristotle too.[21] His philosophical choices were usually dictated by his exegesis of the scriptures, which was his constant starting point, an aspect that Porphyry, a disciple of Plotinus, found especially objectionable in Origen.

None of the ancient Platonists would recognize Origen as one of their school: he was too invested in the particularity of God, the material significance of a divine incarnation, and the specificity of divine revelation as the source of truth, for that to be possibly the case.[22] But he felt that as a servant of divine Wisdom, it was his right to assess all the ancient schools and affirm them wherever they coincided with the biblical tradition. If one ever wishes to grasp "where Origen is coming from" on any point, the answer is almost always: the entire biblical tradition, but refracted closely through the special lenses of John and Paul and the Psalms.

Origen's own lectures at this period formed the basis of what he would shortly publish as the opening chapters of his great treatise (one of the earliest composed) of Christian systematics, which he called *On First Principles* (Περὶ Ἀρχῶν). He also started to travel to other cities at this time and engage in public disputations, a sign that he now saw himself as a significant *didaskalos*-philosopher in his own right. In 212 he visited Rome and sat in on the lectures of the Christian theologian Hippolytus, who drew the attention of the audience to the presence of his distinguished visitor.[23]

His growing fame is also attested at this time by the way the Roman imperial governor of Arabia, under Caracalla, sent letters in around 213 to the prefect of Alexandria asking him to send on Origen to his palace, accompanied by an official litter and bodyguard, so that he could learn more about the Christian movement from a leading exponent.[24] The Empress Julia Mammaea, Severus's mother, also sent for him and listened to his exposition of the Christian religion.[25] This was an invitation traditionally rewarded by a significant sum of gold to honor the professor. All of this growing fame exacerbated the friction with his bishop, who did not expect a minor cleric to adopt such independent ways, at a time when it was still considered the primary (sometimes exclusive) role of the city bishop to expound doctrine.

Whatever had been the unease so far with his bishop, it was Origen's decision to publish the first chapters of his *On First Principles* that caused the gathering storm to break. Demetrios was alarmed by many aspects of the speculative metaphysics Origen discussed there and by his statement—standing on his own authority as a *didaskalos*—about what the church's tradition had definitively covered, and what it had not, thus allowing for further speculation, regardless of the local bishop's opinions or preferences. Origen's lifelong belief was that the Holy Spirit inspired all Christian's into a "priesthood of insight," that is, a specific penetration into the mysteries of God, according to the level of their own spiritual and intellectual refinement, as achieved through their moral and ascetical life, and not simply gifting the charism of theological teaching solely because of a Christian's position in the hierarchy.[26] The real Christian "high priest" was the saint-sage-savant, and this was the state to which all Christian leaders, in particular, had to strive to achieve, not simply presume they already possessed it by virtue of the grace of their ordination and status. This was surely a red rag to Demetrios's bull.

Origen had made only a brief visit to Arabia, but he included the Holy Land on his return and made important church contacts. He greatly impressed Alexander, the bishop of Jerusalem, who gave him the example of how a church ought to have its own library, and he also provided him with a tour of the Holy Land, where Origen encountered and made friends with the learned bishop Theoctist of Palestinian Caesarea. Both hierarchs invited Origen to give discourses while he was there. When news of this came back to Alexandria, Bishop Demetrios felt affronted and sent a delegation with letters demanding Origen return home immediately. He had only just returned to Alexandria when, in the winter of 215, a large-scale riot broke out there.

The emperor Caracalla had made a visit to the university city, and a crowd of students had mocked him. In his fury the emperor set loose his imperial guards to kill protestors on sight, executed the city governor, and allowed his soldiers to attack and scatter all the faculty teachers they could see. It made perfect sense for Origen to lie low, but at the same time it seems that Bishop Demetrios continued to censure him for daring to teach about speculative theological matters and for breaking the canons of the church for presuming to teach theology even though he was not in holy orders. Any prospect of leaving the notoriously volatile city for good must have been tempting. The Palestinian bishops meanwhile seem to have sent letters back criticizing Demetrios for not recognizing what a great asset his church had. What also seems to have been an invitation from the friendly hierarchs to come and settle with them decided Origen to relocate to Caesarea, where he was soon ordained to the priesthood and added to his scholarly labors the liturgical duties of offering homilies on the scriptures several times a week to the ordinary believers in Caesarea.[27]

Demetrios's fury pursued him, even to the point of the bishop writing to the Roman Pope Pontianus, accusing Origen of dubious teachings. A short time afterward, when he was in Athens on a book-collecting trip to stock his new school's library, a Valentinian philosopher named Candidus engaged with Origen in a public disputation based on elements of his new book *On First Principles*. The discussions turned on stock arguments of the time about free will and predestined fates (within the Christian movement these were key friction points between the Valentinians and the orthodox). Origen had suggested that God would never condemn a soul to an endless series of unremitting punishments for faults committed within time since this pain could have no restorative or educative effect and so was nothing more than vindictiveness and thus was an "unworthy thing" to attribute to the beneficent deity.[28]

Then how come scripture teaches about an eternal punishment? To this Origen answered that the punishment spoken of by Christ was literally "of the next age" (Matt. 25:46, κόλασιν αἰώνιον) and did not mean a space of endless time (since time was not applicable in the next age—eternity never means simply an endless "space of time"). Moreover, God's care for our restoration was so extensive that all defective sinfulness would have a chance of being redeemed, even if it took a vast passage of ages (αἰώνια) to achieve this. Under the terms of the debating rules of that era, it was legitimate for an opponent to attribute to any disputant ideas that he had never voiced but which you could "deduce" might be logically implied by his earlier propositions. Candidus triumphantly seized on Origen's remarks about progressive ongoing restoration of souls and concluded that Origen was teaching the ultimate salvation of Satan, a thing that no Christian authority had ever countenanced.

Origen protested he had never said or intended to say any such thing, and the debate ended with both sides claiming to have won the day. When garbled versions of this debate reached Rome and Alexandria, making gossip of the fact that a young theologian had taught "the salvation of Satan" and ultimately that of all fallen creatures, both churches took a very dim view, and for the rest of his life Origen was engaged in damage-limitation exercises, claiming this was never part of his doctrine or his intention[29]—that, in fact he was just musing on Paul's apostolic teachings on God's ultimate victory in the eschaton as set out in 1 Cor. 15:28.

Demetrios was undoubtedly complaining about Origen on more than grounds of personal offense—that he had been ordained by alien clerics and abandoned his native church to serve elsewhere. This is certainly what Eusebius tries to say in his account, making it seem that the Alexandrian bishop was simply jealous. But it is more likely that the root of the complaint against him to Rome concerned aspects of his doctrine, and considering what he had already published in Alexandria,[30] it was likely the censures related to his speculations on when souls originated, to what extent there is an *apokatastasis* or general restoration, and the nature of what he meant by a "spiritual resurrection" of the body. The episode at Athens, however, began a series of charges against him—often based on loose or careless readings of his *On First Principles*—that would dog his reputation for generations to come. Much later, in the sixth century, a series of "excerpts" of what were allegedly Origen's errors were appended to the canons of the Fifth Ecumenical Council (553) (after the event) by clerics who wished to cause the ultimate damage to his reputation as a theologian. Not one of the list of these propositions was actually written by him at all (they were predominantly taken from the writings of Evagrius of Pontus, as we shall see later), but this was a hammer blow that censured his name in a most severe way. And, very typically, it stood on no intelligent basis whatsoever, certainly not based on any properly "ecumenical" grounds, given that ecumenical councils are meant, first and foremost, to be judicious ecclesiastical trials and, as paradigmatic church-court trials, ought to consider only accurate and unprejudiced evidences on which to base their canonical sentences.

Despite these third-century grumblings, the Palestinian bishops stood by him and highly respected him. In Caesarea Maritima, Origen built his school, expanded his library, completed the masterpiece of his *Commentary on John* that he had started in Alexandria, and began a series of commentaries on scriptural books that would more or less annotate every single major biblical text. Never before had anyone, Jew or Christian, worked so extensively or consistently on the body of scripture. To provide reliable scholarly texts (for Jewish–Christian dialogue in the Holy Land), he collated all the various "versions" (Hebrew and Greek) that were extant in a six-columned massive manuscript called the *Hexapla*. Already in Alexandria he had taken Hebrew lessons from a Jewish master,[31] and in Caesarea he shows a close awareness of the work of the rabbinic school of Tannaim currently working in Caesarea.[32]

His scholarly bishops now asked him to assume the role of theological *peritus* at local church synods that were being held. His work *Dialogue with Heracleides* is one treatise that emerges from this activity. The text was only rediscovered in 1941 as part of the Tura papyri finds.[33] Origen carefully and gently persuades an old Arabian bishop that he could not just take the Old Testament literally and demand that all his church follow him in it. Heracleides had seemingly taught a form of modalism (not quite sure of the distinction between the Father and the divine Son—and whether this meant there were two gods or one). The Arabian churches around him also seem to have taught, on the basis of Old Testament literalism, that "the soul is the blood." With great tact, and care that neither Heracleides nor the other local bishops lose face, Origen here engages in a discussion that leads them to see that the Old Testament ideas have to be subordinated to the evangelical and apostolic teachings.

The *Dialogue with Heracleides* presents an excellent example of how subtle Origen was in debate. When he concludes that to believe "the soul is the blood" reductively materializes a spiritual element, one of the bishops present explains to a newcomer, "Brother Origen teaches the soul is immortal." To this Origen immediately replies that the truth is it is both immortal and nonimmortal; in other words, the soul is only conditionally immortal since it holds its being dependently from God.[34] Another notable Arabian synod he spoke at, as chief theologian, was the one where the very famous Arabian bishop Beryllus of Bostra had, very sensitively, to be brought to heel. Beryllus was an advocate of a form of monarchian theology (the deity in Jesus was a gift from God).[35] He too, apparently, was persuaded by the force of Origen's words, that the divinity of Jesus was eternally preexistent not temporarily gifted to a charismatically graced man.[36]

One of Origen's Caesarean students named Theodore has left a speech of encomium about his teacher. He tells how all of Origen's studies were religiously rooted. Beginning with logic and dialectic, the curriculum moved on to cosmology and natural history, followed by ethics and then theology proper. Theodore describes meeting his teacher:

> It was like a spark falling in my deepest soul, setting it on fire . . . . It was at the same time a love for the holy Word, the most beautiful object of all that, with an irresistible force, attracts all things to itself by its ineffable beauty. And it was also love for this man [Origen] the friend and advocate of the holy Word, that caused me to give up all other goals so that I had only one remaining object that I treasured and longed for—philosophy; and that divine man who was my master of philosophy.[37]

Church tradition says that Theodore was later renamed (at his baptism or ordination perhaps) as Gregory and became the apostolic bishop who evangelized the Cappadocian region, earning such a reputation for sanctity that he gained the sobriquet θαυματουργός, "the worker of marvels."[38]

Soon after Origen had settled in Palestine, around 235, a palace revolution overthrew Emperor Alexander Severus, whose reign had so far proved hospitable to Christians and scholars. Maximin the Thracian assumed the purple and purged the old guard, initiating persecution against Christian leaders. In Rome, Pope Pontianus and Hippolytus were exiled and sent to the mines, and in Nicomedia Ambrose was arrested, while at Caesarea the archpriest Protoctetus was arrested. Origen went into hiding in Caesarea, in the house of the Virgin Juliana, but while there wrote a treatise, *Exhortation to Martyrdom*, encouraging his friends not to be afraid.[39] It immediately became the church's greatest work of resistance literature and has been read over many generations of suffering since then.

When the persecution blew over, Origen resumed his work alongside Bishop Theoctist, and sometime between 238 and 244 he traveled to Athens once more, staying some time, as when he was resident there he completed his *Commentary on Ezekiel* and began his famous *Commentary on the Song of Songs*. He also speaks of having visited Nicomedia, where his friend and patron Ambrose (having survived his arrest) still resided.[40] It is also possible that he paid a visit to the lecture hall of the great neo-Platonist teacher Plotinus, the only philosopher of that age who could rival him in significance, who was himself another pupil of Ammonius Saccas in Alexandria.[41] This would have been either in Antioch or Rome.

The synods that Origen attended as an expert, with local bishops disputing in a debate format, seem to have taken place during the reign of the emperor Philip the Arab (244–249). If that emperor was not a Christian himself,[42] he was certainly a patron and protector of the Christians of Palestine and Arabia, and when he was assassinated those associated with him (his clients and his sympathizers, and particularly Christian notables) were in danger. Decius, who took the throne, was determined to restore the fortunes of Rome and felt passionately that a return to the cults of the old gods was a major starting point of the regeneration policy. He began a pogrom against the church in which the clerical leaders of Palestine suffered conspicuously.

Pope Fabian was martyred at Rome, and Bishop Alexander of Jerusalem, Origen's close friend, was arrested and martyred at Caesarea, as was the great bishop Babylas at Antioch. The authorities deliberately sought out Origen, hoping to score a great propaganda coup if they could make this most renowned Christian intellectual renounce the faith publicly. He was arrested, and his imprisonment was specially designed so that the torture would not kill him until he had apostatized. He was put in an iron collar and regularly stretched on the rack. Eusebius tells his readers (who would know exactly what he meant in those days) that he was made to endure four spaces of the machine.[43] This meant the ratchets that were turned on a gear wheel to pull apart his leg and arm joints. After this amount of torture, it is clear that Origen would never have been able to walk or use his arms again. But the pain was rationed because on the order of the governor of Caesarea his torturers were commanded to make sure he did not die before he renounced the faith.

Even so, he endured as a Christian confessor for two long years. Dionysius, the learned bishop of Alexandria, himself a fervent admirer and perhaps even former pupil of Origen, now composed, in his honor, his *Encouragement to Martyrdom*. Emperor Decius himself was assassinated along with his children in 252, and his persecution came to an end as swiftly as his dynasty. The Caesarean church immediately gathered up Origen and looked after him. But by this time and by ancient standards, he was already a very old man at sixty-nine.[44] His health was so extensively broken that he died shortly afterward in 254,[45] but not before he had spent his last months writing letters of consolation to the many believers who had suffered in the persecution.[46] In 2012 a set of lost homilies (chiefly on the Psalms), including one *On Pentecost*, were discovered in the State Library at Bavaria by the archivist Dr. Marina Marin Pradel and published by Lorenzo Perrone.[47] In these late writings Origen shows he has lost none of his acuity or spiritual fire. Discussing the fiery tongues that fell on the first disciples, he reminds his own contemporary faithful that this is their destiny too, to become so assimilated to Christ that they share in his own presence and grace, like his contemporary apostles.

Jerome tells us that Origen was buried in the city of Tyre.[48] The crusaders, much later, told that they had seen his tomb set into the back of the sanctuary wall of the great cathedral at Tyre. This would have been a high honor indeed—meant to signify a canonization of a saint. The cathedral they speak about was not built in Origen's day, and no trace remains of anything they saw.[49] That Origen died as a brave confessor, and "not exactly" a martyr,[50] was one of the reasons his later critics felt justified in winnowing his works, when later standards of orthodoxy made him sometimes an uncomfortable fit for the theological controversies of later times. But his reputation for sanctity and for faithful churchmanship, his renown as the real founding father of Christian exegesis and mystical theology, and his place as one of the most profound architects of Christological soteriology meant that no commanding power was able to suppress the great passion of the church, manifested in the way his works were copied and recopied over the centuries.

What now follows is a very brief account of why continuous generations of Christian scholars have fond his work compelling. It will continue, in chapter 2 of Part 1, by discussing Origen's theological architecture, and then go on into Part 2, considering the various historical phases, to the present day, during which his influence has waxed and waned and waxed again, making him one of the very important figures who have mapped out the Christian tradition over the course of most of its history.

NOTES

1. Cited in the medieval *Suidae Lexicon*, ed. Ada Adler (Leipzig: Teubner, 1935), 3:169.

2. See J. A. McGuckin, "Caesarea Maritima as Origen Knew It," in *Origeniana Quinta*, ed. R. J. Daly (Leuven: Peeters, 1992), 3–25.

3. Eusebius writes this about fifty years after Origen's death. He has many of Origen's original manuscripts before him as he does so, including a hundred personal letters (Eusebius, *Church History* 6.36) and short treatises of justification that Origen wrote to his complainants, which are now no longer extant. Most important here are the *Autobiographical Letter* (Eusebius, *Church History* 6.19.12–14), which Eusebius had and we have lost, and the *Letter to Friends in Alexandria* (partly preserved in Rufinus, *De adulteratione librorum Origenis* 8, and in Jerome, *Apologia contra Rufinum* 2.18–19, and mentioned in his *Letters*, 33 and 84). So overall, Eusebius's work is very authoritative—but it is also subject to many typical authorial speculations of the writers of ancient biography. He tends to make things up, if he has gaps in his knowledge, on the basis of what he thinks "likely." So his version of things (especially chronologies and attributed motives) needs some caution in interpretation. See P. Nautin, *Origène: Sa Vie et son Oeuvre* (Paris: Beauchesne, 1977), and J. A. McGuckin, *The Westminster Handbook to Origen* (Louisville, KY: Westminster

John Knox Press, 2004), 1–2. Material about Origen in the later writers Socrates Scholasticus and Epiphanius of Salamis is much less reliable. In the ninth century the learned scholar Photius kept a voluminous record of his reading (*Bibliotheca*) and has a chapter there (118) that gives his remarks about (now lost) works of Origen he had read.

4. Eusebius was moved to do this in imitation of his spiritual teacher Pamphilus the Martyr, who had also composed an "Apologia for Origen" (now largely lost). Eusebius had been the research assistant for his imprisoned mentor and was thus very familiar with all the Origen archive in the library at Caesarea.

5. Eusebius, *Martyrs of Palestine* 11.1.

6. I.e., patristic.

7. Eusebius, *Con. Marc.* 1.4.3; *Ec. Th.* 1.14.

8. Referring to T. Graumann, *Die Kirche der Väter: Vätertheologie und Väterbeweis in den Kirchen des Ostens bis zum Konzil von Ephesus (431)* (Tübingen: Mohr Siebeck, 2002), 17. Vinzent here notes: "This was an argument developed in the debate between Asterius, Marcellus of Ancyra and Eusebius of Caesarea." See M. Vinzent, "Origenes als Postscriptum: Paulinus von Tyrus und die origenistische Diadoche," in *Origeniana Septima*, ed. W. A. Bienert and U. Kuhneweg (Leuven: Peeters, 1999).

9. M. Vinzent, "Jewish Christian Relations: A Painful Split," in *The T&T Clark Handbook to the Early Church*, ed. I. L. E. Ramelli, J. A. McGuckin, and P. Siejkowski (Edinburgh: T&T Clark, 2021), 37.

10. Jerome, *Epistle* 39.22.

11. Eusebius, *Church History* 6.2.11.

12. Eusebius, *Church History* 6.2.7.

13. Eusebius, *Church History* 6.2.8–10.

14. Eusebius, *Church History* 6.3.4–5 and 6.4–6.5.

15. *Historia Augusta* 17.1 (on Severus). Severus was alarmed at the spread of the Christian faith among court and government circles, and his rescript of 202 had forbidden conversions to Judaism or Christianity—which probably started a series of waves of mob violence against the churches and synagogues, especially in Alexandria, over the next decade.

16. One of which was the right to be executed by decapitation in lieu of torture.

17. Eusebius, *Church History* 6.3.3.

18. Eusebius, *Church History* 6.2.13–14.

19. Eusebius, *Church History* 6.2.13.

20. Eusebius says (*Church History* 6.6.) he was a disciple too of Clement of Alexandria, the Christian theologian. This is probably a false deduction from Eusebius's (wrong) supposition that the Catechetical School of Alexandria was a formal establishment and Clement had belonged to it before Origen.

21. See R. M. Berchman, *From Philo to Origen: Middle Platonism in Transition* (Chico, CA: Scholars Press, 1984).

22. See M. J. Edwards, *Origen against Plato* (Aldershot, UK: Ashgate, 2002).

23. Reported in Jerome, *De Viris Illustribus* 61.

24. Eusebius, *Church History* 6.19.15.

25. Eusebius, *Church History* 6.21.3–4.

26. See J. A. McGuckin, "Origen's Doctrine of the Priesthood," *Clergy Review* 70, no. 8 (August 1985): 277–86; no. 9 (September 1985): 318–25.

27. Eusebius, *Church History* 6.23.4.

28. For a recent consideration of antique *apokatastasis* concepts, see M. J. McClymond, *The Devil's Redemption: A New History and Interpretation of Christian Universalism*, 2 vols. (Grand Rapids, MI: Baker Academic, 2019).

29. Part of his exculpatory *Letter to Friends in Alexandria* on this subject is preserved in Jerome's *Apology Against Rufinus* 2.18–19. See also McGuckin, *Westminster Handbook to Origen*, 15. Origen claims to his Palestinian bishops and his larger circle of friends that the opponent had circulated a mutilated text of the debate, falsifying and misrepresenting his own statements within it to make it appear he had clearly lost the debate.

30. While resident in Alexandria, Origen issued *On First Principles* and the first five books of the *Commentary on John*, books 1–8 of his *Genesis Commentary*, books 1–15 of his *Psalms Commentary*, a *Commentary on Lamentations*, two books *On the Resurrection*, and ten books of *Miscellanies* (*Stromata*). Much more would follow in Caesarea.

31. Origen, *On First Principles* 1.3.4, 4.3.14.

32. In the preface to his *Commentary on the Psalms*, he tells us that he consulted with the rabbinic Patriarch Ioullos on points of interpretation. The Talmud speaks of Origen discussing matters with the rabbinic scholar Hoschaia Rabba. See McGuckin, "Caesarea Maritima"; McGuckin, *Westminster Handbook to Origen*, 11n62; and J. A. McGuckin, "Origen on the Jews," in *Christianity & Judaism*, ed. D. Wood, Studies in Church History 29 (Oxford: Blackwell, 1997), 1–13.

33. This was a major discovery in 1941 of a cache of Christian manuscripts, including works by Origen and Didymus the Blind, among others. Origen's fragments included his *Homily on the Witch of Endor* and his *Dialaogue with Heracleides* and parts of his *Commentary on Romans*, *Discourse on Pascha*, and *Against Celsus*. See L. Doutreleau, "Que Savons-nous aujourd'hui des papyrus de Toura?," *Recherches des Sciences Religieuses* 43 (1955): 161–93 (with photographs).

34. The whole text is available online at https://sites.google.com/site/demontortoise2000/Home/origen_dialog_with_heracleides.

35. Eusebius, *Church History* 6.33.1.

36. Eusebius, *Church History* 6.33.2–3.

37. Gregory Thaumaturgos, *Panegyric on Origen* 6.

38. Eusebius, *Church History* 7.14.

39. Advocating flight and avoidance if possible (c.f. Matt. 10.23) but willing acceptance of martyrdom once arrested.

40. He mentions this in a letter to the Christian scholar Julius Africanus, who had consulted him on questions of literary interpretation. See McGuckin, *Westminster Handbook to Origen*, 20.

41. McGuckin, *Westminster Handbook to Origen*, 21.

42. Eusebius thinks he was. *Church History* 6.34.

43. Eusebius, *Church History* 6.39.6.

44. Eusebius, *Church History* 7.1.

45. Eusebius's dates are distorted here. Although he puts the death in the reign of Gallus, it was most likely in the early years of the reign of Valerian.

46. Eusebius, *Church History* 6.39.5: "After these things were over Origen left many words of comfort, full of sweetness, to those who needed assistance, as can be seen from so many of his epistles." (Now, sadly, lost to us.)

47. In the GCS series of patristic texts. A translation by J. W. Trigg has appeared as *Origen: Homilies on the Psalms*, vol. 141 of the Fathers of the Church Series. Trigg discusses the texts in the July 2020 issue of *Commonweal*.

48. Jerome, *De Viris Illustribus* 54.

49. On the medieval writers' accounts, see B. F. Westcott's article "Origenes," in *Dictionary of Christian Biography*, ed. W. Smith and H. Wace (London: John Murray, 1887), 4:103.

50. The early church believed that those who died under their wounds at the time of persecution would be assured of a place in heaven and ought to be venerated by the church as great saints. See J. A. McGuckin, "Martyr Devotion in the Alexandrian School (Origen to Athanasius)," in *Martyrs & Martyrologies*, ed. D. Wood, Studies in Church History 30 (Oxford: Blackwell, 1993), 35–45.

Chapter 2

Aspects of Origen's Thought World

PROLEGOMENA

In the remainder of this first part of the book, I will try to give a picture of Origen's thought world under four headings: his concept of God's outreach as saving Trinity; his understanding of the centrality of scriptural revelation; his impact on (indeed foundation of) Christian spiritual theology, sometimes called ascetical theology; and lastly aspects of his church dogmatics that had a large impact (both positive and negative) on succeeding generations of Christian theologians in antiquity. In trying to summarize such a vastly spacious thinker as Origen, I have to use very wide brush strokes here, which may annoy some Origenian specialists, but which I do for the sake of introducing our subject comprehensibly and somewhat comprehensively. In that light, for me, it seems that Origen's greatest long-term importance as a Christian theologian is first of all his theological architecture about salvation: how he conceived God's being and how that being reaches out from divine "impassibility" to the world of created beings, which stands in so much need and in such deep suffering. This is the largest of all canvases a Christian theologian can ever put on an easel. In assembling his "story" about God and God's outreach, Origen gives a stunningly beautiful account of the divine Trinity, the incarnation of the eternal Word, the gift of the Holy Spirit, and the impact this has on humanity. It is a story he roots in the soil of the Bible, but one he addresses to his contemporary Greek world. He believes first and foremost that when Christians confess the Son of God as the eternal Logos of God (the reason, rationale, and wisdom of the deity, which is seeded as the substrate and goal of all created life), they are thereby committed to the fundamental "faith" that all life is rational, all theology is rational, and therefore in accord with all (true) philosophical or scientific insight. The putting together of cosmology, scripture, and theology, therefore, is not for him some academic's pet project but a fundamental response that evangelical faith demands. His overarching motive was to make the church attractive for intellectuals—in the sense of offering a mission to his generation in Alexandria (and throughout subsequent history) and yet protecting the apostolic tradition from the ravages inflicted on it by mythmakers on one side (how he saw the Valentinian gnostics) and fundamentalists on the other (whom he called anthropomorphite simpletons). But here he makes a screeching departure from one of the most sacred "givens" of Hellenistic religious philosophy. For Origen, God is not impassive. The divine impassibility (which is truly his because he is immaterial and self-activating) is nevertheless open to the pleas of all creaturehood, and he "sympathizes with" and helps the creation that he loves with passion.[1] No Hellenist would ever thus define God, making his mercy a quintessential aspect of his impassible majesty. This too is why the Logos is sent by the Father to rescue creation, and why the Logos himself, like the divine Father whose image he is, is moved to the process of salvation by a passion of love that results in his Passion of suffering.[2]

If we accept that Origen is first and foremost an expansive architect, laying out the ground plan for Christian soteriological theory, we can then see how other important axioms follow straight afterward. The first of these, in my opinion, is how he shapes all subsequent Christian approaches to the holy scriptures. That he invented the concept and nomenclature "Old Testament" and "New Testament" may give one the sense of how fundamental he was to later biblical commentary—both for those who liked his style and those who disapproved of it. For both parties he had, in a real sense, set the ground rules. Our chapter therefore follows up Origen as a biblical interpreter. But when we look into this, it becomes immediately apparent that he sees the entire scriptural account as a coherent whole, totally dedicated to the divine task of teaching humans how to live in God. Again, in my opinion, all Origen's work can be classified as a theology of *paideia*: God teaching us always, in every manner and every encounter. This master theme especially emerges in the way that most of what Origen is concerned about is called, in the modern age, "ethics" but was called in antiquity "ascetical thought." Asceticism is the repentant turn back to God, which Origen envisages needs to be done both individually and collectively. For him the Logos is the supreme pedagogue, but since his teaching is ultimately concerned with bringing humanity back to the realization that it is a race that is not simply material, but one that is possessed of a psychic destiny to be united with the Logos, and thus through him with God, then this whole track of his thought could equally validly be called the mystical theology of Origen. Indeed he is without question the first great Christian mystical writer, and his thought in this domain (how the soul can find union with God through Christ in the Spirit) preformed the architecture of every major Christian writer who followed. After treating these three macro concepts, our treatment will then look at smaller, but equally influential, aspects of his overall system that deal with the means and measures of his great design: the infrastructure, as it were, of the larger architecture. So the final section will deal with aspects of Origen's ecclesial dogmatics: his ideas about the sacraments or the state of the afterlife, and other ideas of his that had a long posthistory in Christian disputation.

These are the four areas that, however briefly treated, might give an accurate account of what this ancient thinker was up to and how he considered that all aspects of his thinking coinhered and cross-referenced each other at all times. In respect to all of these four major ideas, each of numbers two through four could just as truly be regarded as extrapolations of number one: who God is and how he reaches out to his world for its salvation. And that is where we shall now begin.

THE OUTREACH OF GOD TO HIS WORLD: A SOTERIOLOGY OF LOVE

God's outreach to creation is the deep core of all Origen's theology. He calls the task of speaking about God "a dangerous thing, even when one is speaking the truth about him,"[3] an axiom his later disciple Gregory Nazianzen expanded on in a masterly way in his famed *First Theological Oration*.[4] It is clear enough that Origen's thought on God was colored by the Greek philosophical debates of his own time, most particularly the concept of the problem of the one and the many: the immensity and the singularity (absolute oneness) of God "as opposed to" the fragile particularity of the material world, and its apparently chaotic multiplicity. Could there be any relation between the two, the immortal and changeless creator's unapproachably absolute person and the mortal evanescence of created things? Relating the "one" and the "many" was one of the great religious questions of his day, and the Valentinian gnostics of Origen's Alexandria had offered a resolution to it that, by means of mythic cosmological narratives, married a generic Hellenistic scheme of the ascent of pure minds to the ineffable deity (something Plotinus did much better in his *Enneads*) to surface elements of the Christian tradition. Origen knew about them well enough but was determined not to follow their path of using mythological schemes to buffer emanating spiritual aeons (heavenly powers) between the divine one and the created many. Even if Aristotle had thought that "the friend of myths is in some sense already a philosopher,"[5] Origen radically disagreed. He had only mockery for those who adopted a mythical methodology to search for divine truth.[6] Moreover, Origen, for all his awareness and respect for philosophical clarity, is first and foremost a biblical theologian not a Greek philosopher, and this is exactly why he follows the Hebraic biblical tradition in affirming that God, who made the world, loves and cherishes it, rather than despising and distancing himself from it. He approaches the biblical text as harmonious oracles that fill out and give substance to philosophical deduction. He is, therefore, one of the very first theologians who adopt the method of approach that "faith gives fullness to reasoning."[7] He did share, however, with many of the Hellenistic thinkers the concept that God was most closely linked to humanity by the rational power of conscious reflection. For Origen it was more than just "like is known to like" (an epistemological axiom of the Platonists), for he saw the biblical account of the divinity making mankind in its own image and likeness as a symbolic pattern for how the Logos (the very image of God himself) made mankind in his own (i.e., the Logos's) likeness. So there is an ontologically deep bond between human consciousness and the divine presence that the Logos left in humanity when he created it. As Origen phrased it, "There is a certain affinity between the mind and God, of whom the mind is an intellectual icon, and this is because of the fact that the mind, especially when it is purified and distanced from physical materiality, is able to enjoy some perception of the divine nature."[8] Philosophy, logic, and literary criticism were all, for Origen, "handmaiden sciences" to the exegesis of scripture.[9] With this synthesis, guided by the hand of scripture, the open heart and the pure mind would be given by God the grace to see the truth. For him the approach to God was not quintessentially a matter of epistemology, as it was for many of the Greeks, but one of repentance: the urgent need to find the restoration to communion with the Father that gave humans life in the first place. For Origen, once humanity lost the clear-sighted connection with God, it also lost its grip on the springs of life, and declined into ignorance and then death. For Origen, the knowledge of God was no less than union with the creator's life force, and thus, for him, this restorative learning process (what we moderns often call the "search for God") is rendered into a matter of ontology, a question of the root of being. Following the biblical tradition, Origen corrects the basic Hellenistic preconception about God/the gods, namely, that divinity shuns and abhors the fallibility and error of the material world. Rather, union with the godhead is something God intended and established from the beginning of creation, he argues, and the collapse of this union is a matter that the divine power seeks always to remedy.

Restoration, making fresh, is entirely what divine revelation is all about, therefore, and can be seen, when correctly understood, to be entirely soteriological, that is, salvific, in purpose. There is, for Origen, a material human nature (into which we have fallen and which was not our original purpose from God) and that "higher and more divine nature into which God shall change us, and indeed keep us in this state, if only we shall show God, by our conduct, that we wish to be so kept."[10] The material human "nature" that materialist reductionists so focus on as a fixity, therefore, is not the true nature of a human being. God makes illumined creatures ascend to their true nature: the stability of such entry into the divine being provided only by God to those who enter into the relationship. This is a radically new definition that this Christian philosopher brings to the concept of human nature.

Origen's starting point in theology proper is that the true God is entirely incorporeal.[11] Nothing material applies to him. This has to be understood at every level, especially when interpreting the Bible's many material images, which are *always* symbolic. The human mind gives the best model for God's incorporeity. It needs no perceptible dimension and can range freely where it wishes; so too God is like infinite intellective power and cannot be discerned by any of our physical senses.[12] When scripture speaks of "seeing" God, it means only by the soul or by the heart (which for him are both synonyms of mind-conception).[13] The account of God's revelation at Sinai tells us that God lies hidden in thick darkness (Ex. 20:21; Ps. 18:11), which is a symbolic way of telling us that no speech can access him,[14] and all human knowledge of God depends utterly on God's self-revelation through the Son. The Son of God fulfills this task perfectly, being the eternal Logos, with God from before time, and through whom the Father made the world of created beings. The Logos came to earth as a teacher of fallen souls, and for this end was made a man. Origen echoes (it is merely an echo not an endorsement) the neo-Platonic method of learning higher truths "by way of ascent."[15] For him, however, the path is wholly Christocentric: "One ascends from knowledge of the Son to knowledge of the Father."[16] Origen treats all the Christological titles in the scriptures as stepping-stones to understand the true significance of Jesus: beginning with the ideas of "the way" and the "door" and opening the mind and heart to the salvific teaching force of the Logos-Pedagogue, who like a good teacher of pupils with learning difficulties has stooped down from on high in the flesh to engage us in the necessary ascent from the humanity of Jesus to the divinity of the Word. As the Word is, himself, the archetypal "image" of God (the only image of the invisible),[17] so those who follow and are illuminated by his teaching become the "likeness" of the image, and drawing close, like to like, are enabled through the Son to stand in relation with the Father.[18] While this has all the hallmarks of good Greek pedagogy, it is clear on a patient reading that it is a pure and highly creative reworking of Paul's doctrine of inherited sonship, and the cosmological Christology of Colossians and Ephesians, synthesized with the Johannine Logos doctrine. Often, a very careless reading of it all has resulted in commentators dismissing Origen as someone who has diluted Christian faith with Platonism, which is a world away from the truth.

This is not to say that all aspects of Origen's thought accorded with later orthodox thinkers. While he stresses the absolute transcendence of the Father, who is one and wholly simplex,[19] the Son is described as related to the world of multiplicity because of his creative and salvific work.[20] He, the Logos, is therefore the essential link between the one and the many, the eternal mediator. His mediation begins from the dawn of creation and is merely continued, not initiated, in his salvific work as incarnate Lord. The Father alone (*monas*) is absolute goodness in itself (*autoagathos*); the Son-Logos is "the image of the very goodness of God."[21] As goodness itself, the Father is the cause of all other goodness, including the Son's goodness, which is the fountain for all of creation's.[22] The Son and the Holy Spirit, to an unimaginable degree, exceed in goodness all other created realities, but the Father exceeds them in an even greater degree than they exceed us.[23] God is not only goodness but Being itself,[24] and Being is goodness (Origen is one of the first thinkers to make this equation). So there is a very strong degree of subordination in Origen's concept of the Trinity, even though he sees the Son-Word and Spirit as eternally related to the divine being, not creatures. Exegeting John 1:3, "All things were made through him and apart from him nothing was made," Origen concludes that this "nothing," which was spoken of, was evil, which does not derive from God or his Logos and thus, ultimately, has no place in the divine schemata either of existence or salvation.

The primary act of outreach from God's being, therefore, was to his Son and his Spirit. But the secondary act was through the Son-Logos, who fulfils the Father's command to make the world order. This cosmic order itself was accomplished in two major acts: the first creation and then the second creation,[25] the latter of which is the present (material) world order we observe.[26] It is the second created order that is spoken of in Genesis.[27] For Origen the first unfolding of creation was an entirely spiritual order. *Noes* (that is, rational spirit entities, or intelligences) are issued from the Logos, and by the power of contemplation of his being, they are enabled to form a chorus of communion around him and thus stand before God the Father. The first creation *noes* are in ranks of honor, uppermost being "divines," then thrones and principalities, and the lowest (what will eventually become human) souls (*psychai*).[28]

Through a cosmic catastrophe, a fall that Origen describes as being as incomprehensible as any evil (but suggests it was because the lowest ranks of *noes* started to lapse in their contemplative union with the Logos, and thus defected from the source of being), the perfect communion of this first order of creation was disrupted. This was why the Logos instituted the second material order of the world, precisely to harbor the fallen souls, who had so "cooled off" from their original spiritual condition that they were now materialized into a bodily form in a material world that was at one and the same time their means of rescue (by repentance) and their punishment designed to purify them (their prison). So it was that the fallen souls were embodied, while other *noes* continued the praise of God as the bodiless angels. While the Logos provides the union with God directly to the angels who surround him, for embodied souls the Logos had to undertake a long and painful *paideia*: offering remedial guidance to humanity, calling to it to rise back to wisdom, offering the law as a guide, and finally appearing on earth as a man in order to accelerate the return to God of all the lost souls, for whom he retained a passionate longing. Salvation would be offered in the form of a return to true being, humans realizing their destiny lay far beyond this material realm, and that communion with Jesus, established through repentance, was actually far more than moral obedience to a teacher of virtue, but a mystical union that revealed the ontological key to all things: namely, that humans could ascend stage by stage, through deeper and deeper communion with Jesus, who himself opened out into the mystery of the Logos,[29] the creator of all souls (*noes*), and who still offered to fallen souls the prospect of returning to perfect union with God, through repentance and wisdom.

It has to be said, however, that this scheme of the "fall of souls according to Origen" is not so consistently and systematically set out in the ancient *magister* as this previous synopsis might suggest. When one reads accounts of what Origen said on the subject, a great deal depends on whom one trusts to give an account of what he actually said. His idea of (a) a premundane creation of rational intelligences (*noes*) and (b) the cooling off and falling from an undifferentiated state of closeness to God into several differentiations of states (ranks of being) became items that in the late fourth and sixth centuries were almost hysterically argued about, though they had probably been offered by Origen originally as eschatological speculations or aporias. So the texts that make him out to be most dogmatic about the fall of preexistent intellects (into becoming souls) and the fall into varied ranks of beings (angels, heavenly bodies, humans, and demons) are largely supplied "outside of Origen"— by which I mean from the records of his enemies, chiefly the scribes of Justinian's court and Jerome, neither of whom prove on close examination to be particularly careful accountants. An earlier and popular edition of the *De Principiis* prepared by G. W. Butterworth out of Koetschau's edition of the text elevated these external text witnesses to the core of the edition under the rubric of "Greek" (falsely suggesting it was Origen's own Greek we were able to read here). We can return to this issue when we discuss the attacks made on Origen in later centuries. It is, nevertheless, clear that in the beginning of the *Peri Archon* Origen did want to start by considering the fall of the creation in the context of how God started it (intended it).[30] Ideas of the Fall (for which he places individual moral consciousness at the core) are found extant in undisputed parts of Origen's *Peri Archon*, as well as paralleled in other writings of his.[31]

In this grand and expansive schematic, Origen plays on all the scriptures as if they were a great multikeyboard organ and sets out a fundamental architecture of theology that had a very dramatic impact on most thinkers who followed. He has made a doctrine of God that explains the issue of the one and many (stressing God's oneness, absolute goodness, and aseity) as well as underpinning an extensive cosmology (doctrine of creation) that is simultaneously a theory of good and evil as well as being a doctrine of salvation (soteriology). Its architecture is like that of the original pyramids—with a vastness of scope and a perfection of detail (like stones between which one could not insert a knife blade). Many later Christian thinkers would dismantle large parts of it and even reject elements Origen regarded as critical to the logic of the whole narrative, and that aspect we shall look at shortly, but there would be very few in the history of the church who could ever match his fundamental and comprehensive vision that all things proceeded from God through love and issued out to the world in a divinely appointed invitation to ascend to union through repentance both in and motivated by the incarnate Lord. It was this macrostructure, elevated out of reading Paul and John in particular, that made the church read Paul and John back through its lens ever afterward. And that is precisely why Origen, despite the many revisions the later church made to his work, was (and arguably remains) the most important Christian theologian after the apostles, for he synthesized these two greatest apostles.

Before we leave this aspect of Origen's envisaging the outreach of God through the Logos to creation, and the yearning of earthbound souls to return to union with God through the Logos, let us note that this is, in fact, one of the first articulations of the rationale of the doctrine of the Holy Trinity: God's being as his mode of outreach to other spiritual entities. Origen made trinitarian theology coterminous with soteriological thought, and in this aspect of his foundational architecture for Christian theology he was very sure-footed. All subsequent attempts to articulate the Trinity that have lost sight of this fundamental insight have come to grief in desiccated abstraction.

DIVINE SCRIPTURE: MYSTICAL CHARTER OF SALVATION

Origen does not make up this schema from fresh air. It is fundamentally his (very dense) summation of all that the holy scripture teaches. He regards the entirety of the scriptures (which he divides into Old and New Covenants—he himself made up the term "Old Testament") as the divine Logos's charter for effecting the restoration of fallen souls, working through a long history from the appearance of embodied souls in the material world (created especially for their rehabilitation after their fall from spiritual life), through the rise of civilizations, to the high point of the special covenant with Israel, and on to the consummation of the Logos's plan of teaching and accelerating the turning back (repentance) of souls, namely, the appearance of the Logos himself through the incarnation of Jesus. For Origen every word of the scripture, Old and New Testament alike, is correlated and bound together as one mystical and oracular text that speaks the selfsame story: the lapse into sin and death, and the means of return to union with God.

To the modern biblical reader, accustomed to looking at texts from their atomized historical perspectives, this makes no sense, and it is important, so as to understand Origen's approach, to realize that he does not see the text as historically conditioned. Rather, any given text or episode is set within a certain history (King David, or the life of a prophet, for example) but positioned there by its true author, the Logos (never any mortal vessel such as a prophet), in order to chart out in advance the entire and vast scheme of salvation in Christ. So all the Bible is one text, albeit one with several levels of meaning and significance embedded within it. The story of Abraham's son, Isaac, carrying the wood of his sacrifice up the mountain (Gen. 22) refers to the historical patriarch, of course, but it has a deeper significance for those who know more of the mind of the Logos, as a symbol of the ascent of Jesus of Mount Calvary carrying the wood of his own sacrifice. The text announcing that "the virgin is with child" (Isa. 7.14) can refer to a princess giving birth in the court of Hezekiah, but it also has a deeper significance in the story of salvation as referring to the birth of Jesus from the Virgin Mary. Origen talks of how Jesus speaks in the Gospels to some people in the valleys, to others on the plains, and to a few on the mountaintops, and that this is a symbol of several levels of initiation in the scriptural text: Some things are for slower, more material minds and deal with basic moral matters. Other passages concern higher wisdom. Still more are mystically freighted and understandable only by the more advanced disciples who have purified their minds and can grasp the mysteries of salvation hidden inside the letter of the text: the spirit within the letter Paul spoke of.[32]

For Origen the key point is that the divine Logos is the single eternal mind (author) issuing the totality of scripture. Altogether it serves as a mysterious and complex unity, but not one that gives its meanings easily. He offers the analogy that each scriptural text has a key lying in front of it. But it is not necessarily the key to that particular door, and one has to take the key and find the correct door/text to open up the proper interpretation. There is a proper sequence to the reading of the doors and texts. Like a supreme pedagogue (for so Origen primarily approaches the divine Word's principles of salvation), the Word makes the (human) reader work for the mystery embedded in the text.

But there are certain rules a divinely inspired teacher (such as Origen himself) can reveal for the use of those who wish to read the mysteries aright and ascend in spiritual depth. One of these is that there must never be, in any biblical exegesis, anything at all that is "unworthy of God." To interpret passages that speak of God's anger, or his bodily parts, or his hatred of Egyptians, or such like, in a literal way and deduce from them aspects of Christian dogma is, for Origen, the height of foolishness and blasphemy. Those who stick close to the literal meaning, thinking they are performing a service to God, are, he argues, like those dim souls who never ascend out of the valleys (the Pharisees and other opponents of Christ) and can never hear the teaching of the Word that he gives on the mountaintops: his deeper mystical initiations to those he loves and instructs.

As we have already noted, he offers the concept of God "eternally" (an endless stretch of time being envisaged) tormenting sinners in hell as an idea that is unworthy of God's majesty as a merciful teacher. In the first place, he says, when scriptures talks about eternity, it uses the word for *aeons*, which signifies a different age not a long-drawn-out stretch of time, and secondly since God is a teacher, all punishment he inflicts must be remedial (end driven) in the divine intent, and inflicting endless pain has no value in this regard.

Other rules were applied consistently, and some of these are explicitly discussed in a very influential passage in his *On First Principles* 4.2. It would be too much to go into them all in detail here, but these have been extensively studied in recent years and the image of Origen as some crazed allegorist wildly trampolining off the biblical text has been shown to be no more than a careless caricature.[33] For example, Origen erects a starting premise of levels of authority in the whole text of scripture. Not everything carries the same weight in the overall totality. Some earthly transmitters of scripture (the prophets or apostles, for example) were much better (more fully initiated by the Word and Spirit) than others, and we ought to prioritize the most elevated way beyond the lesser visionaries. So the two primary authorities in all scripture stand as John the Evangelist and Paul. Next, along with these high authorities, come the Psalms, which are like the prayer book of the Logos himself looking forward over all salvation history. After that come the other apostles with their respective gospels, and then the ranks of prophets—with great souls such as Isaiah and Jeremiah obviously being superior in weight to lesser souls such as Zephaniah, and, as such, having much more in their teaching that reveals the coming salvation of the incarnate Word (Isaiah's suffering servant texts, for example).

Another important principle of his exegesis is the manner in which he demanded that scriptural exegesis should never be "atomic" (pericopes taken out at random and isolated) but always cross-referenced. One chief way he did this was to put together in a nexus of associated verses, passages that seemed to speak of the same thing, either by a shared keyword or a shared symbol. This manner of making associated chains (*catenae*) of texts to be taken together in exegeting a certain passage of central focus established itself throughout the ancient Christian world as a standard method immediately after him. Many of these chains of reference can still be seen today, for example, in the church's hymns and scripture readings associated with great festivals of the liturgical calendar.

Origen's exegetical system has often been caricatured as excessively symbolistic. There were times when even his most admiring disciples later "toned down" some of his specific interpretations, and many of the Syrian exegetes of the patristic era consistently argued for a less ideologically driven system of exegesis. But in the end it was the overall approach of Origen, albeit moderated, that held sway for many centuries, even into the modern age of Christianity. Critics who accuse him of not having sufficient regard for the literal and historical reading of any given passage of the Bible have often not read him carefully enough. Beginning his life as a trained grammarian of the Roman schools, Origen never (throughout a life that saw him comment extensively on almost every single book of the Bible) neglected a very close observation of the tense, literal meaning, and historical location of the verses he was considering.

It is simply that while moderns may consider the Bible to be a historically conditioned text, to be interpreted historically before anything else, he understood it from the outset to be an eschatological text, to be read according to its genre, that is, read eschatologically, not historically, or we might more carefully say, not in a historical-reductionist way that excises the eschatological out from its narrowly linear understanding of history. Very few moderns were able to appreciate his processes of interpretation (basically ancient ones of literary philosophy derived from the litterateurs of the Great Library of Alexandria) until the advent of postmodernist literary theory allowed wider horizons of literary interpretation and threw a dazzling light on Origen's true purposes. Within the church, one can already see the general adoption of the Origenian exegetical process in the Cappadocian Fathers of the late fourth century (duly moderated in terms of controversial highlights) and in the more simplified system Pope Gregory the Great set out for the entire Latin church in his sixth-century *Pastoral Rule*.

A MYSTICISM OF LOVE: ORIGEN'S ASCETICAL THEOLOGY

If, so far, all of this sounds either highly intellectualist (the ascent of the mind to union with the Logos) or soberingly grim (the constant path of repentance and purification the soul must traverse), I have given the wrong impression. Origen is, in many ways, the father of Christian mystical theology; or, to put that in another way, everything to do with God he sees as a story of love seeking to return to loving union what had been lost from loving union. He is (because he finds this story radiant in the scriptural texts) the first internationally significant philosopher in the world (the very first significant Christian philosopher of history) to elevate a metaphysics of love as the root cause and final purpose of the entirety of all phenomena: the "single theory," as it were, that explains all things. For Origen, God, in love, created the cosmos through the patterning of the Logos, and the Spirit reworks and refreshes that patterning, where it has failed, in order to restore the springs of being within his creation. Union with the Logos, now incarnated for a fallen world by the Spirit, not only is the moral salvation of creatures but also their ontological stabilization. In union with God, a creature finds the root of the principle of life. But this itself turns out to be a union of love: united to the source of all life (the Logos who gave us and continues to give us being), creaturehood finds that the love of God is itself the power and energy of life. Where love abounds, there too life develops and ascends. Where love is cool, life and meaning ebb away. Before the making of this present material world, it was, Origen surmises, a cooling of love among some of the *noes* that brought about the Fall. Now, the rediscovery of the love of the Logos will cause spirits to ascend on high and flourish once more in the love and life of God. He expresses this theory of a metaphysics of love across his writings but most especially, perhaps, in his exegesis of the *Song of Songs*. In approaching the text this way, he becomes the grandfather of a massive series of later Christian writers who follow his lead.

The *Song of Songs* describes in vivid poetry a woman who runs through a vineyard searching passionately for her lover. Origen says that this is a text of high mystical symbolism. Far from being a simple epithalamium verse, it gives, in deep symbolic order, the story of the defection of spirits to their present earthy condition. The soul of all creatures, for Origen, is depicted in the passion of the Shulamite woman for her royal lover (Solomon). The woman represents the soul; the king represents the divine Logos. Having the love of the Logos as the very principle of its life, it finds that all its hope and joy, all that it desires and seeks after, is contained in him. Those who recognize this run after the Logos in all they do: the passion to be united with him configures their entire being. Even those who do not understand have the longing for God rooted deep within their souls, and unless it is found and acted upon (running after God) their lives will be frustrated and miss the mark. By using this image of the lover and the beloved hurrying into the bridal chamber as the central cipher of the relation between the soul and God, Origen transforms the entirety of the Christian doctrine of salvation into a wonderfully warm and intimate story that cuts across academic and literary sophistication to have a force that can attract even the believers who would never normally open a book. But this story will draw them:

> Let him kiss me with the kisses of his mouth, for your love is more delightful than wine. Pleasing is the fragrance of your perfumes. Your name is like perfume poured out. No wonder the young women love you. Take me away with you. Let us hasten. Let the king bring me into his chambers. We rejoice and delight in you. We will praise your love more than wine. How right they are to adore you.[34]

For Origen, the Logos who reaches into the soul of every person in order to instruct and reform them turns out to be the king who loves them and wishes to admit them back to their lost royal status as intimate companions of his chamber. That all this depicts the cosmological fall and return of the soul is like turning on the electric garden lighting that transforms a sophisticated scene into a magical one. Origen thereby makes his metaphysics of love a warm and loving message, one which he fills out extensively by his constant advocacy of prayer and meditation, devoted scripture reading, and genuine moral effort, all of which combine to make his mysticism of love a deeply personal path of faithful discipleship: a mysticism rooted in ethics.

Origen is surely speaking from his own personal experience of God when he writes in his *Commentary on the Song of Songs*:

> Next the Bride looks for the Bridegroom who, after revealing himself, has disappeared again. This kind of thing often happens throughout the Song. Someone can only understand this who has experienced it personally. Often, and God is my witness here, I myself have felt that the Bridegroom was coming near, indeed that he was as near as could be to me: but then he has suddenly gone away: and I could no longer find what I was seeking. Once more I set myself to long for his coming and then at times he returns. And when he has appeared to me, so close that I could hold him in my hands, once more he escapes me and once more vanishes; and I have to start over again to look for him. He does that often until I hold him fast and rise up, leaning on my well-beloved One.[35]

This notion that the lover (God) wishes to meet with his beloved (the soul) makes all of Origen's thought a "world apart" from Platonic metaphysics, which spoke of the intellective ascent of the soul from sublunar imprisonment to the higher realms. Origen's Logos incarnate in Jesus does not merely wait for souls to ascend, in passionate and sacrificial self-emptying (*kenosis*)[36] he comes more eagerly to us in condescending compassion (*katabasis*) than we are ready to run to him.

ORIGEN'S CONTROVERSIAL DOGMATICS

On my home bookshelves I have a guidebook to Rome that, on the recto side of the page, shows the ancient ruin sites as they presently appear to the potential visitor, but on the verso it has a see-through plastic cover sheet that has printed on it a ghost of what those ruins once looked like in imperial Rome. The act of flipping over the superimposition onto the recto page is startling. Waste ground with a few random stone blocks on it suddenly appears as a magnificent palace or temple. So it is with the thought of Origen. When we make the effort at situating him in his own context, literary and intellectual, he emerges as a startlingly original thinker.

He was certainly a master architect of a theologian. His understanding of the principles of Christian life was vast in scope and of deep religious passion. As he was the first ever to attempt to put all the disparate Christian elements together in a systematic form, he may be forgiven for some "off-key" moments in his symphonic composition. Later generations of Christians, however, were not so ready to allow that any *magister* could have lapses at any time.

Accordingly, his reputation suffered posthumously when, by the standards of later orthodox councils, his decisions (many of them expressed merely as suppositions worthy of discussion in a seminar group rather than strongly held teachings) seemed contradictory to more widely accepted Christian dogma. The arguments that sprung up about and around him over the three hundred years that followed his death were so intense in the early church that eventually his books were proscribed. Many still read them, of course, and, more importantly, the positive substance of most of what he had said had already been "moderated" and incorporated by some of the greatest theologians of the early age: St. Basil the Great, St. Gregory the Theologian, St. Gregory of Nyssa, St. Dionysios of Alexandria, St. Cyril of Alexandria, St. John Chrysostom, St. Jerome, St. Ambrose, St. Gregory the Great, St. Maximus the Confessor, and St. John Damascene. In this way, of course, Origen's legacy, despite his posthumous censure, entered into the heart of the Christian tradition as an enduring and authentic way to articulate the apostolic tradition, and through these great Fathers of the Church (as well as through his own surviving extensive fragments) Origen came to have a permanent place in all subsequent forms of Christian tradition up to and through the Reformation era.

Even so, the "moderation" to his schemata was significant. Origen himself had certain universalist tendencies. In his own lifetime he got into trouble with the Alexandrian and Roman hierarchies when his rival Candidus reported to Bishop Heraclas of Alexandria that during a disputation at Athens he had taught the rehabilitation of the Devil himself after a sufficiently long duration of reform. Origen himself always denied he had ever said this, but other aspects of his teaching maintained that God, eternally merciful, would never inflict an endless punishment, and since moral defect was always a matter of choice, it could always be remedied by repentance. Perhaps this is what Candidus meant: that in debate, when Origen had insisted on this point, it was logically tantamount to saying, "Everyone, however evil, can find repentance and salvation." Origen had originally made the argument to deny the fatalism of the Valentinian gnostics, an early form of "predestination to evil" theory, which Origen found totally obnoxious. Mainstream opinion in the early church, however, despite great thinkers who recognized Origen had a point about purgative stages of reform for erring souls after life, generally insisted on the eternal fixity of hell for unrepentant sinners, and always remained more than cautious about universalist ideas of salvation.[37]

Another of his speculations that caused the ire of ecclesiastical authorities to fall on his head was his concept of the present world as a "second creation," the first being a purely spiritual cosmic order before souls had fallen into material form and required a terrestrial dwelling place to work out their salvation and ascent. In shorthand, this has been called Origen's "doctrine of preexistence."[38] This was an early casualty and had already been largely rejected by the second generation of Origenian disciples. In Origen's day, and regarding himself as a philosophical teacher in an academic environment, Origen felt that some degree of speculation was legitimate for a theological teacher. By the second generation of his Christian successors, the majority of theological teachers in the early church were now bishops, not so much academic professors but pastoral leaders of the liturgical preaching, and by then such degrees of speculation were not felt to be a good idea in case they scandalized the faithful at large.

Perhaps the main reason his reputation was damaged posthumously, however, was the manner in which he formulated his Christology. Near his own time, in the mid-to early second century, elements of what we would call subordinationism (that the Son and Spirit were, somehow, not as great as God the Father) were not out of the ordinary in many places. Some of the most rigid forms of subordinationist thought, such as represented by the adoptionist monarchians, had been systematically attacked and exposed by the school of Logos theologians (such as Hippolytus and Tertullian), a school of thought to which Origen also belonged.

But Origen wished to insist that, although the Son-Logos was eternally begotten from the Father and was divine, he was "a second god as it were" (δεύτερος θεός) and was not to be mistaken for "God Himself" (αὐτοθεός), whereby he meant the Father. His understanding of the dynamic of the Trinity was that the Son and Spirit were as far below the Father (yet truly divine because they made him known to the world and because of the intimacy of their eternal relationship with the Father) as we creatures were below the Son and Spirit. When the Arian crisis blew up in the early fourth century, almost a century after Origen's death, it turned around this enduring problematic in his theological system. He had taught the eternal deity of the Son, and the current bishop of Alexandria, Alexander, and his deacon Athanasius stressed that this was the most important aspect of what Origen had to say. If the Son was divine, then he was completely divine, divinity allowing no degrees, and was thus "God of God, light of light, true God of true God." But we must remember that this clarity was available only after the Council of Nicaea established it in its creed to refute Arianism.

Arius, however, an Origenian disciple of sorts, leaned more heavily on Origen's statements that the Son was somehow less than the Father and could not be confused with God, if the concept of God was taken absolutely. Arius saw the Logos as something like a superior angel of God, but not divine in the full sense of that term: a second-class kind of god. So both sides of the Arian dispute were taking different parts of Origen's more ancient Christology and laying different stresses on them. At the Council of Nicaea in 325, the Western theologian Hosius of Cordoba advised Emperor Constantine that the phrase "*Homoousios* [co-natural] with the Father" could be used as a blunt instrument to refute and expose Arians, and so it was adopted into the Nicene Creed. Alexander and Athanasius agreed to this, mainly because it flushed out Arian dissidents, though they preferred the more precise phrase *tautotes tes ousias* (the Son has an identity of essence with the Father), and this because their articulation avoided the problems of ascribing *ousia* ("material form" in some understandings of the word) to the wholly immaterial godhead (a doctrine of Origen's they wished to defend).

At the time of Nicaea, the leading theologian bishop of the Origenian school was Eusebius of Caesarea. He mocked the Nicene *Homoousion*, precisely on the grounds that it flew in the face of Origen's hard-won insistence that God is totally incorporeal. To put into a key clause of the creed that he was of the same substance, or "stuff," as God the Father to him was simply ridiculous. However, in those days (as today!) such precision of theological nicety could often be misread—and Eusebius's unease with the Nicene Creed was widely taken by the Nicene party as proof that he was a closet Arian who was attacking the divinity of the Word. When all the dust of battle had subsided by the beginning of the fifth century, there remained a lingering taste in the air that "Origenism" leaned to the side of Arianism, and so he was tainted by what Arius had said. This was a very anachronistic position to hold, but then again it was a fairly widespread sentiment among many bishops who were suspicious of "clever theologians." Saints Gregory of Nazianzus and Basil of Caesarea (later to be called Gregory the Theologian and Basil the Great) both deliberately collaborated at this time to produce an anthology of "the best of Origen," which would be called *The Philokalia of Origen*. This was meant to serve both as a rehabilitation of their mentor's reputation as a strong defender of the eternal divinity of the Word and as a handbook to introduce the basic principles of his exegesis to future generations of bishop-preachers. On the strength of their joint reputations as great fathers in later generations of the church, Origen's influence survived this first test.

Origen's broader core of significant followers (the longer list of great saints named earlier) had to work hard to make the case that this association of Origen with Arianism was unfair and inaccurate. In the end they managed to do it largely by incorporating the best of his thought into their own works, though in the process they tended to "piecemeal" the coherence Origen himself thought he had constructed. Instead of a great systematic stretching from "first principles" of creation to the final eschaton, Origen's works became a stone quarry where significant theologians came to chip away blocks of various size to incorporate into other architectural plans.

Origen's very strong insistence that God is wholly spiritual and totally immaterial earned him the enmity of many of the very simple monks of the desert, men who read their Bible in very limited ways and took it very literally, so that when it spoke of God's anger it just meant God was angry and needed appeasing quickly. There is still a marked tension within the churches even to this day between those who take the biblical authority as a set of literal instructions and those who read it as a complex of poetic, historical, and prophetic symbols. Origen's taking head-on issue with literalism is a battle still very much present.

His insistence on reading all things for the higher spiritual sense also made him tend to treat the scriptures as sacramentally more important than the eucharist. Origen once berated his congregation in Caesarea for being very scrupulous in making sure they dropped no crumb of the eucharistic bread to the floor while communicating, but at the same time being more than careless in listening to his exposition of the scriptures. We presume some wandered off during the sermon and others were shuffling and talking at the back of church. Did they not understand, he said, that communion with the Word took place just as much when the sacred scripture was heard as when the eucharist was consumed?[39] To take the words of Jesus, "Unless you eat the flesh of the Son of Man and drink his blood, you have no life in you," in a deeply literal way, he argued, was the worst way of approaching the scripture with a "literalism that could kill the spirit."[40] At the time, this must have disturbed many of the "simpler believers" in Caesarea where he was the priest, especially if we work on the premise that then (as now) they were the majority in the church. He gave this opinion in several asides rather than in any formal doctrinal statement, but it would rise up once more in the time of Reformation eucharistic disputes.[41]

At that stage it was part of an argument that had been running on since Carolingian times: should Christians observe a "realist" doctrine of the eucharistic sacrament or a "symbolist" one? This transposes Origen's argument into a very anachronistic context. In fact, Origen was not as far away from the belief of the simple folk of his church as he seemed in his criticism. He simply wished the faithful to have as much reverence for the scripture readings and expositions as they did for the reverent consumption of the eucharistic elements (which he took for granted as a right and proper thing). In his own mind, as a philosopher-theologian, Origen believed passionately that a symbolic sign was actually more real than a material sign, but it was a stance ordinary folk did not share with the same passion. Even so, many of Origen's critics have found him to be less than satisfactory in terms of understanding the material potency of the sacraments as a logical corollary of the incarnation. Patristic thought after him would make up for this deficit. Perhaps it was a weakness brought into Origen's system because he introduced a distinction between the Logos and Jesus when it came to incarnational thought?

One last aspect of controversy he introduced was the manner in which he regarded all authority within the church as conditioned on the spiritual sensibility of the one who presumed to claim it. For him the true priests of the Christian church were not those who claimed to have ordained status in the ranks of hierarchy and, because of their rank (presbyters or bishops), demanded that they alone should have the right to teach theology to the faithful. Origen's starting point here is that only those who have been initiated by the Logos and the Spirit have the right to teach about God. They do so by their (divinely) illuminated wisdom and especially by their lives of evident holiness. Without such wisdom and devoid of this holiness they are clearly not "priests of the Most High" and should be quiet. This was clearly and inevitably, *ab initio*, going to raise the ire of a bishop, and in the case of his own early hierarch, Demetrios of Alexandria, a man highly conscious of his rights and privileges, it led to a bitter and damaging rivalry. Origen obviously claimed the right to teach in the church, despite all Demetrios's attempts to silence him, because of his innate wisdom and his ascetic lifestyle. He sensed in himself the deep gift of the Spirit. Many bishops around him he did not rate highly. He was one of the very first (Hippolytus of Rome was another) of those Christian theologians who clashed with institutional church authorities as represented by the orders of the hierarchy claiming authority to teach by virtue of their "office." He may have been the first—he would certainly not be the last.[42] For this he has earned scorn in no small degree, perhaps from significantly smaller minds. True to add, however, he has also been the darling of some of the church's greatest bishop-theologians across the ages.

NOTES

1. Origen, *Homilies on Ezekiel* 6.6: "The Father himself, God of all the universe, is 'long-suffering and full of mercy and pity' [Ps. 86:15]. Must he not, therefore, be open to suffering? So you must realize that in dealing with Mankind he suffers the passions of humans: 'For the Lord God supports your ways even as a man supports his own son' [Deut. 1:31]."

2. Origen, *Homilies on Ezekiel* 6.6: "The Saviour came down to earth out of pity for human kind and deigned to assume our flesh, and endured his passion and sorrows before he suffered on the cross, for without sufferings he would not have entered into full participation in human life . . . . And what is that passion which he suffered for us? It is the passion of love."

3. Origen, *Select Commentaries on the Psalms* 1.2.

4. Gregory Nazianzen, *Oration* 27.

5. Aristotle, *Metaphysica* 1.9.982b, 18f.

6. Origen, *Series Commentary on Matthew* 38 and 46; *Commentary on Matthew* 1.7.33; *Homilies on Ezekiel* 2.2; *Homilies on First Kings* 1.13; *Commentary on Romans* 5.1.

7. Once again, his disciple St. Gregory the Theologian summarized it in the axiom, "Faith, in fact, is what gives fullness to our reasoning" (Gregory Nazianzen, *Oration* 29.21).

8. Origen, *On First Principles* 1.7.

9. Gregory Thaumaturgos, *Epistle to Origen* 1–2.

10. Origen, *Against Celsus* 5.23.

11. Origen, *On First Principles* 1.1.1–4, 3.6.1f.

12. Origen, *On First Principles* 1.1.8, 2.4.3; *Commentary on John* 19.146.

13. Origen, *On First Principles* 1.1.9.

14. Origen, *Commentary on John* 2.172; *Against Celsus* 6.17.

15. See Plato, *Symposium* 210a–212a; Albinus, *Epitome* 10.5–6. One begins by contemplating materially beautiful objects, then ascends by means of increasing abstractions to the concept of Beauty itself, and thus to the Good.

16. Origen, *Commentary on John* 19.35–39.

17. Col. 1:15; Origen, *Against Celsus* 7.42–44, 6.17.69; *Homilies on Luke* 3.1.

18. "If you knew me you would know my Father also": Origen, *Commentary on John* 19.39.

19. Origen, *On First Principles* 1.1.6; *Against Celsus* 7.38.

20. Origen, *Commentary on John* 1.119; *Against Celsus* 7.38.

21. Using Wisd. 7:26; Origen, *On First Principles* 1.2.13; *Commentary on John* 13.151–153, 254.

22. Here based on Mark 10:18. Origen, *On First Principles* 1.2.13; *Commentary on John* 1.254.

23. Origen, *Commentary on John* 1.151.

24. Origen, *Commentary on John* 2.95–96.

25. Origen, *On First Principles* 3.6.7; c.f. Philo, *De Mundi Opificio* 16–37; Plato, *Phaedrus* 79A–B.

26. Origen, *On First Principles* 1.4.3–5, 2.1.1.

27. Gen. 1:6–10. Origen, *Against Celsus* 6.50–51; *Commentary on Genesis* 1.2.

28. Origen, *Commentary on John* 1.216.

29. Origen's Christology was complex in that he envisaged Jesus not as personally synonymous with the Logos (this would be the hypostatic synodical Christology of the late fourth century) but rather as one of the original *noes*—created souls—who first attended the divine Logos before the making of the present material world, and who did not fall along with other *noes* (including all mortal humanity in the end) but in fact grew closer and closer to the Logos so as to become "one soul" with him. It was the choice of the great soul Jesus to be incarnated for the sake of salvation that allowed the Logos to descend with him to earth, using him as his spiritual vehicle and medium. It was this Christology that chiefly damaged Origen's reputation in the fourth century when the Nicene theologians were articulating their refutation of Arianism's subordinationist theology.

30. This is because he is predominantly influenced by Paul's eschatological conception in 1 Corinthians that God's will for the goodness and beauty of creation can never be ultimately frustrated, and so there must be a return to wholeness as part of the eschaton.

31. Throughout *Peri Archon* 1–2 and *Commentary on John* 1.92, for example; or the making of satiated souls to fit a material world, in *Peri Archon* 2.8.3, 1.3.8, and 1.4.1, compared with *Homilies on Gen*esis 1.13 and *Commentary on John* 1.95; or the lack of attentive contemplation leading to the fall of *noes* to lower states of communion, in *Homilies on Exodus* 6.4 and *Homilies on Jeremiah* 12.2–6, 28.1.

32. Origen lays out this threefold system in *On First Principles* 4.2.4. He does not always follow it to the letter himself.

33. See the masterly work of K. Torjesen, *Hermeneutical Procedure and Theological Method in Origen's Exegesis* (Berlin: De Gruyter, 1986).

34. Song 1:2–4.

35. Origen, *Commentary on the Song of Songs* 7.

36. See Phil. 2:6–11.

37. A new defense of the old issue has been recently mounted by D. Bentley Hart, *That All Shall Be Saved: Heaven, Hell, and Universal Salvation* (New Haven, CT: Yale University Press, 2019). Ilaria Ramelli's fine study *The Christian Doctrine of Apokatastasis* (Leiden: Brill, 2013) presents all the patristic evidence, with special reference to Origen and his influence throughout history on this matter.

38. Origen, *On First Principles* 2.9.2–8.

39. Origen, *Homilies on Exodus* 13.3.
40. *Origen, Homilies on Leviticus* 7.5.
41. See L. Lies, *Wort und Eucharistie bei Origenes: Zur spiritualisierungstenden des Eucharistieverstandnisses* (Innsbruck: Tyrolia-Verlag, 1978).
42. See McGuckin, "Origen's Doctrine of the Priesthood."

PART TWO
Origen's Contested Legacy

Chapter 3

Prolegomena

In his lively study of Origen, Joseph Trigg reflects in this way on the long-term legacy that Origen achieved within Christianity: "The inclusiveness of Origen's interests, the extent of his accomplishments, the coherence of his thought, the breadth of his influence, and the intensity of the controversy that has continued to surround him, make Origen a figure of unquestionably great historical importance."[1] This section of our study will now consider the main features of that legacy. As Trigg points out, it is a legacy that almost at every stage has involved controversy among the successive generations of the church. For his massive biblical achievement, bringing scriptural commentary into the forefront of all subsequent theological method, Origen achieves the rank of one of the greatest of all Christian thinkers. And yet his method of symbolic interpretation was felt by many to be a system that departed too much from historical contexts and meanings. For his laying down of the architecture of Christian dogmatics on God, Christ, and the Holy Spirit, his achievement is equally profound. Yet in each case the later Christian generations had major qualifications to make on, and at times bitter contestations to advance against, his literal propositions.

Adopting an architecture and yet reacting against it can leave a strange sense of disorientation on the ground. I felt something of the same thing once when touring the great church of Hagia Sophia in Istanbul (the ancient Christian capital of Constantinople). As Justinian's impressive Christian basilica, it was orientated toward Jerusalem, and the whole building leads one to move to the focal point of the easternmost apsidal bay, where once the great silver altar stood. After the fall of the city to the Ottomans in 1453, the church became the mosque of Sultan Mehmet II, and at that point the Islamic Mihrab was introduced, reorienting the worshipers' focal attention away from due east and toward Mecca.[2] The several degrees of reorientation that this involved are, architecturally speaking, quite jarring when one stands in the eastern end.

So it is with the history of Christian theology. One can often sense Origen's presence very strongly in major intellectual matters, and yet equally sense the shock waves of major departures from viewpoints that were caused by sharp reactions to some of his propositions as they were fought over in later disputes. In one sense (as at Hagia Sophia), the radical departure from a prior architecture is as much a testament to indebtedness as a close obedience to it. So whether Origen's ideas lasted or were thrown out by later Christianity, he still matters. We remember how St. Gregory Nazianzen called him "the sharpening stone of us all,"[3] and in another image (one that recognizes that all were not disciples as devoted as Gregory) he might well be called "the spoon that stirred everyone." He definitely stirred up everything, in his own lifetime and afterward.

In this second part of the book I would like to discuss some of that contested legacy in greater detail: how it was that Origen "mapped out the tradition" for later generations of the church. To organize this topic in a succinct way, I will divide the treatment into four parts, covering chapters 3 to 6, the first two dealing with his contested legacy in antiquity, and the latter two considering first his late medieval and early modern reception and then his modern reevaluation from the eighteenth century through the present day.

ORIGEN'S DISCIPLES AND IMMEDIATE SUCCESSORS

Origen's First Followers

Many of Origen's first disciples have not left a literary record behind them, for the simple reason they were martyred. So many of his elite private students were executed as Christians during the time of persecution, each time being accompanied to the platform where they were beheaded (as befitted their rank) by their teacher, Origen himself, that the crowd started to whistle and boo him whenever he appeared. His own lack of noble birth (his father had citizen status; he, as a result of a mixed marriage outside the class of *nobiliores*, did not) made him legally unfit for the capital sentence that had been laid only against those of higher birth who had converted to the church.

Eusebius records the names of several of those first disciples who were martyred. Two brothers, Plutarch and Heraclas, moved across to Origen after spending five years previously studying with Ammonius Saccas, the renowned neo-Platonist.[4] Plutarch was martyred while Origen stood by him to give him courage. Heraclas survived and joined Origen as his assistant, later supplanting him in the favors of the bishop Demetrios when Origen moved to Caesarea and assuming the episcopal throne at Alexandria himself after Demetrios's death. Eusebius records that in his own career he became "greatly distinguished in philosophy and other Greek learning."[5] The city prefect eventually posted guards of soldiers around Origen's lodgings in order to stop any new subscriptions to his classes.[6] Even so, no less than seven of his class were executed for adherence to the faith, or, as Eusebius describes them, "who were arrested and then perfected by martyrdom."[7] He lists them as Plutarch; Serenus, who was burned and "who through fire gave proof of the faith he had received"[8]; Heraclides the catechumen and Hero the newly baptized, who were both beheaded; another Serenus, who was beheaded after enduring great tortures; and two women disciples, Herais the catechumen and Potaimiaena, whom Eusebius describes as being "in the full bloom of her youthful beauty, both in body and in mind."[9] Dionysios was also a student of his in Alexandria and stayed in the city after Origen left for Caesarea. In his turn, Dionysios achieved a great reputation for learning and eventually succeeded Heraclas as bishop. He never forgot his first master, and when news came that Origen had himself been arrested in Caesarea during the Decian persecution and sentenced to torture,[10] Dionysios composed for his benefit his treatise *Exhortation to Martyrdom*. While we have no surviving works from his hands, we also have to remember Ambrose and his wife, Tatiana, two immensely wealthy Alexandrian Christians. Origen had converted Ambrose from the Valentinian gnostic community, and Ambrose supported his ministry in both Alexandria and Caesarea, paying for multiple stenographers to take down his drafts of the *Peri Archon* as well as commissioning several other works from him, most notably the *Commentary on the Gospel of John*.[11] Origen was as devoted to Ambrose as Ambrose was to his teacher. Jerome later elevated their friendship and common rule of life together as a perfect model of spiritual friendship: "They never took a meal together without having something read aloud, and never went to bed until some portion of the scripture had been brought home to them by a brother's voice. Night and day were so organized that prayer only gave way to reading and reading only gave way to prayer."[12]

The University School at Caesarea

To found a school, a purely Christian *schola*, had been a sense of mission that burned in Origen from the time he grew up in Alexandria and saw what prestige the philosophical and literary schools enjoyed, clustered around the world-class project of the Great Library at Alexandria. Theirs was not merely the mission to collect every significant book ever produced (the librarians, we remember, forced every incoming ship or camel caravan to hand over any copies of literature they possessed—for purposes of copying); they also wanted to create the world's greatest gathering of scholars and make definitive commentaries on the classical (and sacred) texts. Origen too wanted to build a library and gather a community of scholars around it (and around himself—as "head of school").[13] His friction with Bishop Demetrios of Alexandria clearly made that city an unlikely home base in which to build the dream. The Alexandrian hierarch was set on a path that would make the episcopal claim to occupy the "head of school" not based on philosophical or rhetorical acumen but on the fact of institutional ordination as *episcopos*. When, in his Old Testament exegeses, Origen turns his attention toward the idea of priesthood, he is withering about the merits of this claim, concluding that God recognizes priests who are filled with wisdom and grace, not simply those who occupy offices and exercise power.[14] For him it is the charismatic grace that allows someone to "speak for" the church. So when Bishops Alexander and Theoctist of Palestine invited him to come and work in their territories, the two chief cities of Caesarea Maritima[15] and Jerusalem, he jumped at the chance.

We know from surviving records that he soon became an acknowledged church expert, being called in by the bishops to speak at local synods and settle conflicts over theology and pastoral practice. He was also invited by the bishop to preach regularly at the midweek liturgical assemblies,[16] and there he interpreted the scriptures more generally than he did in his own school. The latter we would today regard as a private higher educational establishment, chiefly inhabited by the wealthy who paid for instruction in rhetoric and philosophy. One of those was the later apostle of Cappadocia, St. Gregory Thaumaturgos, who made Origen's fame renowned in the church of Cappadocia, as we shall shortly see. Before he adopted his episcopal name of Gregory, he was known as Theodore. Son of a wealthy Christian family, Theodore came to Caesarea, with his brother, looking for a good school. In a surviving "graduation homily,"[17] he gives thanks for having found Origen as the best of teachers and offers us a short record of the broad curriculum over which Origen presided: rhetoric, cosmology, literature, but above all the significance of the sacred scriptures and how they were to be read as the guide to life.[18] Theodore gives us an interesting window onto Origen's character as a teacher. He says that as a young man it must have been his guardian angel who led him to Origen, "a man possessed of a rare combination of a certain sweet and graceful persuasiveness, allied to a strange and compelling power." He adds that his first meeting made him feel as if "some spark had fallen alight into the depth of my soul."[19]

While Origen was alive and teaching in Caesarea, the rabbinical school, also based there, was beginning the slow transformation of Judaism from a temple-sacrifice-based religion to the modern form of scripture-focused rabbinic Judaism.[20] The two schools, the rabbinic center and Origen's academy, were thus set in a highly productive rivalry, each claiming to be the authentic inheritor of the traditions of ancient Judaism, each claiming to have the correct "key" to the inner mysteries of the scriptural text and its enduring message for contemporary society.

Origen's *schola* building seems, originally, to have been located near the Augustus temple in the town center, a venue that also served as a town library.[21] We know from Origen's surviving fragments of letters to friends that while he was based in Caesarea he went on several book-buying trips: at least one to Athens, and one to Jericho, where he seems to have purchased one of the jars with ancient versions of scripture within it that had turned up (undoubtedly) from the Qumran caves that would only be rediscovered in the mid-twentieth century. This he used in compiling his monumental and multicolumned version of biblical editions known as the *Hexapla*. His gathering together of a library at the heart of his school was the first known instance of a purely Christian academy of higher learning, what today we would call a university college. Origen saw this foundation as part of the essential mission of the church in the world, the dissemination of wisdom being synonymous with the *kerygma* (proclamation) of the gospel of the incarnate Logos.

Those who came after him continued his academic work, and up to the late fourth century Caesarea Maritima was led by a series of highly scholarly bishops who continued to amplify the library and built Caesarea's reputation as the most learned Christian city in the world. Its scriptorium became legendary, and when Constantine the Great wanted pandects[22] for his newly built churches, it was to Caesarea that he gave the commission.

One of the first great devotees of Origen at Caesarea was Pamphilus (d. 310). Eusebius, the later bishop of Caesarea and great church historian, was a dedicated disciple of his, and tells of his life and martyrdom in his book *The Martyrs of Palestine*. Pamphilus was an aristocratic scholar born in Beirut who moved to study in Alexandria under the priest-theologian and scholar Pierius.[23] Pierius was a renowned biblical preacher and ascetic in his own time, devoted to the work and memory of Origen and using it and popularizing it extensively. Bishop Agapius of Caesarea then invited Pamphilus to come as a priest to his diocese in Palestine and take up the mission there of reinvigorating the school and library of Origen. While developing the school, he also opened a scribal bureau of copyists at Caesarea and began the dissemination of texts of scripture to the churches, as well as making copies of important theological literature. Chief among these book-publishing exercises must have been the dissemination in a far wider range of the writings of Origen himself.

Pamphilus followed Origen in seeing the scriptures as a guide to mystical union with the incarnate Word and set this as the first distinguishing mark of an "Origenian" approach to theology, moving his influence, as it were, further out from his actual text and into a style of theologizing spirituality. The persecution under Maximinus Daia was especially bitter in Palestine. Pamphilus was arrested in November 307 and held in prison until his execution, by decapitation, in February 310. Pierius and Eusebius immediately wrote two separate biographies of the martyr, unfortunately now lost, though Eusebius's references to him in the *Martyrs of Palestine* and in the *Ecclesiastical History* survive.

During his two years of imprisonment, Pamphilus reviewed the state of the church under immense stress and concluded that one of the worst threats was not the violence of the emperors but the intellectual laziness of the senior hierarchs, manifested, as far as he was concerned, in the very careless conclusion that since several Arians had used Origen's works in the aftermath of Nicaea to fight against the Nicene movement, then all the work of Origen had been exposed as heterodox. Bringing to his side his disciple Eusebius (shortly to be elected bishop of Caesarea), the two set to work to compose an extensive *Apologia for the Cause of Origen*. It was to be in six books. Pamphilus did not live to compete the sixth, though Eusebius finished it.[24] Unfortunately, only book one of the work has survived, in a Latin translation made by the Origenian scholar Rufinus.[25]

Pamphilus dedicated this work to the confessors, those Christians of his church who had not been executed but sent, instead, to work as slaves in the terrible ore mines (*damnatio ad metalla*). It is one indication how he felt that this intellectual labor was not an effete ivory-tower exercise in academic theology, but rather a serious fight to secure the deep and experiential theology of the gospel that was in danger of being diluted by a creeping anti-intellectual attitude. For Pamphilus, Origen was a prophetic interpreter of the mystical path to union with Christ, and if one did not understand the relationship of theology to the spiritual life, mediated through the close reading of scripture, then the whole inner balance and energy of Christianity stood in danger of being dulled down and rendered sterile.

In his *Apology*,[26] Pamphilus set out the first considered response to two critical questions about Origen's posthumous reputation, both of which needed to be addressed with urgency. The first was why Origen could not be quoted in every instance as a clear example of the core teaching (*dogma*) of the church; the second was why this did not render him useless—and, following from this, why he remained of enduring importance for the church's theological tradition. Almost all the greater Greek Fathers of the Church who continued to defend Origen, following after Pamphilus, more or less repeated the arguments of the *Apologia*. When the West rediscovered Origen in the early modern period, Pamphilus's arguments were recirculated by the likes of Pico della Mirandola, the Renaissance publisher Merlin, and Erasmus of Rotterdam and so had a second large impact.

The writings of Origen's lesser-known advocates from this time have been lost, but Photius, the ninth-century theologian bibliophile, tells us that they were many.[27] It was their collective reputation for saintly wisdom, as martyrs, confessors, and great hierarchs, that managed to save Origen's legacy through, and even after, a series of synodical condemnations in the later centuries. Pamphilus gave the reader a method for approaching Origen. He explains (very insightfully) that the way Origen theologized was part of the ancient academy's style of learning: by means of setting out hypothesis and antithesis to the students so that they could get to the core of the wider issues involved. This method that the earliest Christian theologians adopted from the Hellenistic academies set out to give students tools of logic rather than notes that they had to reproduce and learn by heart. By having to work out the problematic from the present puzzle (*aporia*) offered to them by their teacher, the class would be enabled, by the end of their education (so it was hoped), to solve all other similar problems themselves in later life.

This was a very important point to make for his generation, because at the time Pamphilus was writing, the Christian church was fast moving away from that (relatively brief) moment it had shared in the zeitgeist of Late Antique philosophy. The time in which the great churches such as Rome and Alexandria had scholars they looked toward, to match and emulate the pagan teachers in the philosophical schools, was coming to an end, and the church was entering an era where the Christian bishops were generally less educated and increasingly more suspicious of the intelligentsia, who thought Greek philosophy was a useful tool for elucidating Christian thinking and sacred literature.

By the end of the fourth century, Gregory of Nazianzus, who was devoted to Origen's work and who was also one of the most learned men of his generation, lamented bitterly (and with scathing satire) the generally poor level of education that he witnessed among the episcopal class. Gregory was really one of the last of a group of earlier hierarchs who, in a period stretching from the third through to the mid-fourth century, mostly shared the same formative history of education: a study of the *progymnasmata*, where texts would be used to set out *problemata* to the class as exercises they were expected to resolve by discussion—even by argument and debate—as open questions.

By the end of the Arian crisis, in the late fourth century, and largely because of it, theology was no longer regarded as a suitable topic for approach as a set of aporias. So, in a sense, Pamphilus is appealing for some leeway to be given to Origen as an antique teacher in a new (less tolerant because more public) environment. As well as explaining why the older theological method was "different" in his own age, Pamphilus is also sounding a note of warning that this relative "closing of the mind" among the clerical elites spelled troubles for the future. What they wanted was no longer consideration of issues but rather certainty of a dogma proclaimed with unarguable force.

Pamphilus points out, therefore, that Origen often set out a teaching and then offered, alongside it, a contrary view. Since he wanted his advanced pupils then to worry it all through in a seminar setting, he often did not bother to resolve the dichotomy he had set up by pointing out clashes and contradictions in the biblical database. In his magisterial *Commentary on John*, for example, as his treatment goes on, he more and more stops filling in the conclusion to arguments, expecting his students (or readers) to be able to do this for themselves. Arriving at the account of the Mystical (or Last) Supper, he tells his readers, more or less, "I have done enough now," and he abruptly concludes.[28] This use of open-ended aporia or demonstration of method as a didactic device can often lead him to leave arguments hanging. So, for example, in his writings he can both teach the uncreated status of the Holy Spirit and the created status of the Spirit. How can that be done without inconsistency? Well, in the one instance (in the *De Principiis*, where he is talking about the apostolic tradition and its teachings), he considers the Spirit's work of sanctification and deification among the faithful, and concludes that he cannot deify others if he is not of divine status himself. In the second case, he considers the opening of the Gospel of John where it says, "All things came to be through him" (the Logos), and asks whether this means that even the Spirit came into being through the creative work of the divine Son. This was setting out both the hypothesis and the antithesis. Theologians of later centuries who were arguing passionately over the divine or nondivine status of the Spirit (namely, the late fourth century) could not bear this method that took uncertainty and ambivalence as its very starting point. It wanted to go straight to the answer. Of course, that meant that some of Origen's readers concluded that he was an early witness for the divinity of the Spirit, while others pointed to another set of texts and concluded, rather, that he was "on their side" and against it. Since the different sides were so bitterly divided in the Arian crisis (not just over the Spirit but also over the status of the Logos), Origen tended to have massively devoted followers on the one hand and passionate enemies on the other, with only a few (generally those who were much more educated) arguing for a more moderated understanding of the history of Christian tradition.

Pamphilus made the case that Origen had to be taken as a guide, not as a dogmatician, but that what he had to offer the church (his profound biblical sensitivity, his deep mystical and spiritual doctrine, and his all-encompassing sense of God's salvation in Christ) was far too important to pass over or, even worse, to jettison outright. All in all, Pamphilus argued, Origen was deeply attached to the orthodox tradition (as his structure of the *De Principiis* showed, and as he himself had stated time after time), and in cases of doubt, the wider tradition (*paradosis*) of the church had to be followed obediently.

To underscore his point, Pamphilus then offered a series of texts where, passage by passage, he addressed head-on the charges that Origen taught heretical things about the Trinity, the Incarnation, the historicity of scripture, the nature of the soul, the possibility of reincarnation, the issue of whether punishment after death was everlasting, and the state of the risen body. All these precise arguments that he raises were the equally specific objections that his contemporaries had so far raised as evidence that Origen was heretical. This caucus of Origen's opponents in the third and fourth centuries comprised Methodius of Olympus, Peter of Alexandria, and Eustathius of Antioch. The focus of the unrest with Origen's theology to date had centered on a core nexus of ideas: questions Origen had raised about the soul's possible existence before its earthly appearance, whether the end of all things would mirror the beginning (the doctrine of *apokatastasis*), the nature of the risen body (would it be material or immaterial?), and whether the creation was eternally open-ended. Once all these thoughts had been prized out of the larger context of Origen's questioning and set up on their own terms, as it were, and treated moreover as if they were indeed what Origen was dogmatically asserting, it was inevitable that the wider Christian tradition set them aside as having no solid scriptural foundation, and thus as "heretical ideas." It was a small circular step then to decide that these were the heretical ideas propagated by Origen—simply because he had discussed them—and thus, in a leap of bent logic, that Origen must therefore have been a heretic.

Jerome, once a dedicated follower who later was one of those who publicly wished to consign the writings of Origen to the shredder (though he is now proven to have continued to use the writings "very heavily" from his own secret copies even when overtly denouncing him), was so annoyed by Pamphilus's arguments, and the spiritual and intellectual status the latter had for making them, that he widely spread the opinion that the *Apology for Origen* was not his work at all but rather that of the "crypto-Arian"[29] Eusebius of Caesarea. It is now established that only the sixth and last book had been penned by Eusebius, but Jerome's attitude shows the turn away from serious intellectual debate and toward arguments from authority, which often verged into arguments that turned on who shouted the loudest or who could cast more aspersions on character than another.

After Pamphilus's execution as a martyr, the Origen school at Caesarea was at a high-water mark in terms of reputation. The learned cleric Eusebius (c. 260–340) became the bishop and head of school in around 314. Eusebius was passionately devoted to the memory both of Origen and of Pamphilus. He even adopted the latter's name as part of his own title, being known as Eusebius Pamphili (Pamphilus's son, Eusebius). Eusebius was regarded as one of most learned men of his generation, skilled in both biblical and dogmatic theology, and was destined to become a significant player in the debates surrounding the great Arian crisis that consumed much of the fourth century. The emperor Constantine rated him very highly indeed, and in many respects Eusebius served as a kind of Christian court rhetorician, providing encomiastic texts in praise of the emperor's Christian virtues. For this he has earned the opprobrium of generations of Reformation divines who regard him as one of the first great sellouts to the "imperialization" of the church. In his defense it ought to be said that his rhetoric is typical of how people of this era addressed emperors—to their face at least—and after having experienced several generations of bitter and bloody persecutions (during the last of which he lost many of his closest friends to the violence of nasty political oppressors), the advent of Constantine (the toleration, financial reparations, and advancement of the bishops as magistrates that he orchestrated) must have seemed like a God-sent miracle to most Christians of Eusebius's generation. The emperor rewarded his loyalty by the rise in prestige that attended the school and diocese of Caesarea, and by offering support to the institution as an organizing center of church operations in Syria, where it matched Antioch and Alexandria for a brief time. Eusebius was regarded as an "expert" voice to be heard in the synods that started to accumulate after Constantine's *vicennalia*[30] in 325.

The Arian crisis that exploded at this time became so intractable partly because the emperors tried to use the synodical system to resolve it. Provincial synods had been held since the middle of the second century at least as a way of resolving Christian disputes that had a more than local significance. With the Arian dispute, turning as it did over very significant questions of the divine, or less-than-fully-divine, status of the Son of God, Emperor Constantine took the counsel of his ecclesiastical advisor Hosius of Cordoba and tried to resolve the argument by airing the whole matter (at first it had only seemed to be a falling out over obscure theological issues between Alexander of Alexandria and one of his learned clerics) at a series of province-wide synods. Eventually, because the conflict seemed to deepen and grow even more divisive, he used the occasion of his imperial anniversary in 325 to call the largest convocation of Christian bishops ever seen, to his palace at Nicaea. When they arrived here, Hosius and the Alexandrian theologians (Alexander and Athanasius) were content to use the word *Homoousion* (consubstantial or co-essential) as an adjective added to the profession of faith, in order to sideline Arian sentiments that the Son of God was not eternal and not "properly speaking" divine as the Father was. But when Eusebius of Caesarea came to the council, he came as someone who had already been censured by an earlier synod for heterodox beliefs, and he had to spend a lot of the time less in arguing the broader theological case and more in trying to save his reputation and remove the penalties imposed on him. It was at the Nicene council that Eusebius more or less gambled away most of the prestige that had formerly attached to his school as a center of theological refinement. Here, and for years afterward until time of his death, the "Nicene" party, supporting the consubstantiality of the Son, regarded "the Eusebians" as more or less Arian in spirit.

Eusebius, being devoted to the memory of Origen, had claimed to be the living spokesperson for what Origen really meant, but in fact he interpreted the third century theologian in a rather wooden and reductionist way. He had taken syllogisms out from Origen's works and advanced them into dogmas, when Origen himself had predominantly offered them as discussion points. Disastrously, as far as the Nicenes were concerned, Eusebius had insisted on the subordinate, or lesser, divine status of the Son (a subordinationist trend of pre-fourth-century Trinitarian thought that was still strong in Origen but was in the course of being set aside in later theology since divine status can admit of no degree), and adding to this position, he also claimed that Origen had taught that the Spirit was not God (overlooking those places where he clearly taught he was unquestionably divine in character). Athanasius of Alexandria's classification of him and his teaching as "the Eusebians," who were part of the Arian cause, led to his reputation being clouded over in a very significant way, and along with Eusebius, the cloud of suspicion over crypto-Arianism overshadowed Origen's memory too, to no small degree because Eusebius had publicly identified his very narrow and dogmatic "Origenism"[31] as the authentic article, which in no sense of the word it was.

But Eusebius was much more than a dogmatician. His positive reputation in his own lifetime (and beyond as history would show) was as an exegete and a historian. He is in fact the first truly great historian the Christian church produced, and his monumentally important *Church History* provided the paradigm for almost all Church history texts and manuals that were to be written for the next two millennia.

Church historians today often find much to fault in Eusebius: they object to the manner of his value judgments, to the way he writes history with the main emphasis being on "the good versus the bad." But this is what he learned not only from his classical Greek predecessors (history is the account of one's people's "honor") but more so from the entirety of the Hebrew scriptures, where the covenant's development and progress is described (as, for example, in 1 and 2 Kings) as being advanced by the good and hindered by the wicked, but all the while moved by God's overarching hand. In other words, Eusebius wrote his *Church History* as an extension of salvation history, following Old Testament paradigms and also the example of St. Luke in his Acts of the Apostles. He had the historian's instinct to put down in print many of his sources, and since these (often primary documents in his Caesarean library for him to consult at leisure) have otherwise largely disappeared from the record, Eusebius's writing is irreplaceable, and still a gripping read to this day.

So right from the start this *Church History* became a major event in the church. And within it Eusebius devoted all of chapter 6 to the praises of his hero Origen. However much, in later times, Origen might be attacked and discounted for some of his theories (undoubtedly heterodox by later standards), there was always this chapter in one of the church's "most read" books that praised him to the skies, as the church's greatest exegete, its noblest theologian, its cleverest thinker, and one of its most holy members. This, when added to the also known fact that most of the church's greatest saints who were also intelligent thinkers themselves felt the same way about Origen, conspired to preserve his work and his saintly memory even though he was posthumously condemned by emperors, synods, and popes alike.[32]

In one sense Eusebius's chapter 6 of the *Church History* did much to repair the damage he himself had done to his hero's reputation by claiming that Origen would never have approved of the *Homoousion*. Of course, this latter complaint was hopelessly anachronistic. Origen's point on this topic was that applying material terms such as *substance*, *shape*, or *size* to the purely spiritual divinity was bad theology. What the fourth-century *Homoousion* was really arguing was that the Son of God was eternal and possessed the selfsame divinity of the Father, not that the Son was "made of the same stuff" as the Father. Eusebius was incorrect in using Origen as an authority against the Nicene movement. Indeed, Athanasius and Alexander were both able to employ Origen in their own positive theology because of his arguments that the Son was indeed eternal and uncreated.

Athanasius undoubtedly admired Origen's character and works, selecting the most favorable aspects of the whole system in accordance with Nicene orthodoxy—not anachronistically, as much as this was his testimony to the orthodox spirit of Origen, who had always maintained that he wrote only in defense of the church's evangelical tradition. Athanasius described him as "that labor-loving Origen" (*tou philoponou Origenous*). He quotes him several times in his *Defence of the Nicene Definition* as an important witness of the faith.[33] This support Athanasius offered, along with that of other notable scholar-saints such as Gregory Thaumaturgos, Pamphilus, Macrina, Basil the Great, Gregory the Theologian, Gregory of Nyssa, and Theotimos of Scythia,[34] is a major reason the later historian Socrates Scholastikos is scandalized by the manner in which later bishops (especially Epiphanius of Salamis) have tried to censure the great confessor's name and writings posthumously, as if he were some heretical thinker.[35] If Athanasius and other major saints of the church regard him with respect and reverence, then condemnation is hardly an ecclesial response, so runs the argument, but rather the lead should be taken from the witness of what those great saints did in response to some erroneous or overspeculative statements in some places:

namely, to correct and pass over, in acknowledgment of the magnificent parts of the outstanding majority of his work.

Eusebius died in 340. In the same year his disciple, the theologian Acacius (the "One-Eyed"), became bishop of the see of Caesarea, in succession to him, and was himself a highly active and influential theologian, especially esteemed by the emperor Constantius. His position was also in opposition to the Nicene *Homoousion*, and Acacius did much to establish Constantius's imperial policy as radically setting aside the creed of the Council of Nicaea. Acacius was more of a church politician than Eusebius and chiefly wanted a compromise position to be adopted as a midway between the Nicenes and the radical Arians, both of whom he regarded as being "extreme" parties, and in this cause he suggested that the Logos should be confessed as "like the Father in all things." His party was known thereafter as the *Homoians*, but they were regarded by the Nicene party as no different from the Arian collective in denying the full sense of the divinity of the Son.

Acacius also went on record explicitly denying the divinity of the Holy Spirit. Jerome, in his book recording the academic achievements of outstanding Christians,[36] gives honor to Acacius for his indefatigable work continuing to build up to international standard the library Origen had founded almost a century and a half beforehand, and he notes how Acacius, despite all his involvement in high ecclesiastical politics, had time to author a seventeen-volume *Commentary on the Book of Ecclesiastes* and a six-volume treatise *Answers to Various Questions*. The path set before him by Eusebius, to advance Origen's reputation in the cause of attacking the Nicene *Homoousion*, a continuation of the main approach of Eusebius that Acacius so fervently adopted and pressed in what turned out to be the high-water mark of the Arian controversy, did another set of lasting damages—by association—to Origen's reputation for orthodoxy, and this for the same reasons as with Eusebius. For to claim Origen was an opponent of the *Homoousion* was a very serious matter for the fourth-century arbiters of orthodoxy.

Precisely because Origen's remarks about the fallacy of using "substance language" about God had been widely taken up by Arian opponents of the *Homoousion*, it was widely felt, especially in the Latin West after Jerome, that Origen could no longer be relied on as an authority. And in the East, Athanasius's scorn for the Caesarean theology of the Eusebians ran on into the Cappadocian Fathers' with their out-and-out rejection of the Christology and pneumatology of Acacius. This marginalization of the formerly prestigious "school of Origen" cast such a shadow over Origen posthumously that, at the same time as opposing Acacius, the leading Cappadocian Fathers, Gregory Nazianzen and Basil of Caesarea, felt it necessary to defend their ancient hero and launch a rehabilitation, as it were, by publishing a "best of" collection of his works called the *Philocalia Origenis*,[37] a selection that majored on Origen's exegetical insights, demonstrating his mastery, while leaving aside much of his dogmatic statements.

And so the advocacy of the Caesarean school, by the time Acacius died in 365, had left Origen (wholly anachronistically it has to be said)[38] tarred and feathered as an enemy of Nicaea among the broader, perhaps less educated, members of the episcopate, even though those who had read him closely, such as Alexander of Alexandria, could understand that he was actually an advocate of the uncreated eternity of the Logos (the fundamental point the pro-Nicene theologians were arguing for). This tarring of his reputation as a friend of Arians was something that his fourth-century (and after) orthodox admirers felt dismay about, and there were several attempts to reclaim him for the Nicene movement. The most important of them was initiated by the Cappadocian Fathers, Basil the Great, Gregory the Theologian, and Gregory of Nyssa, and it is largely thanks to these three that Origen's reputation and writings survived in the long term. But that activity of rehabilitation was begun even earlier, in Alexandria, and it is to this, Origen's birthplace, that we shall now return.

ORIGEN'S REHABILITATION AT ALEXANDRIA

Origen's three earliest and most devoted followers at Alexandria were Dionysios[39] (bishop of the city in 248), Theognostos,[40] and Pierios.[41] All of them were senior theologians with international reputations directing the major Christian theological *schola* or *didaskaleion* there, heirs of Clement and Origen in the prestige they brought to the school.[42] Theognostos was director between 265 and 280. His works have not survived, but his writing is highly praised by Photios, his ninth-century reader, for both his style and his religious spirit. Photius tells us that in his opinion Theognostos's treatise *Hypotyposeis* was a very close copy, perhaps even a synopsis for students, of Origen's *Peri Archon*. Photios criticizes him for this[43] (we remember he is a senior churchman after the time of the Justinianic condemnations), but as far as Athanasius was concerned this veneration of the old master was not a matter for fault but for praise, and Athanasius was determined that the Arian party would never be allowed to claim Origen for their cause, pointing out his spirit of allegiance to the Church's tradition and his defense of the eternity of the Logos.[44] Theognostos is one of the first to have nuanced Origen's ideas about divine substance, for he argued that the Son's *ousia* certainly did not originate out of nothing (as a creation of the Father) but was derived out of the Father, as a mirror reflection derives from the light, or as steam derives from water. The Son is thus the emanation (*aporroia*) of the *ousia* of the Father, and thus, logically, *ek tes ousias tou Patros* (of the being of the Father), as Nicaea would phrase it.

Pierios was Theognostos's immediate successor.[45] It was Pierios who taught Pamphilus and passed the Origenian tradition back to Palestinian Caesarea—still in that classical didactic tradition of working through the text (in this case scripture, or the writings of Origen) from aporias—or questions posed to the reader that they were supposed to solve by logically thinking through and applying "principles." He was a priest under Bishop Theonas of Alexandria and noted for his ascetical life and the elegance of his scholarship. He was so devoted to his intellectual mentor that, following Jerome,[46] his contemporaries called him "Origen Junior." He died at Rome some time after 309.

This earliest *catena*, or chain, of teaching disciples of Origen, who in turn became the standard-bearers (or *diadochoi*, "successors") of his tradition and directors (*scholarchs*) of an "academy" devoted to his principles, was critically important in establishing Origen's long-lasting influence over Christian thought internationally, for it is clear that without these powerful immediate "successors"[47] and advocates (and we might here also include another, Didymus the Blind at Alexandria,[48] who continued this tradition), Origen's work might have simply been archived and occasionally referenced, as happened with many another ancient Christian thinker before his time. And when this was the case, undoubtedly the vast majority of the corpus of the text was lost over a century or so simply because the labor involved in copying it was not seen as justified in present circumstances. But here, with this establishment of Origen's memory as a magisterially inspired theologian, a true Origenian school had been established immediately after his death, one that was rooted in the two leading academic centers of the ancient church, Alexandria and Caesarea, one that had *scholarchs* to protect and sustain it and copyists to propagate it. This is clearly borne out by the massive extent of the surviving library of Origen's work, even allowing for the many texts that have been fragmented and lost.[49]

Yet, just as it was with the tradition of Plato (already venerable by the time of the Christians), the original "master" was regarded as a source of wisdom that not everyone could appropriate without interpretive guidance. After Plato's death, a series of school directors were nominated for his Academy.[50] These first *scholarchs* were Speusippus (347–339 BC), Xenocrates (339–314), Polemon (314–269), and Crates (c. 269–266). Archesilaus of Pitane, the next *scholarch* in succession, is widely regarded as having departed so significantly from the master's tradition that his incumbency is taken as having ended the original period of Platonism. But, even so, the later forms of the Academy's principles were taken on by self-identifying intellectual heirs called the Commentators.[51] There are five major figures in this later tradition of the intellectual transmission of Platonism: Syrianus, Proclus, Calcidius, Damascius, and Olympiodorus.

In the case of the transmission of Origen's thought and works, it was Caesarea that tried to maintain the closest parallel with the Academy (a school and library where the purity of the tradition was maintained and taught), since Alexandria had partly lost out, in terms of location, by not having the bulk of Origen's own library and also by having a "hit and miss" attitude to his memory by various bishops of the city. Demetrios prosecuted Origen while he was alive. His successor, Heraclas, continued the complaints against his former colleague. The following bishops, Dionysios, Maximus, and Theonas, were glad to see their city develop Origen's idea of a high-level school of theology there, but Peter of Alexandria (300–311) was hostile, and his attitudes probably led to Pierios taking refuge at Rome.

Leontius of Byzantium (c. 485–543) hinted that Alexander of Alexandria was less than pleased with Origen's theology, but that may be simply his retrospective view of the troubles that Alexander's dialogues with Arius had caused him. It is clear enough that Alexander can be said to have initiated the great dispute with Arius over the eternity of the Son, precisely by strongly advocating the ideas on the Logos's unique participation in the eternal godhead found in Origen's *First Principles*. Athanasius, Alexander's close disciple and successor, bears out this more positive estimate of Alexander's advocacy because such was basically his own position. Athanasius was consistently an advocate of his Alexandrian theological predecessor, while always being careful to make significant changes in the Origenian Christology[52] so as to obviate Arius's stress on the subordination of the Son in an ontological sense.[53]

All the while, Athanasius insisted that Origen, whatever he might have appeared to have said about order and procession within the Trinity, certainly did not intend to teach the ontological inferiority of the Son of God. In his *De Decretis* (27), Athanasius points out that the church must interpret this great man "generously." He implies by this that the Arians, particularly the Eusebians, are not his best advocates and are woodenly pressing points that Origen's overall intent (his *skopos*) clearly did not intend. To this end, Athanasius defended Origen as having taught the divinity of the Holy Spirit and praised his name as one of the church's theological heroes.[54] Although the doctrine of the *Homoousion* was not particularly Athanasius's preferred formulary for the ontological union of the trinitarian persons,[55] he recognized Origen as teaching the same core doctrine, even though the latter was located in an entirely different context to that which had sprung up in the Arian dispute. Origen himself did not much care for the term *Homoousios*, as he felt it had been misused by the monarchians of the previous generation to himself as a key argument for a monist vision of God. His own focus was all on the importance of the divine mediation of the Logos and the Spirit within the deity of the Father. In the time of Athanasius, Eusebius of Caesarea, maintaining that he was the doyen of contemporary "Origenists," had himself also decided that he would "disapprove" of the Nicene favoring of the *Homoousion* and carried this through until he was forced to admit the legitimacy of the term within the Nicene creed.

His reluctance was continued, however, as soon as Constantine himself started to turn his support away from the Nicene party and take more guidance from Eusebius of Nicomedia (d. 341). This spread a wide belief among the less educated that Origen himself had been an opponent of the *Homoousion* and thus a proponent of the Arian position of the Son's dissimilarity to the being of the Father. Athanasius was a clear and significant voice in disputing this, in defense of Origen, reclaiming him for the wider tradition of orthodoxy. It was long felt, especially after the fifth-century Origenist anathemata, that Athanasius must have done this simply as part of his arsenal of arguments against the Arian cause in general; that is, he was defending Nicaea, not Origen as such, but recent scholarship has clearly shown that this is not the case. Indeed, Origen himself clearly advocated the absolute ontological unity of the trinitarian persons, which was basically the core point of the fourth-century term.

Although it had often been presumed earlier that Origen's positive defense of the *Homoousion* (intending to assert the ontological closeness of the Logos and the Father) was a piece of retrospective wishful thinking foisted onto him posthumously by Rufinus and Origen's other Nicene supporters,[56] Mark Edwards has recently made an unimpeachable case that Origen originally did teach the *Homoousion* (once again anticipating the agenda of generations after him). The word was not a favored term of his (for two reasons: he wished habitually to assert the great "transcendence" and *monarchia* of the Father even while denying the monist ontological conclusions of the earlier monarchian theologians, and he also wished to avoid terms that implied material substance in the godhead), but he certainly used the term himself, as an analogy, and (as Edwards argues) with the specific intention of asserting that the Son is truly and entirely divine, not a creature and not temporal.[57]

It was primarily this positive advocacy of Athanasius, later reinforced by the Cappadocian Fathers and Maximus the Confessor, that gave Origen an unshakeable place in the church's universal tradition despite the great resistance that was marshaled against him in the time of the emperor Justinian.

The overshadowing of the Caesarean school, after the Arian crisis, meant that the second wave that took up Origen's tradition released itself from the aspect of school location (Alexandria and Caesarea) and became, in that process, more liberal in its approach. These were the Nicene intellectuals that wished to keep Origen's greatest achievements while subordinating his thought to the overall prescripts of Nicene orthodoxy. They were the truly significant "Commentators" and were major theologians in their own right, as well as achieving reputations for high sanctity, the Cappadocian Fathers: Basil the Great, Gregory the Theologian (of Nazianzus), and Gregory of Nyssa. It is to this "neo-Origenian" school, as it were, that we shall now move.

ORIGEN'S ADAPTATION BY THE CAPPADOCIANS

There were actually seven Cappadocians who figured highly in the defense of Nicene Christianity in the late fourth century. They were all interrelated by ties of family or close friendship. The full list is Basil of Caesarea, his younger brothers Gregory of Nyssa and Peter of Sebaste, their sister Macrina, Basil's friend Gregory of Nazianzus, the latter's cousin Amphilokius of Ikonium, and Gregory of Nyssa's deacon Evagrius of Pontus. The four outstanding theologians in that company, who each left a large written archive, were Basil, the two Gregories, and Evagrius, and it will be on them that I concentrate.[58] Each of them were reverent disciples of Origen, though in varying degrees of attachment. Gregory of Nazianzus seems to have served as a higher tutor to both Gregory of Nyssa and Evagrius in their youth, and when the former was composing his renowned *Theological Orations*[59] in Constantinople in 380 (to prepare the ground for the great Council of Constantinople in 381, which took back the church in the capital from the Arians and reasserted the faith of Nicaea), Gregory of Nyssa sent Evagrius to his older namesake to serve as his secretary and theological assistant. All three were deeply devoted to Origen's thought. Basil was indebted too but less willing to embrace him so enthusiastically. Yet he regarded his church as being rooted in the tradition of their "Cappadocian apostle," St. Gregory Thaumaturgos,[60] who had been one of the original disciples of Origen in Caesarea Maritima, and he saw it is his core task not only to defend Nicenism but also to preserve the ancestral traditions of his metropolitan see, and Origenian spirituality was one of the foundational parts of their church tradition.

Gregory the Theologian

It was Gregory of Nazianzus[61] who probably encouraged Basil's devotion to Origen. He had spent the best part of ten years studying rhetoric, philosophy, and theology in the university city of Athens, much of that time in the company of Basil. Their teacher was the Christian philosopher Prohaeresios,[62] an Armenian originally based in Caesarea who also taught Eunapius and Julian. Basil was glad enough to leave Athens and moved on to study monasticism in Egypt before returning home to Cappadocia, where he decided to take up the ascetical life rather than a public career in law. Soon enough, of course, he was caught up in the administration of the great episcopal see of Caesarea and would eventually become the archbishop there with the assistance of Gregory and Gregory's old father, who commanded immense weight in the province. In Athens his friend Gregory expressed immense regret at Basil's departure, and soon afterward he too decided to return home to Cappadocia, intending to live the retired life of an ascetic (a learned scholarly type of monastic seclusion rather than a common, or cenobitic, life) in the company of close friends and relatives. Gregory had not counted on the fact that his father was the local bishop and magistrate, however, or that his word carried weight in both imperial law and ecclesiastical law. The elder Gregory commanded his son to be ordained priest (it was an age where forced ordinations were not all that rare), and his son knew well enough that, once ordained, a presbyter was under the beck and call of his bishop and could not plead "monastic retirement" as a way of escape. In the immediate aftermath of his ordination, he was immensely distressed by what he saw as the torpedoing of his career hopes (in fact, it gave him his greatest platform and made him one of the most renowned Fathers of the Church), and he fled in protest from the town of Nazianzus to take refuge with his friend Basil.

Basil had been writing to him in glowing terms about the way he and his sister Macrina[63] had transformed their country estate in Armenian Pontus into a monastic commune. Gregory Nazianzen had returned replies pouring gentle scorn on the kind of lifestyle Basil was commending. He regarded the cenobitic style as too bound up with obedience to an abbot and too concerned with physical labor, to the detriment of time for study. His preferred idea of monasticism (and it would be an idea that flourished greatly in later Byzantine times) was that of a more scholarly seclusion devoted to contemplative and literary activity. Now, however, in the shockwaves attendant on his outrage at having been forced into parochial service by his father, Gregory decided to take refuge with Basil at his estate in Pontus. When he got there, the community eventually persuaded him that it would be the best thing to return to the Nazianzen church and serve there as a theologian, but in the several months that he spent there, he engaged with Basil to make a compendium of the works of Origen, chiefly as they pertained to scriptural exegesis. Many years later when Gregory was the archbishop of Constantinople, Jerome was present at one of his liturgies and heard him preach. The latter records that he never heard anyone interpret the scripture like him. Not much formal commentary on the Bible has survived, but all of Gregory's writings (everything in fact that he ever penned) is drenched in biblical reference throughout, and he shows a very deep knowledge of, and respect for, Origen's work.

Knowing that the reputation of the great Alexandrian was being contested because some had accused him (anachronistically) of being hostile to the *Homoousion*,[64] and also that he had been associated with several leaders of the Arian party, Gregory persuaded Basil that they needed to repair the damage quickly. And it was probably at this time in the retreat at the Annesos estate that together they made a selection of the major passages of Origen's work (chiefly from the *Peri Archon*) that spelled out principles of exegesis. This collection was in the genre of a Byzantine florilegium, sometimes called a *Philokalia*.[65] It very carefully avoids all the controversial points of Origen's teachings (the doctrine of *apokatastasis*, the possible preexistence of souls, and so on) and sets out instead the method of interpreting texts in varying levels of symbolic understanding (literal, moral, and mystical) and with some of the basic axioms of biblical theology (the entirety of scripture as inspired, all of it teaching the soteriological incarnation, its Logo centricity, and so on).

There is no doubt that the very great prestige of the two names of these Cappadocian Fathers attached to this work, and the centrality of its popularity as a manual of scriptural teaching for ancient episcopal preachers,[66] served to make Origen's reputation "unsinkable" even despite later synodical condemnations. The *Philocalia of Origen* had an immensely long life as one of the chief collections of scriptural guidance in the Eastern churches. In the West, Gregory the Great's *Pastoral Rule* (which also adopted its major ideas) supplanted it somewhat. It was rendered into English first by George Lewis in 1912.[67] It was Gregory the Theologian's endorsement, and especially this collation of the best exegetical notes from Origen, that provided the "flotation device" that made Origen's name and repute unsinkable in the church ever afterward. If it had not been for Gregory Nazianzen (and to a lesser extent Maximus the Confessor), the synodical disapproval of the Fifth Ecumenical Council in 553 would have certainly proved fatal to his name and his manuscript tradition.

Gregory, in his own theological writings, generally approaches Origen's status as a most significant writer without worrying too much whether one has to accept everything he says or reject it all as the work of a heretic. He is much more relaxed, as appropriate for a scholar-theologian who had enough sense to know that Origen often expressed somewhat daring speculations on matters that, in his own day, had not received a formal or definitive treatment by the church traditions. Gregory also still lived in an age and ethos he shared with Origen (albeit a century and a half later than him) in which sophist-theologians, and the higher schools gathered around them, still understood that an aporia, or a teased-out puzzle-question, was meant to be attacked from various angles, in a spirit of "research-testing," rather than set out as a dogma proclaimed pontifically from a pulpit for the obedient consumption of the faithful. The century after the Cappadocians, however, marked a turning point in the history of clerical higher education. It was a transition to a more fixed conception of dogma (the body of appropriate teaching received in a school) and a more rigid understanding of the Christian tradition as a whole.

The background ethos had shifted away from the ever-more-distant Late Antique schools of philosophy presided over by a senior *magistros* who consciously stood in a school tradition, and had moved toward the more prosaic concept of a school of preparation for holy orders, a seminary education presided over by the abbot of a monastery or a large metropolitan bishop systematizing the preparation of clergy for his archdiocese, where adherence to mainstream orthodoxy and canonical exactitude were the key themes of the candidates' preparation. And in this later environment, Origen's methods were both puzzling and alien, and his reputation was doomed to suffer.

The prelude to the medieval Greek manuscript of the *Philocalia Origenis* contains the remarks of a much later clerical editor who is at a loss to understand how two great fathers such as Gregory and Basil, men renowned for their orthodoxy, could have supported a great "heretic" in this enthusiastic way. This little worried editorial note abundantly illustrates the change of mindset from the antique to the medieval church.

One of Gregory's specific arguments in defense of Origen's reputation as a great theologian was that many things in Christian religion have not been fully clarified; indeed, many never can be fully explicated in this material cosmos, especially thing concerning the state of affairs after life has ended: eschatological realities. Did not the Apostle Paul himself tell the church that such matters exceeded human conceptualization (1 Cor. 2:9)? This was Gregory's typically gentle and amiable manner of rounding off the rough corners of theological argument. He knew that by his own day the Origenian speculation about *apokatastasis*, or the belief that in the eschaton God would reconstitute all things to the good[68] (a fundamental part of Origen's system in which the divine Logos worked infallibly and indefectibly as the savior and restorer of the entire cosmos), had become highly controversial. Origen's idea was seized on—many would say entirely bent out of shape—by controversialists in respect to one singular aspect, namely, the assertion of the noneternity of hell's punishments.[69] His later enemies, culminating in the anti-Origenists of Justinian's time, made it out that he taught that hell would not be "everlasting" and thereby that Origen had contradicted Jesus himself (Mark 9:43, 48; alluding to Isa. 66:24). But in fact his works contain both universalist-leaning "suggestions" (if God's omnipotent power determines that all should be saved, then how can some not be saved?)[70] as well as places that affirm that some souls can and do turn away from God definitively and are cast out. This "lack of consistency in dogma" is typical of the way Origen worked by testing hypotheses among his higher students and discussing the aporias contained in the biblical material itself.

He particularly stressed the importance of reading the precise biblical text, and in reference to the teachings on afterlife punishment, he noted that the New Testament tradition of the punishment of souls spoke of it as *aionios*. While this is generally rendered (and understood) as "eternal," it should, in fact, be translated accurately as "of the next age" (*Aional*). Whatever the case, Origen argued, "eternity" cannot be understood in a temporal linear sense of "endless duration of time," which would be to impose chronology falsely onto a timeless state of God's eschaton. His subtleties, however, did not earn him friends in later centuries. Gregory of Nyssa nevertheless felt his views were entirely sensible, while Gregory of Nazianzus more closely followed Origen by refusing to give a definitive answer about *apokatastasis* and thinking out loud about both possibilities—namely, that sinners may be "refined" by postdeath spiritual fires. This of course combines both the teachings of the postdeath punishment and that of the eventual spiritual rehabilitation of all, in a "very discreet" synthesis, which was probably what Origen originally intended.

Gregory Nazianzen certainly endorses Origen's macro thesis, that in reading theology out of biblical bases the overarching principle to ground the interpreter is "to accept nothing unworthy of God." Accordingly, Gregory strongly affirms Origen's assertion that all "punishment" described as coming from God is therapeutic and loving in nature, never vindictive or retributive.[71] Such a "refining" fire Gregory calls "worthy of the One who punishes us." In his renowned *Fourth Theological Oration* (*Orations* 30.6), Gregory speaks of how the son of God took up all of humanity along with its sins[72] "in order to consume in Himself the worst part of us, just as fire consumes wax." Then he goes on to speak of how the divine Word accomplishes the salvific restoration of rational creatures, who have been variable (impassioned and fallible) while on earth. One notes here how he (deliberately) does not specify that *all* rational creatures will be "conformed to God," the very point of controversy Origen had roused when he spoke of the pulling back to divine union of even the wicked spirits in the final *apokatastasis*.

Gregory leaves it open-ended. Those who knew Origen's original point can continue to discuss if they wish (Gregory presumes they will be sensible enough to understand what an aporia is), but those who are less educated in this (or any other debate) can equally take it that he is speaking here simply of the state and glory of the righteous, those blessed souls ascending to union with God in heaven. This silence of discretion is typical of Gregory the Theologian.[73] Here is how he "restates" Origen's point, laundering it for the mainstream orthodox tradition:

> "And God will be all in all" (1 Cor. 15:28) in the time of restoration [*apokatastasis*], when we will no longer be many, as now, with various movements of the

will and the passions; and it will no longer be the case that we shall carry in ourselves only a little, or nothing of God; but then we shall be entirely conformed to God, able to receive God wholly, and God alone. It is to this perfection that we aspire, and it is Paul himself who is our guarantee for it.

It is a very subtle re-presentation of the *apokatastasis* doctrine, leaving it very clear in the mind of the reader which way Gregory is leaning,[74] and at the same time removing all trace of the key points of controversy in the historic argument over the salvation of the devil that had kicked off the whole argument in the third century. Gregory's final point is nonetheless heavily scored: this positive and broad hope of salvation is not one of Origen's invention; it relies on the apostolic testimony of no less than Paul himself.

The Other Cappadocians

Gregory Nazianzen's close friend was Basil the Great. Basil shows, generally speaking, a deep respect for Origen as a biblical scholar and tends to use him exegetically more than he references him theologically. This would be a sign of things to come for the majority of the later Greek Fathers in their approach to Origen, between the fourth and sixth centuries, until Justinian's chancery moved to blacken Origen's name more systematically. In a sense Gregory Nazianzen's subtlety derived from his very high intelligence (he was one of the most educated men of his age),[75] and the general run of Christian bishops were not able to breathe his refined air very often (a fact he himself wistfully observed more than once when he comments on the low state of episcopal education and culture in his time).

Gregory, and his Cappadocian friends Basil and Gregory of Nyssa, although they did not know it, were both the first and the last generation of bishops who could stand within the classical tradition of the Hellenistic schools and also occupy pastoral office in the church. For this latter part of the fourth century, the two worlds came together for a tantalizing moment. This is why the educated Cappadocians completely understand Origen (since he was an antique schoolman par excellence) and also why their later episcopal successors do not have the same language to work with his theology (because they did not have the elite scholastic education offered by the Late Antique world). To put it more simply: the Cappadocian aristocrats read (alongside Origen and their Bible) Homer, Aristotle, Plato, the Greek poets, and the dramatists. The fathers who followed them, by and large, read solely within narrow bands of the prior Christian tradition.[76] Gregory the Theologian read everything he could lay his hands on but did not put all his knowledge into public discourse or text (he did conduct regular *symposia* on his private estate for Christian intellectual friends). The monks, on the other hand, only read Gregory, Basil, and other monks.

Gregory of Nazianzus, being a close family friend of Basil of Caesarea (whom he had named posthumously as "Basil the Great"), was invited by the family to take over some of the later stages of the rhetorical and theological education of Basil's younger brother, also named Gregory. This Gregory would later be elevated to the episcopate of Nyssa in order to assist his brother, and after Gregory Nazianzen's resignation from the conflicted Council of Constantinople in 381, it was the younger Gregory who gained the emperor's ear and rose to high prominence as an arbiter of Nicene orthodoxy in the Eastern Roman provinces. We do not know much of what the elder Gregory taught his younger colleague, but they were close, and when the Nazianzen was preparing his dossier of orations in defense of the Nicene faith at Constantinople in 380, the younger Gregory sent his deacon, Evagrius of Pontus, to work as his assistant, and he himself came to attend some of the public readings of those works (*Orations* 27–31) when the conciliar fathers were gathering in the capital.

Gregory of Nyssa learned from the elder Gregory to appreciate Origen's brilliance, and he seems to have taken to reading him voraciously, for compared to the other two theologians, the Nazianzen and Basil, Gregory of Nyssa has no qualms in advocating some of Origen's more controversial points of doctrine, such as the *apokatastasis* understood as the eventual rehabilitation of all souls (hence the noneternity of hell), and he also endorses the importance of speculation on the state of souls in the afterlife. His concept of the endless progress and stretching out for higher reality (*prokope*) of souls became an accepted view in Eastern patristic thought, and the extensive exegetical structuring of his writings (such as his *Life of Moses* or *Commentary on the Song of Songs*) set an authoritative style for patristic dogmatic writing after him.

But although Gregory Nyssen was a much more enthusiastic and open endorser of Origen than either Basil or Gregory Nazianzen, and even though in his lifetime he probably enjoyed more imperial favor as an arbiter and model of orthodox theology, nevertheless his writings were not destined to enjoy the same massive outreach as either of his other two elder mentors. The Nyssen's *Catechetical Oration* became a fairly well-known text in antiquity and, of course, his saintly reputation was always high, but he was not extensively read outside this popularizing (pastorally useful) treatise. It would not be until the early part of the twentieth century that his works started to receive a more interested scrutiny, one that caught fire among patristics experts as they realized what a searching intellect had lain hidden under the dust for so long. The interest was signaled early on by Daniélou and Völker.[77] But it culminated in the classicist Werner Jaeger's immense labor in organizing the first critical edition of the complete works in what would eventually materialize as seventeen volumes, setting out no less than sixty texts of Gregory, all of which eventually became accessible to modern scholars online. This "rediscovery" of a major Father of the Church who was so deeply invested in philosophical metaphysics served, in its turn, to stimulate yet another revival of interest in Origen himself, a movement that had also started in the early twentieth century. Gregory of Nyssa research was certainly a door for modern scholarship to enter to see the great extent of Origen's influence in the writings of the ancient Christians, even though it had for so long been (falsely) presumed that, following his posthumous condemnations, influence must surely have waned. That story will be taken up in due course.

Gregory of Nyssa's deacon and colleague was the young intellectual from Pontus named Evagrius (345–399). He had started out his church career as St. Basil's lector and then became Gregory of Nyssa's assistant deacon when the former was episcopally ordained. Gregory loaned him to his mentor Gregory Nazianzen when the latter was preparing his *Theological Orations* against the Arians in Constantinople in 380, and Evagrius seems to have stayed on in the capital after the council ended and the lay aristocrat Nektarios was appointed as archbishop, probably serving as Gregory of Nyssa's head of bureau there.

Evagrius's reputation as a theologian in the capital was running high when he became romantically involved with the wife of a leading nobleman, and it was made clear to him by the lady's family that he would be "well advised" to flee the city. In 383 he took ship to Jerusalem and found refuge in the ascetical community of Rufinus and Melania on the Mount of Olives. Following Melania's encouragement, he passed on to the monastic communities of Egyptian Scete, there becoming perhaps the greatest disciple of the renowned Abba Macarius. By the end of his life, Evagrius was reckoned, certainly among the more educated monks, as one of the holiest and most important spiritual teachers of the monastic movement. His ideas, especially as translated into Syriac, became foundational for monasticism there, and they also passed, in moderated form through his admirer John Cassian, into the heartland of the Latin monastic tradition. In the Byzantine tradition, he had extensive influence in terms of his ascetical teachings, but his passionate admiration for Origen's authority, as in such works as his own *Gnostic Chapters*, was curtailed by official rebukes given to his speculations about *apokatastasis*[78] and the soul's potential passionlessness (*apatheia*). The very high regard the monastic tradition had for him as a practical ascetic and saint is shown in the following remark about him preserved in the anonymous *Historia Monachorum*, a text from the late fourth century about teaching heroes in the Egyptian desert:

We also visited Evagrius, a wise and learned man who was skilled in the discernment of thoughts, an ability he had acquired by experience. He often went down to Alexandria and refuted the pagan philosophers in disputations. This father exhorted the brothers who were with us, not to satiate themselves with water. "For the demons," he said, "frequently light on well-watered places." He taught us much else about *ascesis*, strengthening our souls.[79]

That Evagrius frequently debated with the pagan philosophers in Alexandria is a very important detail and something very rare for a normal Christian monastic. From this we are clearly shown (if we had not already deduced from his extant writings) that Evagrius approached his desert retreat not only as a Christian ascetical experience but also in the manner of the ancient sophistic schools, where the quest for wisdom[80] and virtue through aporetic dialogue was a critical part of the ascetic experience of the sage.[81] Evagrius certainly formed a "school" around him, and it was precisely their collective dedicated questions and speculative searchings that fuelled Evagrius's highly eclectic range of research and, in the process, amplified Origen's earlier discussions about metaphysics, prayer, and redemption.

Evagrius's development of ideas he had read in Origen, to whom he was devoted, were chiefly set out in his *Kephalaia Gnostika*, the provocatively named *Gnostic Chapters*,[82] enough to set off the alarm bells of any heresiologist, but equally a clear call aimed at protecting the longstanding ascetical intellectual tradition (shared by many of the more intellectual Christian monks) that the ascetic life was fundamentally the subjugation of bodily passions for the sake of acquiring wisdom and understanding (*sophia* or *gnosis*). Evagrius treats Origen with immense respect, but does so as a major philosopher in his own right, and does not leave the master's thought untouched by any means.

In dealing with the *Peri Archon*, Evagrius places a much heavier emphasis on the principle that the initial unity that creatures had with God shall be the pattern for the final restoration of all things (*apokatastasis*). Evagrius stresses this aspect of Origen's metaphysic, or protology, because he wished to reapply the ideas (which Origen took basically from Paul's insistence that in the end times God would be "all in all") in a more overtly "spiritual" fashion, designed to assist the meditation and struggle of monastics and to focus their prayer life. Evagrius's thinking is rooted in the psychology of the celibate desert dweller, the way thoughts and unruly longings rise up and proliferate, and how to control them by an ascetic regime of life that purifies the heart and the mind (the teeming thoughts: *logismoi*) and leads the higher spiritual awareness (the *nous*) into the lived-out knowledge of God (*gnosis*).

The critics of this "Origenism" read it in a deeply ontological way, while Evagrius intended it psychologically, and Origen had offered it exegetically.

This cast the worst of all lights on what Origen (and Evagrius) had been saying, because by this time a classical education, one that meant that the individual (monk or bishop) had actually read firsthand any of the texts in question, was becoming a very rare thing indeed. So hand-me-down notions held sway, and chief among them was the idea that anyone who had vaguely talked of the same topic had probably said the same thing. Since Plato in the *Meno* had posited that the soul preexisted bodily birth, it was widely presumed that Origen taught this also, being led astray in his views by a blind devotion to Platonic metaphysics. So extensive was this view that even into the twentieth century it has been widely suggested that Origen was "too Platonic" a thinker and by adherence to the Academy betrayed aspects of the scriptural tradition. Nothing could be further from the truth. As Mark Edwards has robustly shown, Origen's teachings at every instance corrects Plato by applying scriptural doctrine, and as Plotinus and Porphyry recognized, he was in effect more an opponent of Platonic metaphysics than any friend of it.[83]

After Evagrius's death, however, few of the ancient critics cared to make any distinction between his or Plato's or Origen's teachings, and the Evagrian exaggerated stresses (Evagrius's arguing that souls were created before their earthly existence, and that all things—including Satan—would be restored in a final reconciliation with God, and that the ascetic soul could achieve passionlessness—*apatheia*—on earth) were all "fathered" onto Origen. Evagrius had wished to develop a system of intellectual ascent, whereby the ascetic would first purify the material irregularity of thoughts and desires, thereby stabilizing the awareness enough to start the deep contemplation of earthly realities and thus understand how the divine Logos was hidden within each soul as its core of being. From practical asceticism (*praktike*), it thus moved to *apatheia* and hence into the state of understanding (*gnostike*), ascending in degree and capacity until it could command the awareness of God (*theologike*).

Evagrianism Becomes Confused with Origenism

It is disputed whether Evagrius didn't transgress the limits of orthodoxy in expressing his ideal of mystical union, especially on the christological and eschatological levels, though the author continually reviewed his own thought and sought to avoid pantheism. Later, in fact, some of his Palestinian and Syrian followers—the so-called Origenists—went further than he had. But it is also likely that the condemnation of 553[84] was due, at least in part, to hostile interpretations by the anti-Origenists in the extremely complicated events that preceded the ecumenical council.[85]

It was basically Evagrius's speculative developments of Origen's systematic and metaphysical thought, applied in the heart of advanced monastic circles (that rapid information-dissemination service of the fourth-century church), that really stirred the hornets' nest of criticism of this whole theological-philosophical movement, which even if bishops up to the end of the fourth century had not approved of had at least understood as part of the common landscape of education in antiquity. But this shared matrix was now passing away, and the criticism started to lead to cries (ultimately unsuccessful) that such speculation among learned circles ought to be firmly shut out from public Christian discourse—named, that is, as a heresy.

Most ecclesiastics were much less vested in philosophical metaphysics than the Evagrian circle of Origenians: first of all, the simpler *fellahin* monastics, but then also some bishops and theologians who, each in their own way, wanted a less open-ended form of Christian dogmatics. The turmoil of the Arian crisis had just been resolved by the late fourth century, and only then by the imposition of the firm hand of imperial control after more than a generation of bitter controversy among the greatest Christian cities. Many leading clerics had no desire to see another wave of speculation start, on any topic, preferring a much more fixed dogmatic system controlled by episcopal chanceries rather than being inspired by charismatic mystics, ascetics, or philosophers. The priest Jerome, albeit a very learned man, is a clear example of this sea change happening.

Jerome had been deeply annoyed by Evagrius's attachment to his avowed rivals in Jerusalem (the Greek bishop John of Jerusalem and the Latins Rufinus and Melania the Younger), and even more infuriated by the way the four of them strongly rebutted his own policy of blackening Origen's reputation (falsely) as a progenitor of Arianism.[86] Jerome makes one of the first moves, as a heresiologist, trying to make out Origen as the founder of a school of heretics including his three hated rivals:

> These heretics have affinities with Gnosticism which may be traced to the impious teaching of Basilides. It is from him that you derive the assertion that without knowledge of the law it is impossible to avoid sin. But why do I speak of Priscillian who has been condemned by the whole world and put to death by the secular sword?[87] Evagrius of Ibora in Pontus who sends letters to virgins and monks and among others to her whose name[88] bears witness to the blackness of her perfidy, has published a book of maxims on *apatheia*, or, as we should say, impassivity or imperturbability; a state in which the mind ceases to be agitated and—to speak simply—becomes either a stone or a God. His work is widely read, in the East in Greek and in the West in a Latin translation made by his disciple Rufinus. He has also written a book which professes to be about monks and includes in it many, not monks at all, whom he declares to have been Origenists, and who have certainly been condemned by the bishops. I mean

Ammonius, Eusebius, Euthymius, Evagrius himself, Horus, Isidorus, and many others whom it would be tedious to enumerate.[89]

Jerome's great subsequent reputation in the Latin church carried this libelous charge abroad widely, despite Ambrose of Milan's attempts to defuse it at the time (Ambrose was a great admirer and user of Origen's works). Jerome had started off life as a theologian profoundly indebted to Origen's works. After he started to denounce his erstwhile hero, he simply continued to use the writings but stopped citing him. However, he was an acerbic rhetor, a very caustic controversialist, and did much, at least in the Latin-speaking world, to damage Origen (and Evagrius) and popularize the offensively inaccurate caricature of the old master as a gnostic heretic of ancient times—when, in fact, he is one of the most sophisticated antignostic theologians the church ever produced.

NOTES

1. J. Trigg, *Origen: The Bible and Philosophy in the Third Century Church* (London: SCM Press, 1983), 244.
2. In 1934, four years before Attaturk's death, the Hagia Sophia was given secularized status as a museum, and in 2020 it was reclassified as a mosque by the populist president Erdogan.
3. *Suidae Lexicon*, 3:169.
4. Eusebius, *Church History* 6.3.1–2.
5. Eusebius, *Church History* 6.31.2.
6. Eusebius, *Church History* 6.3.5.
7. Eusebius, *Church History* 6.3.13.
8. Eusebius, *Church History* 6.4.2–3.
9. Eusebius, *Church History* 6.5.1.
10. Eusebius, *Church History* 6.46.2.
11. Eusebius, *Church History* 6.23.1–2.
12. Jerome, *Epistle 43: To Marcella*.
13. A concept well recognized among the ancient schools of philosophy. The head of school occupied the "throne." In later times—after the fourth century—this idea was taken over exclusively by the Christian bishops. We get the idea of the cathedral from the Latin term for throne—*cathedra*. But in Origen's time the concept of occupying the throne was primarily indicative of being the most famed rhetorician of a given place, a town or area, and thus the one who was entrusted (in civic society) to "speak for" the town in times of need.
14. See McGuckin, "Origen's Doctrine of the Priesthood."
15. On the Mediterranean coast near Jaffa, where the Roman Provincial Governors had their residences.

16. Most of his "homilies" on scripture derive from this practice, and he must have had scribes taking down his sermons as he spoke. Several times he has cause for complaint that the local congregation seems to suffer from lack of attentiveness.

17. Known as the *Panegyric to Origen*.

18. See L. Larsen, "Disciples of Origen," in McGuckin, *Westminster Handbook to Origen*, 88–89.

19. Gregory Thaumaturgos, *Panegyric to Origen* 6.

20. I. M. Levey, "Caesarea and the Jews," *Bulletin of the American Schools of Oriental Research, Supplementary Studies* 19 (1975): 43–78; See also McGuckin, "Caesarea Maritima as Origen Knew It," and "Origen on the Jews."

21. See McGuckin, "Caesarea Maritima as Origen Knew It."

22. The name for a massive, and very rare, manuscript in antiquity, containing all the Bible, Old and New Testaments, together.

23. Pierius the Presbyter (d. after 309) was the head of the Alexandrian *schola* in the time of Bishop Theonas and was called by Jerome "a younger Origen" (Jerome, *De Viris Illustribus* 76). See also Photius, *Bibliotheca* cod. 118–19. Pierius directly continued the work of Origen in Alexandria under Bishop Theonas, but the latter's successor, Peter I, was determined to root out Origenian influence, and in due course Pierius took refuge and resided at Rome.

24. Photiusb *Bibliotheca* cod. 118.

25. Found in *Patrologia Graeca*, vol. 17, ed. J. P. Migne (Paris: Imprimerie Catholique, 1857), 521–616.

26. The text has now been rendered into English by T. P. Scheck, *Apology for Origen, with the Letter of Rufinus on the Falsification of the Books of Origen*, Fathers of the Church Series 120 (Washington, DC: Catholic University of America Press, 2010).

27. He mentions them in the book of notes he made about his reading in ninth-century Constantinople: Photius, *Bibliotheca* cod.117–18.

28. This stoppage does not denote a lacuna; it was just he felt he had demonstrated "how" to make a Johannine commentary by this stage. But what a dramatic ending the work has, with this image: "And so Judas went out and the text says 'It was night': But it is never night for those who lie on the breast of Jesus." See a fuller argument in J. A. McGuckin, "Structural Design and Apologetic Intent in Origen's Commentary on John," in *Origeniana Sexta*, ed. G. Dorival and A. Le Boulluec (Leuven: Peeters, 1995), 441–57

29. As Athanasius's party felt.

30. The twentieth anniversary of his becoming emperor (raised by his troops in 305).

31. *Origenism* is a term sometimes used to distinguish what people said Origen taught, and which they followed, from *Origenianism*, meaning what Origen actually taught and was taken up by disciples later. Most textbook treatments fail to distinguish between Origenianism and Origenism, but Ilaria Ramelli has made the difference abundantly clear in her differentiation of Evagrius's accurate dependence on Origen and his own extension of Origen's thought in new and personal ways. See I. L. E. Ramelli, "Recovering the True Thoughts of the Origenian Evagrius," in *Evagrius, Kephalaia Gnostika*, trans. Ilaria Ramelli (Leiden: Brill, 2015), xi–lxxxviii.

32. Of course, emperors and popes have also lauded him in history, the latest public affirmation being Pope Benedict XVI's addresses on the importance of Origen in his series of Vatican allocutions on the Fathers of the Church.

33. St. Athanasius, *Defence of the Nicene Definition* 6.27, in *Select Writings and Letters of Athanasius*, trans. A. Robinson, Nicene and Post-Nicene Fathers (Grand Rapids, MI: Eerdmans, 1978), 168. Greek text in H. G. Opitz, ed, *Athanasius Werke*, vol. 2.1 (Berlin: De Gruyter, 1940), *De Decretis Nicaenae Synodi* 27.3.

34. Not to mention the Latins who admired and used him, such as Pope Damasus, Hilary of Poitiers, Rufinus, Melania, and even the (allegedly hostile) Jerome. The list would go on through Maximus the Confessor and Dionyios the (Ps.) Areopagite to many other leading Byzantine and Latin saints and scholars.

35. See Socrates, *Church History* 6.12.18–24 and 26–27.

36. *De Viris Illustribus* (On Outstanding Men) c. 98.

37. *Philocalia* is a Greek term for an anthology of favorite texts.

38. Ilaria Ramelli magisterially demonstrates the wrongheadedness of attributing Arian views on the Son as a creature (*ktisma*) to Origen in I. Ramelli, "Origen's Anti-Subordinationism and Its Heritage in the Nicene and Cappadocian Line," *Vigiliae Christianae* 65 (2011): 21–49.

39. E. Prinzivalli, *Magister Ecclesiae: Il dibattito su Origene tra terzo e quarto secolo* (Rome: Institutum Patristicum Augustinianum, 2002), 33–64.

40. M. Simonetti, "Theognostus," in *Encylopedia of Ancient Christianity*, ed. A. Di Berardino (Downers Grove, IL: IVP Academic, 2008), 3:758.

41. See I. Ramelli, "The Christian Doctrine of the Apokatastasis: A Critical Assessment from the New Testament to Eriugena," *Vigiliae Christianae Supplementa* 12 (2013): 223–77; I. Ramelli, "Origen's First Followers in Alexandria and the East, and His First 'Detractors,'" in Ramelli, *Christian Doctrine of the Apokatastasis*, 223–77. Philip of Side's *Church History* places Theognostos after Pierios, but Pierios was driven out of the city by Bishop Peter of Alexandria, who was an anti-Origenist, and would hardly have had Theognostos continue. See also Simonetti, "Theognostus," 3:758; C. Kannengiesser, "Pierius of Alexandria," in Di Berardino, *Encylopedia of Ancient Christianity*, 3:192–93.

42. After Dionysios, the fusion of the "Alexandrian catechetical school" (which Heraclas had last headed up, the predecessor of Dionysios and the coworker of Origen while the latter served in the administration of Demetrios of Alexandria) with the "school of Origen at Alexandria" can, I think, be presumed. By the end of the third century, the Christian schools of various cities were chiefly the circle of disciples around a past or present Christian master, rather than any establishment meant to catechize the baptismal candidates, as was the case in earlier times.

43. Photius, *Bibliotheca* cod. 106.

44. See, for example, Athanasius, *Epistle IV to Serapion* 9–10; *De Decretis* 27.

45. His fragmentary remains are in *Patrologia Graeca*, vol. 10, ed. J. P. Migne (Paris: Imprimerie Catholique, 1857), 241–46.

46. Jerome, *De Viris Illustribus* 76: "Pierius, presbyter of the church at Alexandria in the reign of Carus and Diocletian, at the time when Theonas ruled as bishop in the same church, taught the people with great success and attained such elegance

of language and published so many treatises on all sorts of subjects (which are still extant) that he was called Origen Junior. He was remarkable for his self-discipline, devoted to voluntary poverty, and thoroughly acquainted with the dialectic art. After the persecution, he passed the rest of his life at Rome. There is extant a long treatise of his *On the Prophet Hosea* which from internal evidence appears to have been delivered on the vigil of Passover."

47. That is, Dionysios, Theognostos, Pierios, and Pamphilus.

48. C. 313–398. He composed a lengthy defense and explication of the theology of the *De Principiis* (see Jerome, *Apologia Adversus Rufinus* 1.6). His theme was following Athanasius and maintaining that Origen's trinitarian theology was in accord with teachings about the Logos's coequal, eternal, and divine status. Because Didymus was associated by name, along with Origen and Evagrius, in the Second Council of Constantinople's condemnation of Origenism, his works have suffered devastating losses, including the loss of his defense of the *De Principiis*.

49. Any other Christian writer of antiquity who had endured such opposition by later generations would have been lost almost without trace.

50. See F. Novotný, "Plato's First Successors," in *The Posthumous Life of Plato*, ed. L. Svoboda and J. L. Barton (Dordrecht: Springer, 1977); J. Dillon, *The Heirs of Plato: A Study of the Old Academy* (Oxford: Oxford University Press, 2003).

51. See M. Tuominen, *The Ancient Commentators on Plato and Aristotle* (London: Routledge, 2014).

52. Origen, for example, had implied that the Logos descended to earth not to inhabit the incarnate Jesus unmediatedly but rather to indwell, out of loving association, the "Great Soul" Jesus (one of the angelic order of the first creation—the *noes*), who thus served as the intermediary of the Logos, keeping his Lord distant from actual enfleshment but allowing him to work within the material order more directly than ever before, because of the intimate union that existed between the Logos and the Great Soul Jesus. Athanasius cast aside this mediation theory and made the Logos the direct personal subject of the incarnate Christ; of course, in so doing, he himself began another generation of conflicts over how this could work in terms of both metaphysics and psychology (the Christological conflicts of the late fourth and mid-fifth centuries).

53. See A. R. Teal, "The God-Man: An Engagement with the Theology of Athanasius of Alexandria: Its Genesis and Impact" (Ph.D. diss., University of Birmingham, 2006), 104–32.

54. *Epistle 4: To Serapion* 9–10.

55. He himself preferred *tautotes tes ousias*—an identity of essence (rather than the "selfsame essence," which could suggest monism).

56. R. P. C. Hanson reemphasised this in "Did Origen Apply the Word *Homoousios* to the Son?" (in Hanson, *Studies in Christian Antiquity* [Edinburgh: T&T Clark, 1983], 53–70), stressing how Origen seemed to avoid the term. See also P. F. Beatrice, "The Word 'Homoousios' from Hellenism to Christianity," *Church History* 71, no. 2 (2002): 243–72.

57. M. Edwards, "Did Origen Apply the Word *Homoousios* to the Son?," *Journal of Theological Studies*, n.s., 49, no. 2 (October 1998): 658–70.

58. Macrina did not leave writings, but a fine study of her significant impact has been produced by S. Elm, *Virgins of God: The Making of Asceticism in Late Antiquity* (Oxford: Oxford University Press, 1996). Amphilokius's surviving works are mainly pastoral in character, with a few apologetic works heavily reliant on his cousin St. Gregory the Theologian, whose heritage he shared for some time in his youth. Jerome, Gregory of Nazianzus, and Basil of Caesarea all regarded him as a pillar of faith, and it was Basil who ordained him bishop. See C. Datema, *Amphilochii Iconiensis Opera*, Corpus Christianorum, Series Graeca 3 (Turnhout: Brepols, 1978).

59. The "Five Theologicals" are *Orations* 27–31 in Gregory's corpus. See F. Norris, *Faith Gives Fullness to Reasoning: The Five Theological Orations of Gregory Nazianzen* (Leiden: Brill, 1990), for text and commentary.

60. C. 213–270, famed saint, wonder-worker, missionary, and bishop of neo-Caesarea in Pontus.

61. In the Eastern church he is known as Gregory the Theologian (a title given to him by the Council of Chalcedon in 451) because of his groundbreaking *Orations* (especially nos. 27–31) setting out the Christian dogma of the Trinity.

62. His "Life" was composed by Eunapius in the *Lives of the Philosophers* (text in *Philostratus and Eunapius: The Lives of the Sophists*, trans. W. C. Wright [Cambridge, MA: Harvard University Press, 1921]). Eunapius portrays him as a Hellenistic holy sage in that narrative, but Prohaeresios was a dedicated and ascetic Christian who refused Julian's lucrative overtures to come over to pagan Theurgy. He was invited to Rome and was awarded a statue there with the inscription, "From Rome, the Queen of Cities, to the King of Eloquence" (*Lives of the Sophists*, 492). See also E. J. Watts, *City and School in Late Antique Athens and Alexandria* (Berkeley, CA: University of California Press, 2006), 48–78.

63. Basil never credits Macrina, never mentions her in fact. The omission is repaired by his younger brother Gregory of Nyssa, who composed the *Life of Macrina*, characterizing her as a new Socrates. Macrina and Gregory Nazianzen supervised Gregory Nyssa's early education.

64. The Nicene teaching that the Son was of the "same substance" as the Father (implying as a shorthand that he was eternal and fully divine just as the Father was divine). Origen taught that the Son was divine, and eternal, as the Father's medium and high priest of creation, but unaware of the precisely tooled arguments that would arise seventy years after his death, he found commonality of substance a rather poor theological argument, since God was in essence beyond all substance.

65. A "book for connoisseurs of beautiful things." The now better-known (eighteenth-century) *Philokalia* is just such a compendium of patristic spiritual texts.

66. Gregory sent it to Bishop Theodore of Tyana precisely for this reason, mentioning how Basil had collaborated with him on the project of excerpting Origen's biblical thought. Gregory, *Epistle 115: To Theodore*.

67. G. Lewis, trans., *The Philocalia of Origen: A Compilation of Selected Passages from Origen's Works Made by St. Gregory of Nazianzus and St. Basil of Caesarea* (Edinburgh: T&T Clark, 1911). The Greek text had been prepared by Armitage Robinson in 1893. This has been recently reprinted: J. Armitage Robinson, ed., *The*

Philocalia of Origen (Eugene, OR: Wipf and Stock, 2020). The critical text is the subject of two volumes in the Sources Chrétiennes series, vols. 226 and 302.

68. See F. W. Norris, "Apokatastasis," in McGuckin, *Westminster Handbook to Origen*, 59–62.

69. For a fuller discussion of the whole question, see I. L. E. Ramelli, *A Larger Hope? Universal Salvation from Christian Beginnings to Julian of Norwich* (Eugene, OR: Cascade Books, 2019).

70. 1 Tim. 2:4; see also Ezek. 18:23 and John 3:17.

71. Gregory Nazianzen, *Orations* 45 (*In Sanctum Pascha*), in *Patrologia Graeca* (hereafter cited *PG*), vol. 36, ed. J. P. Migne (Paris: Imprimerie Catholique, 1858), 633; see also *Orations* 38 and 16.6.

72. Origen originally believed that the divine Logos was a separate "person" from the great (angelic) soul known as Jesus, who was the "carrier," as it were, of the divine Logos. He posited this relationship of disjunction so as to preserve the absolute immateriality of the Logos. By the time of Athanasius, orthodox tradition had already quietly disposed of this aspect of his thought, and Gregory simply presupposes this should be left to obscurity. Indeed, it is Gregory who repairs the lacunae this correction leaves in Origen's system by underlining how the incarnate Son of God (Logos enfleshed) precisely adopts our sinfulness in order to heal it. See Gregory's *Epistles 101–3: To Cledonius*.

73. In his poem *Carmen* (1.5.548), Gregory speaks of the soul's experience of either light or fire in the afterlife, depending on its condition. Then he goes on: "But whether or not *All* will later partake of God, let that be discussed elsewhere."

74. Gregory taught Christ's work of salvation was not just for the elect few but for all (*Orations* 33.9; *PG* 36:225B). In his *Dogmatic Poems* 2.76–77 he shares Origen's (and the Letter the to Colossians') truly cosmic vision of the redemption's power: "Christ offered his blood to God and purified the entire cosmos. Undergoing the torment of the cross, he nailed sins onto it."

75. See J. A. McGuckin, *St. Gregory Nazianzen: An Intellectual Biography* (Crestwood, NY: St. Vladimir's Seminary Press, 2001).

76. The significant departures from that rule tend to be the more intellectual theologians, who also tend to be advocates of the value and abiding worth of Origen's thought. Maximus the Confessor is an example.

77. J. Daniélou, *Platonisme et Théologie Mystique* (Paris: Aubier, 1944); W. Völker, *Gregor von Nyssa als Mystiker* (Wiesbaden: Franz Steiner Verlag, 1955).

78. Evagrius (following Origen) taught that the eternal fire spoken of in the Gospels was a purifying "spiritual" fire of the next aeon (eternal—or of the next age—not in the sense of endless duration), and like a fire "burning up the chaff," it was a force that consumed and purified sin, not sinners. See Ramelli, *A Larger Hope?*, 135–37.

79. *Historia Monachorum* 20.15–16, in N. Russell, trans., *The Lives of the Desert Fathers*, Cistercian Studies Series 34 (Kalamazoo, MI: Cistercian Publications, 1981), 107.

80. Not just accumulated knowledge but (especially with the Christians) encounter with the divine Wisdom (Logos).

81. See Pierre Hadot, *Philosophy as a Way of Life*, trans. Michael Chase (Oxford: Blackwell, 1995), and for a general view, J. Adams, *The Religious Teachers of Greece*, Gifford Lectures (Edinburgh: T&T Clark, 1908), available online at https://www.giffordlectures.org/books/religious-teachers-greece.

82. Only published by A. Guillaumont in 1958 from the ancient Syriac translation made of it (*Patrologia Orientalis*, vol. 28.1) and thus recovered from its exile into obscurity. See also Ramelli, *Evagrius, Kephalaia Gnostika*.

83. M. J. Edwards, *Origen against Plato* (London: Routledge, 2017).

84. At Justinian's local synod of Constantinople, preceding the ecumenical council there later that year.

85. J. Gribomont and D. Hombergen, "Evagrius of Pontus," in Di Berardino, *Encyclopedia of Ancient Christianity*, 1:889.

86. Though, as we have seen, Eusebius of Caesarea damaged Origen's reputation by the way he used him during the Arian crisis, Jerome partly started to impugn Origen's orthodoxy in order to annoy Rufinus, John, and Melania, who regarded his theology and his scholarship with too cool an eye for his liking.

87. The lamentable case of the first "heretic"' to be executed for dissidence in the Western Church: Bishop Priscillian of Avila. He was a learned ascetic whom his ecclesiastical enemies handed over to the secular court, where he was sentenced to decapitation for "sorcery."

88. Melania, that is. The name means "black-eyed girl."

89. Jerome, *Epistles* 133.3, in W. H. Fremantle, trans., *The Principal Works of St. Jerome*, Nicene and Post-Nicene Fathers, 2nd series, vol. 6 (Edinburgh: T&T Clark, 1892), 274.

Chapter 4

The Ancient Origenist Crises

In his lifetime, Origen had annoyed his bishop, Demetrios, in Alexandria, along with Pope Fabian of Rome, when he published the treatise *On First Principles*, and after he engaged in open debate in Athens, he had caused "murmurings" because of the issue of whether the devil could ever be saved—with some claiming he had taught this, and he himself insisting that he had never said such a thing. If this can properly be called the first Origenistic crisis, then Evagrius instigated an even noisier one to follow. But it is this one that is more commonly called, in current textbooks, the "First Origenian (or Origenist) Crisis," and a further period of controversy in the sixth century is usually called the "Second Origenist Controversy." We shall treat the issues raised after Evagrius's death under the main protagonists: Epiphanius of Salamis, Jerome, Rufinus of Aquileia, the "Tall Brothers," and Theophilus of Alexandria. We shall treat the sixth-century arguments under the double heading of the monastic disputes in Palestine and Constantinople, and then the state intervention in the form of the councils held under the emperor Justinian.

The Jesuit priest Henri Crouzel, a scholar who devoted his life to studying Origen's works, thought it best to divide the Origenistic crises into six phases, but his essay is one of minute detail.[1] A much fuller study of the various waves of anti-Origen polemic in antiquity has since been undertaken by Elizabeth Clark, whose work remains the fullest treatment of the subject.[2] We shall take a simpler path here by only studying the main lines of the two greatest phases of anti-Origenian argument. One of the problems in the way this concept of "Origenism" has been approached retrospectively—that is, looking back from one age censuring the thoughts and expressions of an earlier period—is that heresiologists are not always the most intellectual of commentators, often quite the opposite. They habitually make the issues squeakily narrow, for having crammed their opponents into narrow vessels of their own imagining, it proves much easier to denounce them and show up their shortcomings against a grid of neatly presented axiomatic points, a checklist as it were. This is what happened to Origen in several phases after his death. And how he was treated by several waves of those who disliked his kind of theological imagination has tended to be lumped together (especially in textbooks and in the minds of heresiologists of all ages) so that "Origenism" itself becomes a sort of heresy and heretical movement, something that in actuality hardly existed outside the imagination of the heresiologists or the pages of second-rate textbooks.

"Origenism" as such arguably never existed outside the rhetorical flourishes of his opponents, and most of what they attributed to him as "wrong ideas" was inaccurately read into his work in any case.[3] This being so, we need to realize from the outset that "Origenism" does not run on through several phases across several centuries but is created *de novo* each time, and there is no necessary commonality in what is thought at any time to be "Origenism," nor that it necessarily has much relation to Origen's own original text or actual agenda. Our approach will look, therefore, at the two illustrative instances, the first in the fourth to fifth centuries and the second in the lead up to the controversy culminating in the synodical condemnations of the sixth century.

EPIPHANIUS OF SALAMIS, JEROME, RUFINUS, AND THEOPHILUS OF ALEXANDRIA

Epiphanius of Salamis (d. 403) is the encapsulation of a new type of systemic theologian in the early church: a monk, then a leader of a community in Palestine (where he came to know and respect Jerome), and eventually bishop in Cyprus. He was someone who wanted to have a simpler biblical fideism than Origen's symbolic exegesis allowed, as the guide to the core Christian life, and he nurtured a profound distaste for the numbers of intelligentsia theologians who spoke of the monastic life in quasi-philosophic terms. His overarching desire was to bring order and clarity into the history of doctrine. It seemed a simple task to state with unarguable clarity, succinct brevity, and impressive authority exactly what it was the orthodox Christians believed. The trouble was that he, like most writers of this era, had little to no sense of historical development.

Lacking finesse, Epiphanius so passionately wanted a simple version of Christian thinking that he bowdlerized the story. For him the main issue was to judge Origen by the way he had contributed to the great issue of his own age, the Arian crisis, and finding that the third-century writer did not use all the Nicene fourth-century formulae was enough to render him unfit to join the ranks of the orthodox. As Crouzel says, speaking of Epiphanius, Jerome, and Theophilus,

They made no systemic studies of Origen's work and based their accusations on isolated texts, taking no account of the explanations often found in other passages in the same book, sometimes only a few lines away.[4] What Origen wrote in the form of exercise (*gymnastikos*) they understood as put forth in the form of doctrine (*dogmatikos*) with a conception of orthodoxy and *regula fidei* which was increasingly being modeled on that of civil law and expressed in "definitions" in the struggle against heresy.[5]

Rufinus, writing under Melania's encouragement at the monastery on the Mount of Olives and witnessing this travesty of criticism that Jerome and Epiphanius were manifesting, tried to make a more scholarly job of the defense. His primary contribution was to make Latin versions of the actual texts of Origen. These would be immensely important in preserving the memory and power of Origen's writings for the Latin-speaking West. Indeed, every revival of Origen's fortunes in the West, from antiquity through to the Renaissance, was made on the basis of Rufinus's Latin versions of the *De Principiis* and selected exegetical works. Rufinus also translated Pamphilus's *Apology for Origen*, and he more or less follows the martyr's own lines of argumentative defense (as did almost all his other Western advocates up to Pico della Mirandola and Erasmus). As he makes clear in his own *Preface to the Apology of Pamphilus*,[6] Rufinus knew that hostility toward Origen was largely based on prejudiced hearsay rather than engagement with the actual text. "Do such people not understand that to wound the conscience of weaker brethren by false accusations is to sin against Christ?[7] For such a reason they should not lend their ears to Origen's defamers, or think to learn about another man's faith from a third party, especially since the means of finding this first hand is possible."[8] This, in a nutshell, was why he prepared the translations. He also makes it clear that the core arguments attacking Origen revolve around a vague belief that he denied the Trinity (i.e., the divinity of the Holy Spirit), the full deity of the savior (the *Homoousion*), and the full fleshly reality of the incarnate Lord and of his resurrection (the corporeality of the risen body). He ends his preface by asserting that Origen confessed all these things in accordance with the Apostle (Paul) and that this is the (Nicene) faith that both his bishop (John of Jerusalem) and he teach and hold to the present day.[9]

Meanwhile, Epiphanius decided the best way to fight residual Arianism was to create a short handbook and manual of all the heresies he could enumerate. It has come to be known as the *Panarion* or *Treasure Chest against All Heresies*. In this he describes the historic heretics in terms like wild animals and suggests the antidote to their various poisons. In this context he mockingly refers to Origen as the "would-be sage" who "entitled himself Adamantius" (completely inaccurately, as this was a title given to him posthumously) and calls him "a toad, noisy from too much moisture which keeps croaking louder and ever louder."[10] He states the reason he opposes "the sect of Origenists" (one suspects he means primarily here Jerome's critics Melania, Rufinus, Evagrius, and Bishop John of Jerusalem) is because of their complex way of understanding the resurrection of the Lord (rather than the simple statement of a bodily resurrection).

His generic suspicion of "Greek learning" comes out loud and clear, however: Hellenistic education is a poisonous venom he does not want to see in the church:

> Taking the Lord's resurrection for a preventive draught, as it were, let us spit out the oil of the toad's poison, and the harm that has been done by the noxious creature. For this is what has happened to Origen with all his followers, and I mourn him on this account. Ah, how badly you have been hurt, and how many others you have hurt, as though you have been bitten by a baneful viper, by which I mean secular education, and have become the cause of others' death. Naturalists say that a dormouse hides in its den and bears a number of young at once, as many as five and more, but vipers hunt them. And if a viper finds the den full, since it cannot eat them all it eats its fill of one or two then and there, but punctures the eyes of the rest, and after they are blinded brings them food, and feeds them until it is ready to take each one out and eat it. But if simple people happen upon such creatures and take them for food, they poison themselves with what has been fed on the viper's venom. And you too, Origen, with your mind blinded by your Greek education, have spat out venom for your followers, and become poisonous food for them, harming more people with the poison by which you yourself have been harmed.[11]

His other treatise, *Ancoratus* (meaning "The Well-Anchored Man"), takes up the attack on Origen more fully. He especially singled out from Origen various propositions about the nature of souls and the state of the final consummation, making the usual alteration of changing Origen's seminar "I wonder if . . . " statements into dogmatic utterances. But more to the point, I think, this controversy into which Jerome had pulled him came in Epiphanius's advanced old age, and it stirred within him very bad memories of how he had been dismissed earlier in his career as something of a recidivist, both in Egypt and in Palestine, when he had served as hegumen (abbot) of a monastic community. Epiphanius had first come across the renowned Tall Brothers when he himself was a monk in the Alexandrian archdiocese. The Tall Brothers had alarmed him by their highly sophisticated circle of monastic admirers, centered on the reading of the works of Origen. The Tall Brothers, with Evagrius in their midst, had a great and internationally resonant reputation and formed the nucleus of a type of monastic mystical philosophy in Egypt that characterized the simplicity of "nonreading" communities (those who felt ascetic struggle was enough if allied with vocal prayers) as a rather ignorant rusticity.

Epiphanius saw himself as the rallying ground for the old style of monastic life: hard labors to tire the body and quiet its needs, and recitation of the hours in long services. He was not an ignorant man per se, although his enemies liked to characterize him this way. But he certainly had no desire to see monasticism mixed up with what he felt was Hellenistic sophism that had caused such massive rifts in the church during the Arian crisis.[12] This made him a hard and dogmatic opponent. When he had returned to visit the Palestinian monks, he learned of Jerome's conflict with the Origenian scholars of Melania and Rufinus's monastery on the Mount of Olives. Evagrius had been converted to the monastic life in that community before he went to Egypt, so there was a close connection between Jerome's "enemies" and his own distaste for the Tall Brothers, who now all seemed to Epiphanius (hearing the tale via Jerome, who flattered Epiphanius as a most learned and multiskilled linguist) to be in a cabal, creating a sect of "Origenist heresies."

Now that he was a senior bishop in Cyprus, Epiphanius decided that he could attack the prestige of Melania's community by causing problems for John, the bishop of Jerusalem, who favored them. Epiphanius visited Jerusalem in 394 and while invited to preach there (a visiting bishop according to canon law had to be invited to do any episcopal acts by his host, the diocesan bishop) embarrassed John by denouncing Origenism in church as a heresy that needed to be rooted out and also by complaining that things in this diocese were not entirely spick and span.[13] He called on Bishop John to formally condemn the writings (all of them!) of Origen. John of course had no intention of doing anything of the kind. In an act of considered scorn, Epiphanius then ordained a priest (a significant scandal to do so in another's diocese—it tacitly signified he regarded John as a lapsed bishop), and what was worse, he did this so that the presbyter could serve Jerome's community at Bethlehem, thus making it independent of bishop John, who regarded both Jerome and Epiphanius as serious troublemakers. Epiphanius then had to make a rapid retreat to Cyprus, but this event caused longstanding ruptures between Melania, Rufinus, and John, on the one side, and Jerome and Epiphanius, on the other. Much of the conflict over so-called Origenism that heats up in the next decade to 399 is about the literary wars between these groups, drawing in Evagrius and the community of the Tall Brothers on the side of John, Melania, Rufinus, and Palladius.

All was well when Evagrius was alive. Theophilus, the archbishop of Alexandria (thus the notional superior of all Christian communities in Egypt, including monastics), revered Evagrius and treated him with honor as the leading theologian in Egypt. Like Evagrius, Theophilus used Origen's writings extensively himself, especially his biblical commentaries. But after Evagrius's death he became offended at the way the Tall Brothers were resisting his increasingly absolutist rule. And who were these Tall Brothers? They were four unusually tall siblings—Ammonius, Dioscorus, Eusebius, and Euthymios—who enjoyed a commanding reputation as ascetics in Egypt and had also been close friends with Evagrius and venerated Origen as not only the leading thinker and biblical exegete of the Christian world but also the most important theorist of the monastic life.

Theophilus had ordained one of the brothers, Dioscorus, as his own adjutant bishop, assigned to Hermopolis Minor. Ammonius was the founder of the second-generation revival of the famous monastic colony at Nitria and the spiritual leader of Kellia[14] (after Amun, its founder). He was the mentor and guide of Evagrius, who came (on the advice of Melania) to live with him at Nitria in 383 before moving to settle permanently at Kellia, twelve miles away. In the 390s there were about six hundred monks living here looking to the guidance of the Tall Brothers, a considerably large ecclesiastic settlement[15] that rivalled Alexandria for prestige as a Christian center, and in some ways outshone it, to the discomfort of the powerful archbishop of the capital.

Theophilus knew his Origen well enough to remember that the old master had taught that spiritual authority in the church derived from the personal spiritual acumen and level of insight of the officeholder and did not arise by virtue of ordination to the office itself.[16] He knew, from the dim view that Dioscorus of Hermopolis had of his style of administration, that he was regarded by the zealous Nitrian ascetics and intellectuals as not being someone they would naturally look up to for guidance.

Theophilus was a powerful career cleric who kept together his vast Egyptian diocese under autocratic control. Each of the almost two hundred other Egyptian bishops was ordained solely on the basis of being his junior assistant bishop and not allowed any independent authority (a state of affairs that contradicted the canonical basis of every other Christian state, where each diocesan bishop was sovereign, subject only to the collective vote of the local episcopal synod, whose president the archbishop was). In his earlier career, Theophilus had intervened in the Palestinian "Origenist" controversy, favoring the orthodoxy of the disciples of Origen. In his own archdiocese, many monks had appealed to him to drive away the intellectual Origenian monastics, who now commanded Nitria and Kellia, because they were disturbing the simple beliefs of the majority of monks by such teachings as that God was "not really angry" when the scripture spoke of his wrath. Theophilus in fact wrote his *Festal Letter* of 399 to rebuke such monks for their literalism, and so, early on, he not only used the works of Origen himself but protected the intelligentsia communities from the grumblings of the simpler peasant communities, who felt that severe penance and manual labor, cycled around the regular recitation of the psalms, were the real cores of monastic life.

In any case, three years after Evagrius's death, Theophilus decided he could kill two birds with one stone. In 402 he decided to issue a decree of exile against the Tall Brothers, and to declare that the "Origenistic" monastics were perverting the health of monasticism. In doing this, he gave all the monastics of Egypt a sharp warning as to how far his authority extended. It sobered all of them, including the simpler communities. But it also pleased the latter by affirming their values and discouraging the intelligentsia communities by the exile of their most famous leaders. He had, in effect, played to the majority.

Jerome, as might be expected, wrote a letter praising Theophilus for condemning the "Origenists."[17] But the Tall Brothers refused to go quietly. They accepted the relatively new canonical order of complaints established in the international church and took their appeal to the imperial capital. Formerly, Alexandria had been the chief legal court of appeal for the whole Eastern church, but since the late fourth century this right had passed to the church of Constantinople. Alexandria alone had refused to accept this state of affairs, so when the Tall Brothers appealed to the archbishop of Constantinople (John Chrysostom) for redress against an unjust sentence, Theophilus regarded this as illegitimate and complained to the emperor that his own archbishop, by taking in the monastic group and sympathizing with them, had broken the canons of the church and scorned his own episcopal rights. The emperor was delighted, at last, to have a potential cause for getting rid of Chrysostom, who had proven to be such a thorn in his and his wife Eudoxia's side, and so he invited Theophilus to come to a suburb of the capital and preside over the Synod of the Oak in 403, which deposed Chrysostom. This allowed the emperor to send him off into (temporary) exile to cool him off a little. Theophilus even invited Epiphanius to come and join the affair, but the latter, who was now in his eighties, took ill while traveling to Constantinople and turned back toward Cyprus, dying en route.

While at Constantinople, Theophilus made up all his differences with the Tall Brothers, and when they all returned home he was very pleased with the way he had so successfully established his reputation as a man to be reckoned with. He had shown all the Egyptian monks who was the boss, and he felt he could now relax his position. From this time onward, he stopped regarding the intellectual monks as "Origenists" and certainly did not consider them heretical deviants. Having reconciled with the leaders of the community at Nitria, he also personally returned to studying the works of Origen and continued using them extensively in his own writings.

But if this controversy sputtered out in the monastic heartland of Egypt (for Theophilus's successor, Cyril, did not permit its continuance), it burned on in the continuing unease that existed between intellectualist monastic communities and those that did not approve of libraries, manuscripts, or theologians. It was, therefore, inevitable that the fight would break out once again, and this time it reached another crisis a generation later, in Palestine, where the lives of the many monastic communities were already in a disturbed ferment over clashing reactions to the decrees of the Council of Chalcedon (451).

THE SIXTH-CENTURY ORIGENIST CRISIS:

The Palestinian Monks, Justinian, and the Councils of 553

This later part of the "Origenistic crisis" ought really to be called the Evagrian crisis, for it has more to do with the fight against aspects of Evagrius of Pontus's theological version of Origen's school than Origen himself. It was sparked off when the Syrian monastic theologian Stephen Bar Sudhaile in the late fifth century composed a treatise called *The Book of Saint Hierotheus*.[18] This was an apocryphon—a treatise masquerading as a work of an ancient from apostolic times, a disciple of Paul, who was the mentor of St. Dionysios of Athens. The treatises of Pseudo-Dionysios the Areopagite, also apocryphally composed at this time in Syriac-speaking circles, have a relation to this work, but one that remains obscure.

Stephen Bar Sudhaili was a mystic, a native of Edessa who lived as a monk in Jerusalem. He composed commentaries on scripture and was a renowned teacher among the Palestinian monastics of his time. His work, however, was heavily based on Evagrius and stressed certain controversial aspects of his teacher even more acutely, taking Evagrius's speculations even further into a mystical direction of pantheistic assimilation. His work discusses the originating emanation from divine primordial essence of the double universes of spiritual and material reality. The spiritual ascent of the monk is then described in terms of an ascentive return to the divine essence. The individual spiritual intellect (*nous*) realizes its synonymity with Christ the Logos. In the end, the Son hands over the kingdom to the Father, and all things are absorbed in the primal Good.

It is this tipping over into a Pantheistic mysticism that alarmed many of the theologians of the sixth century, and which they attributed to Origen of Alexandria (quite unjustifiably) and thus called the "Origenistic heresy." Stephen also reaffirmed quite openly Origen's speculation that since God was pure goodness all his punishments were therapeutic and corrective (and thus could not endure for an endless time). Stephen simply stated (boldly contradicting the New Testament passages that suggested contrary) that the punishments of purgatory or hell would be of limited duration. This idea he had found suggested in Origen but heavily misstated it since Origen noted (as well as his point that divine punishment is meant for a corrective purpose not a penal one) that the concept of duration cannot apply in the eschaton when time exists no more. Because of his stress on the way that the enlightened soul realized its essential identification with the Christ-Logos, Stephen's admirers were also called the Iso-Christoi (Equal-to-Christers). But catastrophically for Origen's reputation, this sect claimed that, far from being the innovators they were, they were simply following the doctrine of old and revered teachers of the eminence of Origen and Evagrius. Many monastics of the time, who had never read any of these original books and who had very little sense of historical development, simply took this at face value and condemned all the writers as if they were one heretical sect enduring from ancient times. This attitude can be seen, for example, in the early sixth-century monastic sages Barsanuphius and John, who warn monks against falling victim to Hellenistic (meaning "pagan" here) speculation: "These are the doctrines of the Hellenes;[19] they are the vain talk of people who claim to be something. Such words belong to idle people and are created through deceit . . . for I bear witness before God that you [reading them] have fallen into a pit of the devil and into ultimate death."[20]

This new doctrine of Stephen's, reminiscent at several points with even older forms of gnosticism, caused two of the leading anti-Chalcedonian theologians of the age (Jacob of Serugh, 451–521, and Philoxenus of Mabbug, d. 523) to send warnings about it to their Syrian communities. But at Jerusalem the teaching also caused a major rift in several of the most important Greek-speaking monasteries in Palestine, especially the Great Lavra and the New Lavra, communities under the spiritual leadership of the Archimandrite St. Sabas.

St. Sabas became alarmed at the way the monastic intelligentsia were developing these metaphysical arguments and tried (vainly) to call for a return to simpler monastic behavior, a time of early ideals of fellahin desert simplicity before this era when monastics acted as philosopher-theologians. The intelligentsia, however, were equally alarmed by his reaction and felt that the condemnation of Stephen was becoming an excuse for throwing out all of Evagrius's writings as well as those of Origen, as if they were all of a similar worthlessness. They attributed to Sabas an anti-intellectual prejudice that caused them to lose faith in the old archimandrite's leadership. The profound instability that this factionalization of the Palestinian monasteries caused (communities splitting and reforming on the basis of it) worried everyone all the way up to the emperor Justinian himself, who regarded the monasteries of Palestine not only as the foundation of the Jerusalem church's orthodoxy but even as the guarantors and practical embodiments of Byzantine control of the Middle Eastern passage from Egypt north to the imperial capital itself and the eastern imperial borders. For the emperor, it was not simply a theological argument at stake here, but a matter of state border security, and to make matters worse it had come on top of the long and bitter arguments that had divided those same monasteries, as well as large parts of Syria and Egypt, because of a concern that St. Cyril of Alexandria's theology had been undermined at the Council of Chalcedon in 451.[21]

Justinian, who saw himself as an informed theologian as well as statesman, decided that another council might be the answer, at which this heresy of the Iso-Christoi could be attacked, the Christology of Chalcedon reexpressed in a way that more clearly showed its role as a subordinate refinement of the Cyrilline theology of the Council of Ephesus in 431. He was hoping that this council (planned for 553 in the imperial city) would thus serve to quell dissent and be the basis of the reconciliation of the prevailing dyophysite and miaphysite schism. After a local preparatory synod organized by the court, a larger meeting was held, which has since gained ecumenical status as the Fifth Great Council, or the Second Council of Constantinople.

The works of Evagrius were closely scrutinized as well as the more recent writings of the Palestinian Iso-Christoi. No one thought to make a close study of the manuscripts of Origen. This was not how scholars of the period proceeded, which was more in the nature of seeking out "dubious propositions" that could be baldly stated and then refuted by an anathema. So in the end, fifteen of these anathemata (condemned propositions) were collated together, which have most unfortunately been titled "The Fifteen Anathemata against Origen"—considering that they were drawn chiefly from the writings of Evagrius and Stephen Bar Sudhaile. They clearly originated as what the conciliar fathers thought "Origenism" meant. A few of them can be recognized, vaguely, from speculations in the writings of Origen—things he asked his seminar students to consider in the course of probing questions, not propositions that he intended them to adopt or promulgate, such as the animation of the sun and other stars (anathema 1); the nature of the final consummation (anathemas 11–12); even metempsychosis, which Origen himself had condemned as incompatible with Christian faith. But where they have a resonance with things Origen wrote about, their appearance in the form of this list, in 553, bears no relation to Origen's own theology but is a distorted form of speculation barely cognizant of it.

One can today reasonably admit that these fifteen propositions, condemned by ecumenical decree, clearly do not to have any place in the orthodox consensus of the faith,[22] but also that the further deduction—that therefore Origen himself had been posthumously condemned as a heretic by an ecumenical decree—fails in its force. The latter implication fails according both to logic, since the doctrines are not those of Origen himself, and to justice, since Ecumenical decrees are first and foremost statements of ecclesiastical law (canon), and ecclesiastical courts of this high stature are not held to lower standards of justice than secular courts, but rather to incomparably higher standards. So both for its faulty reading of the evidence and for its uncharitably harsh attribution of heretical stature to a man who had lived and died in obedience to the *regula fidei* as confessed in his own day,[23] we need to make a distinction between the condemnation of the propositions as such (which were, and still are, for the Orthodox and Catholics not to be considered permissible within the ecumenical consensus of the faith) and the anathematization of Origen himself.

Some scholars have argued of late that the "anti-Origenist" condemnations belong to a local synod of Constantinople and were only later attached to the *acta* of the Ecumenical Council of 553 by subsequent scribal false accounting.[24] Be that as it may, the same arguments stated above apply: a synod is still a council, and the highest standards of justice need apply in its consideration of evidence, especially when making global judgements about an individual. If the evidence is faulted, later standards of accuracy need to be retrospectively applied, which can be done judiciously without in any way affecting the overall synodical and ecumenical judgment that the fifteen propositions so listed are not to be considered part of the orthodox catholic faith of the church (which in fact they never have been).

Here are the fifteen anathemata of 553 that had such a damaging effect on Origen's reputation (especially in the Latin West) and which caused generations of careless readers to presume this was what Origen had actually taught:

1. If anyone asserts the fabulous pre-existence of souls, and shall assert the monstrous restoration which follows from it: let him be anathema.
2. If anyone shall say that the creation of all reasonable things includes only intelligences [*Noes*] without bodies and altogether immaterial, having neither number nor name, so that there is unity between them all by identity of substance, force and energy, and by their union with and knowledge of God the Word; but that no longer desiring the sight of God, they gave themselves over to worse things, each one following his own inclinations, and that they have taken bodies more or less subtle, and have received names, for among the heavenly Powers there is a difference of names as there is also a difference of bodies; and thence some became and are called Cherubim, others Seraphim, and Principalities, and Powers, and Dominations, and Thrones, and Angels, and as many other heavenly orders as there may be: let him be anathema.
3. If anyone shall say that the sun, the moon and the stars are also reasonable beings, and that they have only become what they are because they turned towards evil: let him be anathema.

4. If anyone shall say that the reasonable creatures in whom the divine love had grown cold have been hidden in gross bodies such as ours, and have been called men, while those who have attained the lowest degree of wickedness have shared cold and obscure bodies and are become and called demons and evil spirits: let him be anathema.
5. If anyone shall say that a psychic condition has come from an angelic or archangelic state, and moreover that a demoniac and a human condition has come from a psychic condition, and that from a human state they may become again angels and demons, and that each order of heavenly virtues is either all from those below or from those above, or from those above and below: let him be anathema.
6. If anyone shall say that there is a twofold race of demons, of which the one includes the souls of men and the other the superior spirits who fell to this, and that of all the number of reasonable beings there is but one which has remained unshaken in the love and contemplation of God, and that that spirit is become Christ and the king of all reasonable beings, and that he has created all the bodies which exist in heaven, on earth, and between heaven and earth; and that the world which has in itself elements more ancient than itself, and which exists by themselves, viz.: dryness, damp, heat and cold, and the image to which it was formed, was so formed, and that the most holy and consubstantial Trinity did not create the world, but that it was created by the Demiurgic Nous which is more ancient than the world, and which communicates to it its being: let him be anathema.
7. If anyone shall say that Christ, of whom it is said that he appeared in the form of God, and that he was united before all time with God the Word, and humbled himself in these last days even to humanity, had (according to their expression) pity upon different levels of fallenness which had appeared in the spirits united in the same unity (of which he himself is part), and that to restore them he passed through different classes, had different bodies and different names, became all to all, an Angel among Angels, a Power among Powers, has clothed himself in the different classes of reasonable beings with a form corresponding to that class, and finally has taken flesh and blood like ours and is become man for men; [if anyone says all this] and does not profess that God the Word humbled himself and became man: let him be anathema.
8. If anyone shall not acknowledge that God the Word, of the same substance with the Father and the Holy Ghost, and who was made flesh and became man, one of the Trinity, is Christ in every sense of the word, but [shall affirm] that he is so only in an inaccurate manner, and because of the abasement, as they call it, of the Nous; if anyone shall affirm that this Nous united to God the Word, is the Christ in the true sense of the

word, while the Logos is only called Christ because of this union with the intelligence, and likewise that the intelligence is only called God because of the Logos: let him be anathema.

9. If anyone shall say that it was not the Divine Logos made man by taking an animated body with a soul possessed of logos and nous, that he descended into hell and ascended into heaven, but shall pretend that it is the Nous which has done this, that Nous of which they say (in an impious fashion) he is Christ properly so called, and that he is become so by the knowledge of the Monad: let him be anathema.

10. If anyone shall say that after the resurrection the body of the Lord was ethereal, having the form of a sphere, and that such shall be the bodies of all after the resurrection; and that after the Lord himself shall have rejected his true body and after the others who rise shall have rejected theirs, the nature of their bodies shall be annihilated: let him be anathema.

11. If anyone shall say that the future judgment signifies the destruction of the body and that the end of the story will be an immaterial nature, and that thereafter there will no longer be any matter, but only spiritual Nous, let him be anathema.

12. If anyone shall say that the heavenly Powers and all men and the Devil and evil spirits are united with the Word of God in all respects, as the Nous which is by them called Christ and which is in the form of God, and which humbled itself as they say; and [if anyone shall say] that the Kingdom of Christ shall have an end: let him be anathema.

13. If anyone shall say that Christ [i.e., the Nous] is in no wise different from other reasonable beings, neither substantially nor by wisdom nor by his power and might over all things but that all will be placed at the right hand of God, as well as he that is called by them Christ [the Nous], as also they were in the feigned pre-existence of all things: let him be anathema.

14. If anyone shall say that all reasonable beings will one day be united in one, when the hypostases as well as the numbers and the bodies shall have disappeared, and that the knowledge of the world to come will carry with it the ruin of the worlds, and the rejection of bodies as also the abolition of [all] names, and that there shall be finally an identity of the gnosis and of the hypostasis; moreover, that in this pretended Apokatastasis, spirits only will continue to exist, as it was in the feigned pre-existence: let him be anathema.

15. If anyone shall say that the life of the spirits (Nous) shall be like to the life which was in the beginning while as yet the spirits had not come down or fallen, so that the end and the beginning shall be alike,

and that the end shall be the true measure of the beginning: let him be anathema.[25]

If anathemata of a great council had fallen on anyone else other than Origen, they would have been buried so deep in the obscure dust of Christian history that they would never have been heard of again. None of their works would have survived, or fragmented pieces at best. Yet Origen not only survived, his real thought was read on and studied, and eventually flourished regardless, once it was capable of being read on its own terms[26]—precisely because generations of the largest minds in the church knew that he was both a preeminently saintly witness and an overwhelmingly good theologian, whose works needed only cautious emendation (as St. Gregory the Theologian and many other saints had already argued) but not wholesale rejection or anti-intellectual abjection.

However, the *Letters of Saints Barsanuphius and John* and the instance of St. Sabas (as recounted in the *Lives of the Palestinian Monks* by Cyril of Scythopolis) surely added to the weight of the ecumenical censure of the "Origenism" circulating at this period in the sixth century, an additional and very heavy disapproval from the "holiness tradition." If great monastic saints had opined that anyone reading this material was well along the road to hell, this surely must have had a chilling effect on any monastic library holding the texts in question, and also on that very readership that looked to eminent theologians—monastics themselves. It seemed a long time back that saintly fathers of the stature of Dionysios of Alexandria, Athanasius, Gregory the Theologian, Basil the Great, and Gregory of Nyssa had championed Origen and his writings in the third and fourth centuries. Was there no great saint whose reputation could rise up in this sixth-and seventh-century period to reclaim the utility of the deeper patristic tradition that had adapted and judiciously incorporated the works of the earlier fathers in the unfolding doctrines of orthodoxy?

"Cometh the hour, cometh the man," as the saying has it, and just at this dark moment for Origen's reputation there came along a humble monk, one of the greatest intellects of his day, indeed one of the most brilliant minds of the entire Byzantine period, who renewed the task that St. Gregory of Theologian had taken on in the late fourth century: reconsidering the positive power and merits of the Origenian mystical tradition and adapting it to the needs of the contemporary church. This was the highly intellectual Byzantine saint Maximus the Confessor.

MAXIMUS THE CONFESSOR

Maximus (c. 580–662), the product of a deep and liberal education, had read extensively and was well aware of the currents of the so-called Origenist disputes of the previous generation. He highly valued Gregory the Theologian, whose works he comments on in detail, and adopted Gregory's maxim "Words in the service of the Word," not least in relation to the value Gregory placed on the overall conception Origen sketched out of how all creation moved inexorably toward union with the Logos. Mueller-Jourdan calls this:

> the weltanschauung of Origenism that Maximus knew. It is not irrational today to admit that Maximus inherited the general cosmic vision of all realities introduced by the original inquiry of *On First Principles* . . . . If we can recognize in the metaphysics of Origenism the prime matter of Maximus' cosmic liturgy, particularly the connection between metaphysics and chronological sequences of the general divine economy of creation, it will be obvious that Maximus effected a radical and orthodox reconfiguration of Origen's metaphysics.[27]

However, where Mueller-Jourdan takes his starting point as the generic thought patterns originated by "Origenism" in the fifth century, I would make this important distinction: Maximus went back to the originals.[28] It was not Origenism in the round he was reacting to and correcting; it was precisely the Logocentric mystical coherence of the *De Principiis* and the metaphysics of love contained in such exegetical works as the *Commentary on the Song of Songs* that Maximus developed in close harmony with his reading of Gregory the Theologian and Dionysius the Areopagite. In brief, he synthesized the larger Origenian metaphysics for his own age and—through his witness—on to the Byzantine and modern Orthodox worlds, forging a golden chain of reception and interpretation that ran from Origen through Athanasius, Gregory the Theologian, Dionysius, and Maximus himself, in ways that smoothed and rounded the tradition of a metaphysics of ascentive love so that it was in accord with the ecumenical tradition. Maximus saved Origen for later centuries just as Gregory the Theologian had done earlier. When Maximus censures the style and conclusions of the sixth-century Origenistic sect, as he does in his treatise *Ad Joannem Ambiguum*, it is clear he does so in conscious harmony with his venerated mentor Gregory the Theologian,[29] who censured the way the fourth-century Arians had misapplied him.

Maximus's intention is, once more, to rescue the great worth of what remains of lasting value in Origen's thought.[30] It was also important for Maximus to rehabilitate Evagrius of Pontus, whose worth as a monastic mystical theologian he recognized, though he also knew that Evagrius's speculative theories about the eschaton had largely fuelled the recent Origenistic crisis.[31] His work proceeded by not citing the two writers by name (as he did not wish to be labeled an "Origenist" and he knew his enemies were bent on condemning him for heresy), but his debt is nonetheless evident.[32] In fact, Evagrius's thought world was to be rescued in Maximus's sketching of the "cosmic liturgy," while Evagrius's writings would survive partly by the monastic expedient of being assigned to a venerable sage from the past who had not written anything, and so it was they passed to modern times under the pseudonym St. Nilus, and only in contemporary times has their correct authorship been reasserted and the deep value of Evagrius's spiritual teachings been appreciated in a new light.[33] This pious fraud of pseudonymity was not done so much with Origen himself. In the East his works continued to be read in Greek, but in a corpus that was reduced mainly to his exegetical studies.

These, in any case, had entered into the mainstream of patristic exegetical lore, through such indebted and central exegetes such as Cyril of Alexandria and John Chrysostom, the latter of whom represented a moderating (simplifying) effect on Origen's didactic style. For doctrinal matters, the East was largely content to keep the *Philocalia Origenis*, that dossier of the "best of Origen" that the renowned Cappadocian fathers had collated in the fourth century. Although Maximus had made the most thoroughgoing rehabilitation of Origen's overarching scheme of cosmic salvation, his works were not extensively read until relatively late times, and as he had not cited Origen, it was often not realized how much of the old master had been remade here. There is no doubt, however, that the censures of the Fifth Ecumenical Council did immense damage to the reputation in a global and inaccurate dismissal of the originals. Nevertheless, although the large corpus of Origen's works did take a fairly heavy hit because of it, the one thing that remains astounding about the church's reaction to this call to consign the totality to the flames was the way that so very much was preserved. Of the ancient library of ecclesiastical authors, Origen is in the top three of those whose works have survived. This of course means that generation by generation all those manuscripts were laboriously recopied and repristinated, precisely because they were being read and used as important resources in the regular life of the church. The survival of anything of his would have been remarkable; the survival of so very much is a testament to the wisdom of the great fathers who wanted to prune Origen's tree, not uproot it. As Gregory the Theologian had phrased it (speaking about his attitude to pagan Hellenistic literature), one ought to "clip the thorns from the roses," not consign the entire bush to the flames.

ANTIQUE WESTERN RECEPTION: AMBROSE, JEROME, AUGUSTINE, AND CASSIODORUS

In the West, this "discretionary" reading of Origen did not continue in the same way. By the time of Augustine, it was increasingly rare to find a Latin theologian who could read or speak Greek. So the access of the West to Origen's writings was restricted to a tiny circle of intelligentsia, and more or less only through the medium of the Latin versions made by Jerome and Rufinus, though Ambrose of Milan (c. 340–397) was an exception.

Ambrose of Milan

Ambrose had entered the church as a bishop without significant preparation as a Christian thinker. He had been unexpectedly elected as the new metropolitan bishop by popular acclamation. He remained for most of his life under the influence of his learned mentor, the Milanese priest Simplicianus. It was Simplicianus who also heavily influenced Augustine's decision to convert back to catholic Christianity. Simplicianus was at the center of a circle of Christian intelligentsia in Milan deeply invested in following up the connections between Christian dogmatics and Neo-Platonic thought. Since Ambrose had to learn the craft of being a bishop extremely rapidly after his consecration, Simplicianus guided him to the works of Origen. Ambrose was well able to read directly in Greek and accessed Origen's works with gratitude, especially his exegetical writings. Few in the Milanese cathedral would have known where the learned bishop took his sermon material from, but Jerome's anger was roused against him when he realized his continuing dependence on a theologian he, Jerome, had decided ought to be denounced, and he angrily called Ambrose a "crow dressed up in another bird's feathers" because of it. Nevertheless, many subsequent Latin writers unconsciously absorbed Origen by means of Ambrose.

Jerome

Jerome (c. 347–420) had begun life as a dedicated and zealous follower of Origen, but the mood swing that turned against the old master, perhaps mainly because of the Arian controversies involving the Origenian Academy at Caesarea, shifted his allegiance into a bitter opposition. It was also the sharp rivalry between Jerome's establishment at Bethlehem and the close triad of Melania, Rufinus, and John of Jerusalem in the holy city that embittered Jerome significantly against anything to do with Origen, whom he denounced to the West as a heretic who must be shunned. Even so, and even after his most serious denunciations of Origen, Jerome continued for all his life to use Origen's works heavily, only ceasing to reference him or acknowledge the enduring dependence. Jerome certainly found fault with Origen's doctrines of *apokatastasis*, but he made a travesty of what Origen actually said by claiming that Origen taught there would be an eternally unending series of restitutions of fallen creations (since God alone was unchanging and all potential rehabilitations and judgments could only be relative as far as the creation was concerned). He also strongly distanced himself from other aspects of Origen's work, such as his understanding of the spiritual risen body (based on Paul in 1 Cor. 15) and aspects of his Christology and pneumatology. But in regard to Origen's exegetical writings, Jerome spread them far and wide in the Latin church. Because later Latin ages regarded Jerome as the father of biblical exegesis par excellence, again (without entirely realizing it) the West absorbed Origenian exegetical process and even much of his detailed thought as the staple approach of the whole Latin church.

And so, even as an enemy, Jerome was the sower who disseminated the seeds of Origen to the fields of the West. He did more than establish Origen's biblical theology as a standard, however, for in his early life, and even in his later period of hostility, he set his hand as a master linguist to the translation of Origen's Greek texts. His were the translations (along with those of Rufinus) that allowed the West to read Origen directly, and for many centuries afterward this was the only road of access, yet sufficient to awe generations of later thinkers with the brilliance of the ancient master. In classic studies, Jean Leclerq and Henri de Lubac have both shown the vast extent to which Origen taught the entire medieval Latin West how to exegete scripture[34] and the correspondingly massive amount of medieval manuscripts that contain Latin versions of his works.[35] While listening to Gregory Nazianzen, Evagrius, and Gregory Nyssen in Constantinople, in 380 Jerome rendered into Latin fourteen homilies by Origen on the book of Jeremiah and the same number of homilies on Ezekiel.

At Rome in 383, he made a translation of two homilies by Origen on the Song of Songs, and at Bethlehem in 389, he translated thirty-nine homilies on the Gospel of Luke. Having fallen out very badly with his old friend Rufinus, he set himself to translate the *De Principiis* of Origen, chiefly to show up Rufinus's version as partial. There has been much discussion since as to which of the two is the finest work and which of the two is the most accurate. One thing is clear, however: Rufinus had the better command of Greek. The warring translations had the benefit of preserving one of the chief works of Origen's dogmatics for posterity among Latin speakers, and after the immediate heat of the battle had cooled off in the West, thinkers such as Scotus Eriugena were able to see the Origenian achievement for themselves and reassess its worth firsthand.

Augustine of Hippo

It was long thought that Augustine of Hippo (c. 354–430), being unable to read Greek, was completely unaware of the works of Origen until late in his life, when he asked Jerome what all the fuss was about over the ancient master and (unsurprisingly) got a jaundiced view in return that scared him off. However, more recent study has shown that the influence of Origen had penetrated even into North Africa, and Augustine had indeed been personally influenced.[36] Ilaria Ramelli explains that he, therefore, had two stages in his attitude: the first in his anti-Manichean writings in his early career as a catholic theologian, and the second after he had received an alarming synopsis from Jerome of all that was wrong with the Alexandrian theologian.[37]

Origen affects the great African in two chief ways: the first in terms of the doctrine of *apokatastasis*, and the second in relation to Augustine's doctrine of grace. When he was arguing against the dualistic metaphysics of the Manicheans, Augustine used the concept from the *De Principiis* of how God will restore all things to the good ultimately, so that evil cannot withstand the divine force and can have no independent existence in ultimate terms. This reliance can be seen in his *De Ordine*, the *De Genesi Adversus Manichaeos*, and the *De moribus ecclesiae catholicae et de moribus manichaeorum*. In the latter work, Augustine argues that "God's goodness . . . orders all fallen beings . . . until they return to the state from which they fell."[38] The concept that the goodness of God is the fundamental force that (ontologically) refuses to allow any ultimate success to wickedness is a giveaway to Origen's understanding of Paul's ideas on *apokatastasis*. Between 426 and 427, however, when he wrote his *Retractations*, Augustine had been alerted to the way many regarded his assertion as too like that of Origen's, and he specifically qualifies it in a way that shows he was anxious now to distance himself from the Alexandrian: "It must not be understood as though all beings were restored to the state from which they fell, in the manner in which Origen thought . . . for those who will be punished with the eternal fire do not return to God from whom they fell."[39] Here he reverts to the understanding of eternal fire (*pur aionion*) as "fire of endless duration," despite Origen's arguments that the timeless state of the next age (the true meaning of *aionion*) means that eternity cannot be understood as a sequential, time-bound matter. So it was that by his immense historical influence Augustine turned the compass point in the West away from this important point of exegesis. The problem here was that Augustine did not enjoy a very close reading of Origen[40] and relied for this matter of *apokatastasis* doctrine on Jerome's ridiculous summation of why Origen was wrong. Jerome had warned off Augustine by claiming (falsely) that Origen's *apokatastasis* doctrine relied on the idea of there being an endless succession of aeons that rise up to God and yet fall away again and again, never reaching ontological stability, and he went on to claim (again falsely) that this was tantamount to Origen adopting Plato's idea of a universal salvation based in the nature of souls.[41]

The Pelagian controversy, again later in Augustine's life, was the second occasion when his work crossed paths with what Origen had sketched out earlier. But this time it was Pelagius, making an exegesis in Rome of the Pauline Letter to the Romans, who found Origen's ideas on freedom of will most attractive, and Augustine who found them somewhat alarming. His own earlier statements in the anti-Manichean works asserting the free will of the believer assisted by the grace of God were tightened up in his anti-Pelagian writings, and the ethical encomia that Origen uses so often (the critical importance of a robust and freely willed choice for the good on the part of the soul), were echoed by Pelagius,[42] now seemed to Augustine to underestimate the power of divine grace by placing a human moral energy alongside it—hardly what Origen was speaking about in his own conception of the how the soul is constantly being guided by the Logos of God in its ascentive return to divine communion. Even so, as Caroline Bammel demonstrated, Origen's commentaries on Paul, in their Latin translations, had heavily influenced Augustine, even to the extent of giving him a generic model of how to approach and understand Pauline exegesis.[43]

Ramelli concludes: "Such misunderstandings [of Origen] are reflected in Augustine's anti-Pelagian works, *De haeresibus* and *De Civitate Dei* and were facilitated by his ignorance of the distinction between *aionios* and *aidios*, lost in the translation of both with *aeternus*."[44] Because of this linguistic limitation, Augustine could not appreciate how Origen's *apokatastasis* was anything other than a determinism setting human independence apart from God.

Vittorino Grossi has recently made a detailed note of all the passages where the mature Augustine explicitly references Origen's work.[45] How was it, then, that Augustine, more or less devoid of Greek, came across the writings of Origen? Dominic Keech thinks that before Rufinus and Jerome made their translations there were dossiers of selected Origenian texts circulating in the West, and that Simplicianus in Milan made some of the Origen excerpts available to Augustine while he was resident there.[46] Ramelli accepts this as likely but also thinks he may have had independent library access to partial Latin versions: "That such manuscripts circulated is proved not only by the *Commentarioli in Matthaeum*, but also by Pamphilus[47] who attests that already around 300 CE anonymous manuscripts containing works by Origen circulated."[48] It is abundantly clear, from researches made by Altaner and Studer, that, knowingly or not, Augustine had absorbed a considerable amount of Origen's exegesis across his own biblical work.[49]

Cassiodorus

One of the chief Latin champions of Origen was the monk Cassiodorus (490–c. 585) of the Vivarium monastery near Scylettium (Squillace in Italy today). He was a high-ranking statesman, holding the offices of *quaestor*, consul, and magister officiorum under the Ostrogothic kings and praetorian prefect in 533 under Athalaric. He was also a fine scholar who sensed it was his duty to gather and repair the intellectual heritage of antiquity. In 540 he retired from public life and founded his monastery near his birthplace, placing a scriptorium at the center of all operations. He commanded his monks to exemplify the scholarly life and spend their ascetical efforts in copying manuscripts, but notably both the Christian classics and the pagan works of high art (the poets, historians, and rhetors) so that the Christian religion could be seen not only as the heir of Rome's great and noblest traditions but also as their renovator and developer. His scholarly oversight was able to collate an ample library of exemplars in the Vivarium, to which he brought manuscripts from wherever he could find them. It was his example in this period, often called the beginning of the Dark Ages, that set a standard many other monasteries in the Christian world wished to emulate, thus saving Christianity from being a rigidly prudish and exclusionist religion. His impact on Christian culture is monumental.

Cassiodorus, scholar that he was, came to know the works of Origen through the translations made by Rufinus and Jerome. He valued equally the exegetical works and the dogmatic-philosophical writings (chiefly the *De Principiis*). Bernard Pouderon, who has made a detailed study of the transmission of Origenian manuscripts in the medieval and early modern West, recognizes Cassiodorus as the key figure in the continuing Latin interest in Origen's work.[50] The Latin church continued to read Origen unawares, not realizing how much of Origen's psalm exegesis had been absorbed (often with little change) in Jerome, or how very much of his theology was contained (without attribution) in the writings of Ambrose of Milan, whom it elevated as a pillar of the Latin theological tradition. Cassiodorus knew Origen's Psalm commentary firsthand and also much of Origen's Old Testament exegesis, and he used him extensively in his own Psalm commentary and his Octateuchal writings, where he cites him admiringly. It was largely through Cassiodorus's enthusiastic reviews that Origen continued to be read by the medieval Latins, even though the "condemnation by Pope Vigilius" (as they referred to the anathemata attached to the Fifth Ecumenical Council) was vaguely remembered. Cassiodorus more or less underscored the judgment of Pamphilus, Gregory Nazianzen, Rufinus, and Jerome (in his earlier years) that though some parts of Origen's philosophy and dogmatics were not to be accepted, this was no excuse for an anti-intellectual attitude that wanted to burn the books wholesale or ignore him as a heretic. His is not, perhaps, the widely generous view of Origen's stature as saintly confessor that the earlier Greek fathers held to, but it is a scholar's judicious judgment and a heartening appeal to the discretionary worth of intelligence opposed to denunciation. He writes in his widely read *Institutes*:

> There still exist some immensely eloquent sermons of Origen on the Octateuch in three books. A number of fathers consider him to be a heretic; however, saint Jerome translated several of his smaller works into a very elegant Latin. Apart from the attacks he has received on the authority of many fathers, he was also recently condemned by the blessed Pope Vigilius. Even so, Saint Jerome, in the letter he addressed to Tranquillinus,[51] has shown in a most convincing manner how one ought to read Origen . . . . Accordingly, let us read him with caution and discretion, aiming to draw from him salvific juice, and not the poisons of his perverted dogma, which would be a danger to our life.[52]

In short, Cassiodorus gave the West some scholarly courage in this regard, which buoyed up Origen, who lacked the heavy hitters he had on his side in the Greek-speaking world—those great fathers we have already noticed who deeply admired him and similarly advocated the use of his work, with discretion.

After Cassiodorus, however, it is only at the end of antiquity and well into the dawn of the medieval period that we find any Latin intelligentsia finding their way back to his writings, and surprising themselves at what they find there. That story begins again with Charlemagne's court.

NOTES

1. Written in collaboration with E. Prinzivalli. See H. Crouzel and E. Prinzivalli, "Origenism," in Di Berardino, *Encylopedia of Ancient Christianity*, 2:983–86. See also E. M. Harding, "Origenist Crises," in McGuckin, *Westminster Handbook to Origen*, 162–67.

2. E. A. Clark, *The Origenist Controversy: The Cultural Construction of an Early Christian Debate* (Princeton, NJ: Princeton University Press, 1992).

3. A moderate opponent, Methodius of Olympus (c. 250–311), is a prime example of this. Methodius posthumously castigated Origen for teaching that the resurrected body was not going to be physically the same as the one we now possess on earth (seemingly unaware of the ambivalence Paul himself shows in 1 Cor. 15—a fact not missed by Origen himself). Methodius's whole argument hinges on Origen's use of the term *eidos* (appearance) in this context to mean the appearance of the risen body, whereas Origen was using it as a metaphysical principle about perception. In other words, Methodius more or less completely misread the subtlety of what he (presumably) was reading. Methodius also objected to Origen's theory about the world's

eternity, but overall he also pays his respects to Origen as a theologian who had served the church greatly and whom the church ought to venerate but correct where necessary. He was engaged in a critical but respectful dialogue with Origen, whom he admired, unlike the intemperate critical attitude of Jerome later.

4. This is a sure sign that they were not reading the original text but a manuscript of selected most-damaging gobbets, a deeply unjust and intellectually dubious way to censure a writer, as is apparent to our modern consciousness.

5. Crouzel and Prinzivalli, "Origenism," 984.

6. Text in *Pamphilus: Apology for Origen—with the Letter of Rufinus on the Falsification of the Books of Origen*, trans. T. P. Scheck, Fathers of the Church 120 (Washington, DC: Catholic University of America, 2010).

7. C.f. 1 Cor. 8:12.

8. Rufinus, *Preface to the Apology of Pamphilus* 1.

9. Rufinus, *Preface to the Apology of Pamphilus* 4–7.

10. Epiphanius, *Panarion* 72.3. "Adamantios" was a title of high honor the early church gave to Origen—something like "Man of Steel."

11. Epiphanius, *Panarion* 72.4–8.

12. See M. Villain, "Rufin d'Aquilée: La querelle autour d'Origène (role d'Epiphane de Salamine)," *Recherches de Science Religieuse* 37 (1937): 5–18; and J. Dechow, *Dogma and Mysticism in Early Christianity: Epiphanius of Cyprus and the Legacy of Origen* (Washington, DC: Catholic University of America Press, 1988).

13. He had famously visited a village church and tore down the woven curtain over the main door because it had an image of Christ on it—no images, he said, were permissible in Christ's church. He got into trouble for this as the villagers made him pay for a replacement.

14. The modern Egyptian site of Al Muna.

15. By the fifth and sixth centuries, the monks numbered thousands in Nitria and Kellia.

16. See McGuckin, "Origen's Doctrine of the Priesthood."

17. Jerome, *Epistle 86: To Theophilus*.

18. Its full title is *The Book of Hierotheus on the Hidden Mysteries of the House of God*. It survives in one single Syriac manuscript (British Museum, Add. Mss. 7189) of the thirteenth century. Hierotheus was supposedly the teacher of Dionysius the Areopagite and an immediate disciple of St. Paul. See A. L. Frothingham, *Stephen Bar Sudhaili, the Syrian Mystic, and the Book of Hierotheus* (Leiden: Brill, 1886; repr., Eugene, OR: Wipf & Stock, 2010). The text was also translated by F. S. Marsh, *The Book Which Is Called the Book of the Holy Hierotheus* (London: APA-Philo Press, 1927).

19. I.e., considerations of the *apokatastasis* and the nature and origin of souls. The three writers cited are Origen, Evagrius, and Didymus the Blind, but the amalgam of ideas listed is a hotchpotch of half-read and misunderstood concepts, and the advice is basically to have nothing to do with any literature other than the lives of saints and the sayings of the Desert Elders.

20. See Barsanuphius and John, *Letters* paras. 600–602, in John Chryssavgis, trans., *Barsanuphius and John: Letters*, vol. 2, Fathers of the Church 114 (Washington, DC: Catholic University of America Press, 2007), 179–83.

21. The so-called monophysite controversy. See W. H. C. Frend, *The Rise of the Monophysite Movement* (London: James Clarke, 2008).

22. To which the Orthodox and Catholic churches are committed.

23. Origen's *De Principiis* is all about stating the *Rule of Faith* over and against heretical deviance, and showing theologians where development was needed for the future. He expressed the desire never to deviate from the *regula fidei* ever in his own work.

24. When church historian N. P. Tanner edited his critical edition of the Decrees of the Ecumenical Councils (2 vols. [Washington, DC: Georgetown University Press, 1990]), he did not include any of these anti-Origenist denunciations, saying this: "Our edition does not include the text of the anathemas against Origen since recent studies have shown that these anathemas cannot be attributed to this council" (1:106).

25. Text in Henry R. Percival, ed., *The Seven Ecumenical Councils of the Undivided Church*, Nicene and Post-Nicene Fathers, 2nd series, vol. 14 (Edinburgh: T&T Clark, 1892), 318–319.

26. Before the great eighteenth-century editions of his *opera*, only a very few intelligentsia had access to the manuscripts.

27. P. Mueller-Jourdan, "The Foundation of Origenist Metaphysics," in *The Oxford Handbook of Maximus the Confessor*, ed. P. Allen anf B. Neil (Oxford: Oxford University Press, 2015), 149.

28. And so agree the three most eminent Maximian scholars of the modern era: Völker, Thunberg, and Blowers.

29. See A. Louth, "St. Gregory the Theologian and St. Maximus the Confessor: The Shaping of Tradition," in *The Making and Re-Making of Christian Doctrine: Essays in Honour of Maurice Wiles*, ed. S. Coakley and D. Pailin (Oxford: Oxford University Press, 1993), 117–30; G. Berthold, "The Cappadocian Roots of Maximus the Confessor," in *Maximus Confessor: Actes du Symposium sur Maxime le Confesseur*, ed. F. Heinzer and C. Schonborn (Freiburg: Editions Universitaires, 1982), 51–59.

30. So have argued P. Sherwood, *The Ascetic Life: Four Centuries on Charity*, Ancient Christian Writers 21 (Westminster, MD: Newman Press, 1955), 8–9, 85–91, and J. C. Larchet, *La divinisation de l'homme selon s. Maxime le Confesseur* (Paris: Editions du Cerf, 1996), 30–31, 451–52, 518–20. It is also the position of W. Völker, *Maximus Confessor als Meister des geistlichen Lebens* (Wiesbaden: Franz Steiner, 1965); L. Thunberg, *Microcosm and Mediator: The Theological Anthropology of Maximus the Confessor*, 2nd ed. (Chicago: Open Court Press, 1995); and P. Blowers, *Maximus the Confessor: Jesus Christ and the Transfiguration of the World* (Oxford: Oxford University Press, 2016).

31. See I. H. Dalmais, "Saint Maxime le Confesseur et la crise de l'origenisme monastique," in *Theologie de la vie monastique* (Paris: Aubier, 1961), 411–21.

32. In his own trial, when accused of Origenism (by then a common catchall to accuse a monk of heresy (see P. Hatlie, *The Monks and Monasteries of Constantinople, ca. 350–850* [Cambridge: Cambridge University Press, 2007], 136–40), Maximus

willingly condemned that contemporary monastic movement, even to the point of agreeing to anathematize the name of Origen himself—the latter expedient chiefly, I think, to save himself from his hostile judges, who were seeking any excuse to do what they eventually did, namely, inflict mutilation on him as a traitor. See the account of the trial in *Relatio Motionis 5* in P. Allen and B. Neil, eds., *Maximus the Confessor and His Companions: Documents from Exile* (Oxford: Oxford University Press, 2002), 58–59.

33. Evagrius's most controversial work, the *Gnostic Chapters*, would survive in a Syriac translation.

34. While they knew that Jerome, Augustine, and Pope Vigilius had censured Origen as a somewhat dangerous dogmatician, they also remembered how Jerome had praised him as a great and important exegete.

35. See J. Leclerq, *The Love of Learning and the Desire for God: A Study of Monastic Culture* (New York: Fordham University Press, 1961), 100–102; H. De Lubac, *Exégèse Mediévale: le quatre sens de lécriture*, vol. 1, pt. 1 (Paris: Aubier, 1959), ch. 4, "L'Origène latin." See also A. Siegmund, *Die Überlieferung der griechischen Literatur in der Lateinischen Kirche bis zum zwolften Jahrhundert*, Abhandlungen der bayerischen Benediktiner-Akademie 5 (Munich: Filser-Verlag, 1949), and J. T. Muckle, "Greek Works Translated into Latin before 1350," *Medieval Studies* 4 (1942): 33–42; 5 (1943): 102–14.

36. See D. Keech, *The Anti-Pelagian Christology of Augustine* (Oxford: Oxford University Press, 2012), 23; I. L. E. Ramelli, "Origen and Augustine: A Paradoxical Reception," *Numen* 60 (2013), 280–307; I. L. E. Ramelli, "Origen in the Western Theological and Philosophical Tradition," in *Origeniana Undecima: Origen and Origenism in the History of Western Though*, ed. A. C. Jacobsen (Leuven: Peeters, 2016), 454–58.

37. Ramelli, "Origen in the Western Theological and Philosophical Tradition," 454–55.

38. Augustine, *De moribus ecclesiae catholicae et de moribus manichaeorum* 2.7.9.

39. Augustine, *Retractations* 1.7.6.

40. As Gustave Bardy summed it up, Augustine "connait fort mal les oeuvres d'Origène, et meme ses doctrines caracteristiques." G. Bardy, "Les citations du *De Principiis*," *Augustinianum* 35 (1959): 485.

41. Ramelli, "Origen and Augustine," n59.

42. Overstressing them, perhaps, and in turn being overstressed himself by his disciple Caelestius, whose doctrine, once brought to Africa, was condemned by the African bishops and endorsed by the Ephesian council under the heading of Pelagianism.

43. C. P. Bammel, "Augustine, Origen and the Exegesis of Paul," in *Tradition and Exegesis in Early Christian Writers* (Aldershot, UK: Variorum, 1995), ch. 17. See also J. W. Trigg, "Origen," in *Augustine through the Ages*, ed. A. D. Fitzgerald (Grand Rapids, MI: Eerdmans, 1999), 604.

44. Ramelli, "Origen in the Western Theological and Philosophical Tradition," 458.

45. V. Grossi, "La presenza di Origene nell'ultimo Agostino," in *Origeniana Quinta*, ed. R. J. Daly (Leuven: Peeters, 1992), 558–64.

46. D. Keech, *The Anti-Pelagian Christology of Augustine* (Oxford: Ofxord University Press, 2012), ch. 4, n60.

47. Pamphilus, *Apology for Origen* 12.

48. Ramelli, "Origen in Western Theological and Philosophical Tradition," 458.

49. B. Altaner, "Augustinus und Origenes," *Historisches Jahrbuch der Gorres-Gesellschaft* (Munich) 70 (1951): 15–41; repr. in B. Altaner, *Kleine patristiche Schriften* (Berlin: Akademie-Verlag, 1967), 224–52; B. Studer, "Zur Frage des westlichen Origenismus," *Studia Patristica* 9, no. 3 (1966): 270–87.

50. "Il est certain que Cassiodore fut l'un des principaux acteurs de la transmission de l'œuvre d'Origène en Occident par les copies qu'il fit réaliser de ses traductions latines dans son monastère de Vivarium." B. Pouderon, "La réception d'origène à la renaissance: pour une typologie (version augmentée de textes à l'appui)," *Revue des Etudes Tardo-Antiques* (*RET*). This *RET* version is the amplified online PDF (with full notes) of his digest article "La réception d'Origène à la Renaissance," in *Origeniana Undecima*, ed. A. C. Jacobsen (Leuven: Peeters, 2016), 337–66. It is available online at https://www.researchgate.net/publication/285653423. See also F. Brunholzl, *Histoire de la littérature du Moyen Âge*, vol. 1.1, *De Cassiodore à la fin de la renaissance carolingienne—L'époque mérovingienne* (Turnhout: Brepols, 1990), 35–49.

51. Jerome, *Epistle* 62.

52. Cassiodorus, *Institutes* 1.1.8.

Chapter 5

Origen in Medieval Times and in the Age of Reformation

MEDIEVAL SCHOLARS

Paschasius Radbertus and Ratramnus of Corbie

Paschasius Radbertus (c. 785–865), a disciple of Adalard, abbot of Corbie, and eventually abbot there himself, was one such inquisitive reader who found his way to Origen. He is most famous now for being involved in a significant medieval Latin controversy on the nature of the presence of Christ in the eucharist, establishing, by an important treatise, the doctrine of the real presence as Latin orthodoxy.[1] In this he was opposed at the time by another monk from Corbie, the scholar Ratramnus. In 843 the latter issued a treatise meant as a corrective set of *scholia* on Paschasius's eucharistic teachings, giving it the same title as his colleague's work. It was a piece urged on him by the court of Charles the Bald, who had also asked him to correct the teachings of Gottschalk of Orbais on predestination.[2] Later in his life (c. 867), Ratramnus would also be asked by Abbot Hincmar of Rheims to respond to the criticisms of Latin theology mounted by Photius of Constantinople against Pope Nicholas, and he then composed *Contra Graecorum Opposita*.

This clashing difference on eucharistic theology remained a polite controversy between learned colleagues, which drew no external criticism (anathemata or suchlike) from church authorities.[3] Both men had applied the distinction between *figura* and *veritas* to the eucharist. Were the sacred elements the true body of Christ or a symbolic presentation? Truly the Lord's body and blood, as it were, or sacramentally the body and blood? Paschasius maintained that the elements were "truly" (*in veritate*) the body and blood, while Ratramnus insisted that to be something "in truth" meant that what it purported to be had to be "perceptible to the senses," and since the eucharistic elements retained the appearance and experience of bread and wine, they had to be the *figura*, the symbol or sacrament of the body of God, and could not be called the true body of Christ—or as we might now say, the "actual" body of the Lord. While Paschasius's opinions were largely adopted and would be reinforced over time to become standard catholic orthodoxy, those of Ratramnus would be excitedly rediscovered by several of the Reformers who set out to contest the doctrine of the real presence. The text was first printed in 1532 and became the major early source for Nicholas Ridley's eucharistic teaching;[4] the papacy responding by placing the work on the Vatican's *Index of Forbidden Books*, where it remained until 1900.

This debate strangely harks back to Origen himself, while also looking forward to the Reformation era, when this selfsame question came roaring back to life and this time really did cause divisions, controversies, and anathematizations, being one of the hot questions of the Reformation era. It first arose after Origen had moved as a priest to Caesarea, where the learned bishops Alexander of Jerusalem and Theotecnus of Caesarea employed him in preaching at regular liturgical services and also serving as a theological *peritus* at Palestinian synods, both marks of very high honor for a presbyter at the time. His sermons in the Caesarean church were often quite long (many of them have survived), and in some of them he lets show his impatience at the inattentive reception he was getting.

The problem was that, now speaking to a general church audience including working people from the fields, he was no longer in the select company of his private university students who were dedicated to the philosophical and literary pursuit of truth: ordinary folk in the congregation dozed off, talked while he was speaking, and generally annoyed him by their lack of concentration. In this context of claiming back their attention, Origen complained to them that while they were scrupulously careful about letting no particle of the eucharistic elements, the holy Word of God incarnate, fall from their hands to the floor when they communicated (incidentally giving us a rare insight into third-century liturgical practice), they were, by contrast, very careless indeed in allowing the particles of the Word of God to fall on the floor and be trampled by their crass behavior when the holy scriptures, earlier on, were being read and commented on. This, the presence of the Word among his people, Origen argued, was more mystical and spiritually refined even than the eucharistic reception itself, which (being corporeal) was a concession to more sensory types, while the reception of the Word though the medium of the sacrament of scripture was a very elevated and mystically refined form of communion.

The idea that the scripture was as much, if not more, a sacrament of communion than the eucharist is typical of Origen: an aporia, in a sense, where what is stated hits the mind at first hearing with the shock of something strange and unnerving and then calls out, on deeper reflection, an appreciation of a bigger issue.[5] Origen had always maintained that the scripture was the "body of the Logos" given for the salvation of the faithful. In making this complaining point (he wanted the congregation to be reverently attentive during the readings and the sermon), he was not so much introducing a dogmatic controversy (namely, which is better, eucharist or Bible?); rather, he was trying to point out how the totality of the liturgical experience concurs with the overarching principle that the Logos is purposefully incarnated in the disciples' virtues for the sanctification and salvation of the people of God.

However, it was such a vivid image, and question, that it was bound to be raised in an either/or form sooner or later. In fact, it was to be later. The dialogue between Paschasius Radbertus and Ratramnus served as the slow-burning fuse for this whole question to rise up once more, and then, in the Reformation period, controversialists on all sides really did go back to Origen's text and began to marshal pro and con arguments from what he had to say on several other occasions. Once more, Origen's text was destined to be at the very center of a major crisis about orthodoxy, this time very centrally in the Western church.

Were Ratramnus and Paschasius reading Origen as background material on this point? It is difficult to say so with any certainty. Ratramnus was more likely just reading his colleague and adding *scholia*. Paschasius, in his lifetime, was more renowned for the *Commentary on the Gospel of Matthew* he composed, which without question seems to lean heavily (even at times verbatim) on that composed by Origen, as Vogt has argued and Heine has also noted in his new critical edition of Origen's *Commentary on Matthew*.[6] In this instance, Paschasius probably drew from a collation of patristic exegetical notes (*catenae*), though direct knowledge cannot be ruled out, for the whole ethos of these learned Carolingians derived from Charlemagne's determination to make learning and pedagogy a fundamental character of his administration, and this meant manuscripts circulated freely once more.

Apart from instituting schools, the emperor made the Carolingian court a refuge and gathering place for international scholars. The "Capitulary of Baugulf," which he issued in 787, commanded that all Latin monasteries in his domains must have a library and studious monks within them.[7] Another capitulary, issued in 789, ordered every monastery and episcopal palace to have a functioning school set up to educate the noble youth in reading, chanting, grammar, and mathematics. So the libraries were spreading there, and in communities of scholars even apart from the central court at Aachen, and this meant that original manuscripts were also on the move.

This whole environment drew intelligentsia monastics like a magnet, and as in the Greek East, it was the intelligentsia who found in Origen a theologian to make them open their eyes. Of course, the core issue in the Latin theologians accessing the byways of Origen's thought was, as always, the capacity of individuals to read Greek. But if ever places existed to light the lamp of a revival of Greek learning in the Western church, it was either the Vatican library or the Carolingian monasteries, and one figure—perhaps the most important medieval reviver of Origen's wider thought world—united both places in the course of his life, a man who was very proud of his Irish ancestry.

Johannes Scotus Eriugena

Eriugena (c. 800–877) was a monk known as "John the Irishman, born in Ireland," and was one of the most learned scholars of the Middle Ages. He described his experience of reading the works of Origen (which he accessed not only through Latin translations but also by means of patiently learning Greek) as something that made him "wake up" as if from a walking sleep. When he left Ireland, he settled in the court of Charles the Bald and received the patronage of headship of the palace school of Laon and the role of the king's theological scholar. There grew up a later tradition that he went to the English Abbey of Malmesbury at the invitation of King Alfred the Great, and his pupils there grew so tired of him that they stabbed him to death with their pens, but this rests on a mistaken identification of him with a later scholar "John" made by the historian William of Malmesbury.[8] Still, it is a cautionary tale for all lecturers. William of Malmesbury records another tale about Eriugena, probably authentically sourced this time, which is an early example of a joke against the Irish misfiring.[9]

Like Ratramnus, Eriugena attacked Gottschalk's theology of predestination. His own thinking was inspired by the transcendent vision of the return of all souls to God. He found his Origen through the close study he made of all the major patristic admirers of Origen—Gregory of Nazianzus, Gregory of Nyssa, Ambrose, Dionysius the Areopagite, and Maximus the Confessor—translating them into Latin and making their ideas resonate in the West in new ways. He not only translated the pseudo-Areopagite but also wrote a commentary on his *Celestial Hierarchy*. He translated Maximus's *Ambigua ad Ioannem* as well as the *Quaestiones ad Thalassium*, and the *De Hominis Opificio* of St. Gregory, which he listed under Gregory's original title, *De Imagine*.

This was a typical part of the Carolingian renaissance: trying to repristinate Western thought by a return to the classical Fathers of the Church, whose culture was steeped in an ancient *paideia* and spirit of enquiry that awed these medievals and made them fear that their own period was one of intellectual stagnation. For Eriugena, it was the vast scope of the metaphysics of salvation he found in this Greek tradition that fired his imagination, as well as the teleological drive that Origen had inspired in these important theologians: the way all creation came from God and was destined to return to God, life's origin and final goal (*Arche kai Telos*).

Eriugena approaches Origen most closely by beginning with the root of all theology—to describe what God is not and to insist on apophaticism[10] as the primary theological methodology, since to assert what God truly is, is impossible for a corporeal mind or tongue. The deity for both (just as it was for Gregory the Theologian and Dionysius the Areopagite, other major followers of Origen's lead) is beyond words or human comprehension. Yet this does not mean humanity will be inarticulate in the face of the divine reality. Eriugena asserts, along with Origen, that God is a wholly incorporeal unity, while rational creaturehood (angels and humans) is a corporeal multiplicity. Like Origen, Eriugena asserts that the creation came about as a consequence of the lapse of rational intelligences into sin: because of this, humanity covered up its transcendent nature in the "coat of skin" (Gen. 3:21). The corruptible body that was laid over the human soul, therefore, was not the true and intended nature but the remedy (and penalty) of the lapse to sin. It follows that the slow returning ascent to God will involve also the progressive laying aside of that corporeal medium of the rational creature as it is transfigured into the incorporeal truer reality of its first making. As Eirini Artemi says, "Eriugena was influenced by Augustine of Hippo and Gregory of Nyssa, but the basis of his teaching was, in fact, the theology of Origen."[11]

That tradition came to him especially after 827, when the Byzantine emperor Michael the Stammerer (770–829) sent to the western emperor,[12] Louis the Pious (778–840), a Greek manuscript of Dionysius the Areopagite. At the time, both East and West believed that this was a work by a disciple of St. Paul himself, who had been martyred as apostle to the Franks, and so it had a very high currency among the Carolingians. Louis commissioned Abbot Hilduin to make a Latin translation, but it so closely followed the Greek syntax that it was almost unreadable, and so Charles the Bald then commissioned John Scotus to make a better version. The Greek scholar Anastasius, librarian at the Vatican, who had encouraged John to learn the Greek language at Athens, expressed similar opinions about the quality of John's translation work when sent a copy for him to add *scholia* of his own, but he also added a note saying how great his wonderment was that such a "*barbarus*" from so foreign a land should prove himself a scholar of the classics of Greek literature. Whether or not Anastasius disapproved of the rather wooden translation style, Eriugena, nevertheless, had opened up a very large door for the medieval West by his linguistic mediation. That door would be pushed wider in later generations, encouraged by his pioneering spirit.

Through reading Dionysius, John was led on, in great enthusiasm, to the capacious metaphysical view of mystical ascent to God that he discovered in the related traditions of Gregory of Nyssa, Gregory the Theologian, and Maximus. Origen lay close behind all of this, of course, and by this means, in John's own major work, the *Periphyseon*, he too was drawn into the project of baptizing the neo-Platonists by reinterpreting the ascent of the mind to the Sublime Unity in terms of the soul's mystical return to the Logos.[13] His *Periphyseon* (a Greek title for a Latin treatise) is quite clearly stimulated by Origen's *De Principiis*, which he quotes extensively, and verbatim, in his Latin text, and he explicitly refers to Origen's work by its original Greek title of *Peri Archon*.[14] The similarities are more than passing correspondences. As Ilaria Ramelli writes,

> The overall structure of his *Periphyseon* closely corresponds to that of Origen's *Peri Archon*, the only monumental synthesis of Christian philosophy prior, and comparable, to it. Both works are a Christian systematization of all that is knowable and thinkable .... Both works begin with a treatment of God as universal cause; in both the argumentative methodology is the same: philosophical arguments are always supported by Biblical and Patristic quotes .... The tension of *Periphyseon* toward eschatology is modelled on Origen's thought, all orientated to the ultimate end, in which everything has its perfection. Moreover, Origen's "zetetic"[15] method, at its best in his philosophical masterpiece, reappears in Eriugena's *Periphyseon*, not only for its heuristic format, emphasized by the teacher-disciple dialogue, but also for the continual alterations introduced by Eriugena.[16]

Robert Crouse writes that "In that work [the *Periphyseon*] Eriugena embraces Origen with lucidity and enthusiasm."[17] He is certainly one of the few intellectuals after patristic Late Antiquity and before the later Renaissance who can be said to have appreciated the philosophical subtlety (and overarching theological mission) of the ancient teacher. Crouse concludes: "The *Periphyseon* is certainly the strongest explicit witness to the influence of Origen in the philosophical theology of the Latin West, and it was crucially important as an example of how the doctrine of Origen (and other Greek theologians) might be reconciled with the doctrine of St. Augustine."[18] Eriugena's own version of the angelic hierarchies that he found depicted in pseudo-Dionysius is not a particularly accurate exegesis of the earlier (fifth-century) author's intent. But while pseudo-Dionysius does not himself explicitly reference Origen in this context, his own "project" to baptize and empathetically synthesize the neo-Platonic metaphysics of the post-Proclean era[19] was something that would have gained the approval of Origen himself, and it is also this which inspired Eriugena, making the latter into the first serious medieval Western Christian philosopher after Augustine and Boethius.

Although John Scotus was very careful in not trying to reverse head-on the broader Western tradition of Origenian disapproval, his own works, celebrating the permeation of all creation by the divine energy, called down disapproval of him by later authorities who worried that it had fallen into "pantheistic" sensibilities. What his critics were primarily worried about was his enthusiastic restatement of *apokatastasis* doctrine, which he admired in Origen and had refined by also applying some of the modifications of Gregory of Nyssa and Augustine, as Eirini Artemi and Robert Crouse have demonstrated.[20] Even so, his most important work, the *Periphyseon*[21] (which, throughout, attempts forms of reconciliation between aspects of neo-Platonist and Christian metaphysics), was condemned outright more than three hundred years after his death at the Paris schools in 1220 and again by Pope Honorius III at the Synod of Sens.

Peter Abelard and Bernard of Clairvaux

Abelard and the Burgundian abbot and mystic Bernard have often been seen as opposing forces and styles of medieval theological thought, not least because of the way, at the Second Lateran Council in 1139 and at the Synod of Sens in 1141, Bernard most forcibly opposed Abelard's thought. But in one respect, at least, they harmonized: their application to and reliance on Origen of Alexandria.

Bernard (1090–1153) was profoundly interested in the tradition of the exegesis of the Song of Songs.[22] It was a cardinal point of his own mystical sense of achieved union with God, through Christ, and through him it became the principal text, and tradition, of Western monasticism.[23] Augustine's treatment of the text was meager by comparison, alluding to it only in reference to baptismal initiation and his argument with the Donatists.[24] Origen, by contrast, had taken the three "books of Solomon"[25] as a revelation of the degrees of the soul's spiritual progress into mystical union with the divine Logos. For him, the Song of Songs was the highest, most secret initiation into the perfection of God's love. The motif of the lover seeking restlessly after the beloved, who returns the passion (*eros*) devotedly, is a primary archetype of the way the soul is created to seek always after the love of its maker, the divine Word.

It was largely through Bernard that this motif became central to the Western Christian mystical tradition, with Origen as the grandfather of the whole movement. It was widely known that this tradition had originated with Origen, and this is doubtless why the peak of interest in Origen's Latin manuscript tradition occurred among the monastics of the Carolingian era and especially the twelfth century. Origen believed that the reading of, and immersion in, the sacred scriptures was the primary method the Logos used to reshape the soul's aspirations and realign it in union with him. Bernard took up this idea and, in his very influential work as monastic legislator, made sure to place *lectio divina* (the prayerfully reflective reading of the scriptures and fathers) at the very center of the monastic daily routine. It was Origen, in his *Commentary on the Song of Songs*, who first had sketched out this fundamental theory of how *lectio divina* thus prepared the soul for the gift of divine wisdom. It struck both Augustine[26] and Bernard[27] with great force:

> A person will be able to investigate and discover such things more carefully, provided always that he first seeks and knocks at Wisdom's door, begging God to open unto him and make him worthy to receive the word of wisdom and the word of knowledge given through the Holy Spirit, and to make him a partaker of that Wisdom who once said: "I stretched out my words but you did not hear."[28]

Jean Leclercq, making a close textual study of Bernard's use of Origen,[29] concludes that the reliance is a very deep one:

> [Bernard] does not criticize him, he does not refute him. He does not even cite him. He simply takes his inspiration from him, and more or less consciously he imitates him. He not only preaches on him, but like him. They share the same theories . . . the same conception of the relationship between the Old and New Testaments, the same allegorical exegesis, and above all, the same imagination.

For Abelard, it was not so much the *Commentary on the Song of Songs* that inspired him but the Latin version of Origen's *Commentary on Romans* and Origen's overarching insistence that it is by the ethical life, the persevering quest for moral purity, that the soul most advances. Abelard, like most others in the medieval period, had been prepared to receive Origen according to Jerome's dictum that the exegete was acceptable, the dogmatician not.[30] He even refers to this when he strongly disapproves (for ethical philosophical reasons) of what he thinks is Origen's version of the *apokatastasis*. He denounces what he describes as "that detestable conception of Origen, extending salvation even to the demons,"[31] not properly realizing that this was Jerome's caricature of Origen's thought (which had closely followed Paul's lead) that God's glory could not ultimately be frustrated. But once he engaged directly and personally with Origen's *Commentary on Romans*, Abelard began to think again. This was because he discovered for himself, through the subtlety of the Origenian exegesis, that here indeed was an intellect of considerable strength and acuity. Soon Abelard began to call him "a great Christian philosopher"[32] and even "the greatest of all Christian philosophers."[33] He was impressed by the quality of the Romans commentary and used it extensively in his own version of the same.

Abelard refers to Origen expressly (not always naming him) twenty-eight times—far more than he refers to any other ancient Christian writer.[34] Most of the references come from the commentary, but he is also aware of the *De Principiis*. He is struck by and emulates both the style of the exegesis (a kind of running expositional narrative with reflective excurses) and the recurring emphasis on the freedom of human will as a collaborative spiritual exercise with the grace of God. Abelard follows Origen's theology of the cross and rejects the common medieval "ransom theory" and the concept of "satisfaction for sin." As Bond argues, Abelard speaks of the cross in terms of "God's joining with us . . . . [That] is the atoning work."[35] He also uses the argument of Origen that sin is always a spiritual choice, partly to depart from Augustine's massive influence in the case of original sin.[36]

Abelard is also moved by Origen's example of personal asceticism. He takes it as a real history that Origen castrated himself out of motives of chastity, and while he disapproves of such a thing, he still elevates Origen as an encouragement and an ideal when writing to his former lover, the nun Héloise, to give her encouragement in the life of philosophical asceticism that had been forced on them in the aftermath of his own castration.[37] It has often been something of a cliché in medieval studies to contrast the mystical approach of the monastic movement in the likes of Bernard with the scholastic approach of the likes of Abelard, seeing one as more concerned with scripture and prayer and the other as more interested in philosophy, ethics, and metaphysics. But, as Georges points out, some of the greatest of the medieval philosophers—Anselm, Bonaventure, Aquinas, and Abelard himself—were, of course, monastics and worked through the medium of the scriptures for an end in view which was divine unitive reconciliation, exactly the scope and purpose of Christian theology that Origen himself had first defined.[38]

As Georges notes, it is in the course of writing such encomia to Héloise that Abelard refers explicitly to Origen's exegesis of the incident in Genesis of Isaac digging wells that Philistines keep on filling up with dirt in order to frustrate him.[39] Abelard notes that this well digging is the exercise of "penetrating deeply into the hidden meaning of holy scripture,"[40] but he goes on to characterize it as an image of the application of one's intelligence, despite the many around who wish to discourage the exercise of reason. He knows the passage from Gregory the Great but also knows that Pope Gregory took it from Origen, as he did most of his other scriptural insights:

> St. Gregory, if I am not mistaken had read the *Homilies on Genesis* of the great Christian philosopher Origen, and had drawn from Origen's wells what he now says about these wells. For that zealous digger of spiritual wells strongly urges us not only to drink of them but also to dig our own, as he says in the Twelfth homily of his exposition . . . . So you too, my listener, try to have your own well and your own spring so that when you take up a book of the scriptures you also may start to show some understanding of it from your own perception . . . . Also try to drink from the spring of your own spirit. You have within you "a source of living water," the open channels and flowing streams of rational perception.[41]

It can hardly be missed here how Abelard deliberately juxtaposes the Johannine reference to "springs of living water" flowing out within the human heart (which the evangelist tells his readers is the force of the Holy Spirit) with the rational faculties of a human being. The work of philosophy, for Abelard, is a holy and spiritual effort.

This, of course, was Origen's great insight, that the gift of wisdom and rational perception was indeed the fundamental gift of the divine Logos to humanity, which was why philosophy (signifying rational reflection and analysis) had to be applied to the sacred texts as their explicative method: reason and theology could never be separated, an insight that in Abelard's case once more had reached a crisis point in the church. Origen's celebration of the inseparability of reasons and revelation (the selfsame Logos at the heart of all truth) and what Abelard seems to have learned by closely engaging in his exegetical method, where dogma and exegesis are made one (not according to the facile criticism and *bon mot* of Jerome),[42] seems to have given Abelard renewed courage to publish his views in his Romans commentary. It was received as a highly controversial work, and eventually drew down on his head a second condemnation by church authorities at the Synod of Sens in 1140.

RENAISSANCE AND REFORMATION ERA CONTROVERSIALISTS

The First Printed Editions of Origen in the West (1460–1668)

Origen first made his appearance in printed book form in the West via the Latin translations made long before by Jerome and Rufinus. The first appearance was under the shadow of Jerome, whose complete works were issued at Rome in 1460 by the printing house of Theodorus Laelius and Johannes Andreas. In this edition, there also appeared Origen's *Homilies and Commentary on the Song of Songs*, a work of major importance for the Western mystical revival. Aldo Manutius, the great Venetian printer, subsequently brought out, all unknowingly, the second printed edition of Origen's works in 1503. It comprised Rufinus's Latin translation of Origen's exegetical preached commentaries, namely, the *Homilies on Genesis, Exodus, Leviticus, Numbers, Joshua,* and *Judges*. Manutius commissioned a scholarly preface to introduce the writings, probably written by Jerome Alexander, as Pouderon intimates.[43] Here the stylish intelligence of the works was highly praised, doubtless in part because they were all attributed in the text to Saint Jerome, with whose writings the editor had unconsciously witnessed the profound parallels. The success of this book showed there was a ready market, and soon after, in

1506, Theodore Salodianus, again in Venice, produced a book of Jerome's translations of Origen's important *Commentary on Romans*. The next big movement was the issuing, between 1512 and 1513, of the *editio princeps* of *On First Principles* by the printer Constantius Hierotheus. Another printing, anonymous this time, occurred in 1513 at Venice, of Jerome's Latin translations of Origen's *Commentary on the Song of Songs* and the *Homilies on Job, Isaiah, Jeremiah, Ezekiel, Matthew, Luke,* and *John*.

It was surely the 1512 *editio princeps* of *On First Principles* that marked the moment when Origen the theologian was reborn on the world stage. Hierotheus bolstered his edition with the deliberate publication of the *Apology on Behalf of Origen* by St. Pamphilus of Caesarea. Both works were made from the exemplar of the translations made originally by Rufinus. In the same year, 1512, at Paris, the complete edition of all Origen's works that had so far been translated into Latin was printed at the shop of Jean Petit and Josse Bade, with Jaques Merlin acting as editor. This edition contained an extensive apologia for Origen composed by Merlin himself. In 1536, at Lyons, the work was redone from scratch, with all the translations made by Jerome and Rufinus reassembled under the editorship of Erasmus and Beatus Rhenus. This edition was titled *Origenis Adamantii eximii scripturarum* (*The Most Excellent Comments on Scripture of Origen the Adamantine*).[44]

It would not be until the seventeenth century that the first printed Greek editions started to appear: the *Contra Celsum* in 1605, made by David Hoeschel at Augsburg; the *Philocalia Origenis* in 1618, made by Jean Tarin at Paris; and the *Commentaries on Jeremiah* in 1623, made by M. Ghisler at Lyons. One of the greatest of the early modern Origenian scholars was the French bishop Pierre Daniel Huet (Huetius) (1630–1721), who brought out a major edition of Origen's writings in 1668[45] and whose labors became the basis of several other editions lasting even until the nineteenth-century editions of Abbé Jacques Paul Migne and his Paris publication of the *Cursus Completus Patrologiae Latinae et Graecae*, which tended simply to reproduce all the older editions of the texts but with commissioned Latin translations, where needed, of the Greek texts.

Pico della Mirandola (1463–1494)

Giovanni Pico della Mirandola, the Italian nobleman and religious philosopher who burst onto the world literary scene aged twenty-three with both his *900 Theses* and his *Oration on the Dignity of Man*, was a thinker who wished to revive the esoteric traditions of Christianity. He saw the wisdom of the ancients as the key to renovating the intellectual life of the present. Already learned in Greek and Latin, he also studied Hebrew, Arabic, and Aramaic with the Jewish sage Elia di Medigo in Padua. He also pursued kabbalistic studies with Rabbi Johann Alemanno in Perugia. His friends knew him as *Princeps Concordiae*—the Prince of Harmony—a pun since Concordia (harmony) was one of the noble family's landed estates, and the idea was also at the heart of all Pico wished to do in philosophy, which was to create an active synthesis between Plato and Aristotle, and to harmonize philosophy with the ancient religious systems of humankind.[46] Pico was an early Renaissance advocate of the theory of universal salvation. He adopted Origen's dictum that "eternal damnation" in the New Testament meant punishment for the "other age" (*aionios*) but that it could not be considered as "temporally unending" since God's justice would preclude such a punishment for an offence committed in time and from the basis of limited knowledge. The young scholar enjoyed the protection of the Medicis but also seems to have been poisoned by them when he became an increasing embarrassment. Feeling (ill advisedly) secure in his patronage, he decided to hold a public conference in Rome to debate all nine hundred theses, and he announced that he would defend them against all comers, even paying the expenses of any disputant from any part of Italy who wished to travel to Rome.

This free-spiritedness greatly alarmed Pope Innocent VIII, who in February 1487 halted the conference and appointed a commission of inquiry to look into the orthodoxy of the ideas Pico had published. Initially, thirteen of them were declared heretical or potentially scandalous, and Pico agreed to stop propagating these (though he refused to declare them invalid). Eventually, Rome anathematized all nine hundred theses. One of those rejected propositions was a proposal for a general rehabilitation of the memory of the great Origen and the lifting of the anathemata issued against him in antiquity. George Lewis refers to the episode wryly in the introduction to his edition of the *Philocalia of Origen*.[47]

Erasmus of Rotterdam

The scholar, priest, and "moderate reformer" Erasmus (1466–1536) was one of the great advocates of Origenian thought in the Reformation era, and he worked extensively in his own lifetime not only to make a critical edition of the New Testament in Greek and Latin but also to present good editions of the Fathers of the Church, including Origen's works, which he clearly had studied closely and with great empathy and interest.[48] In his *Enchiridion* (Manual for a Christian Knight), Erasmus ranks Paul, Origen, and Augustine as the three greatest Christian exegetes of all time, and several times gives his post–New Testament exegetical "rankings of intelligences" as Origen, Ambrose, Jerome, and Augustine, perhaps not being entirely aware that Ambrose and Jerome took almost all their biblical acumen from Origen himself.[49] He writes in his manual's "Fifth Rule": "And so, when you bring to light the mysteries of scripture, you must not follow the conjecture of your own heart. What is needed is a rule and some sort of methodology such as those set out by a certain Dionysius in his book *The Divine Names*, or by St. Augustine in his work *On Christian Doctrine*. It was the Apostle Paul who, after Christ, opened up certain springs of allegory. He was followed by Origen, who easily earns the first rank in that area of theology."[50] For Erasmus, it is Origen the exegete who commands his interest. He is content to allow the objectionable metaphysical speculations to remain as set-asides. A similarly positive view of the exegetical writings of the fathers, chief among whom he ranked Origen and Jerome, can be found in the Reformer Zwingli.[51]

Huldrych Zwingli

Irena Backus, who made a magisterial survey of the reception of patristics in the West, includes a close study of Zwingli's (1484–1531) use of the fathers.[52] Along with Luther, Zwingli not only relied on Augustine for their formula *sola scriptura*[53] but generally held a much more positive view of the importance and continuing relevance for the church of patristic exegesis and theology. Backus has shown that Zwingli made a very close and personal study of the works of Origen using Merlin's 1512 edition of his works. In his own copy, Zwingli made numerous marginal notes, and throughout his corpus of writings he has no less than 340 references to Origen. He shows no sign at all of regarding Origen's condemnation as having any lasting merit, but neither does he regard the fathers as authorities in the same sense that they had in early Byzantine times, that is, as theologians who cannot be seen to err even in the slightest.

Martin Luther

By contrast with Zwingli, Martin Luther (1483–1546), who began his ecclesiastical career as an Augustinian monk and New Testament exegete, found Origen's work strongly distasteful, and this chiefly for two reasons. In the first place, it was because of the allegorical process that dominates his exegetical method. It was Luther's own preference for the "simplicity" of scriptural reading that made him regard Jerome and Origen ("Jerome and his Origen," as he says) as examples of people (he also had Erasmus in mind as a target) who "played with" the holy text and created "trifles" (*nugae*) of exegesis. He says, "Jerome and Origen have filled the world with these trifles, and these pestiferous commentaries that have lost sight of the simplicity of scripture."[54] His hatred of allegorical reading (and it has to be said, his more or less total unfamiliarity with the original text of Origen) led him to the famous (and really incomprehensible) utterance: "In the whole corpus of Origen there is not a single word about Christ."[55]

In the second place, Luther began to detest Origen because he saw behind him at every turn the figure of Erasmus, who was his liveliest catholic critic. Erasmus, publishing his own *Treatise on Free Will*, used Origen extensively to argue that the human will remains always free by God's gift. Origen had elevated such a doctrine of human freedom in the face of the gnostics of his own time. Erasmus redirected his master's arguments to undermine Luther's attempt to make his own doctrine of the enslavement of the human will (so he entitled his own treatise, *De servo arbitrio*, replying to Erasmus) the foundation on which he built his case of opposition to Catholicism.[56]

One of the few times Luther appeals to Origen in a positive sense as an exegetical authority is to agree with his exegesis of the "Petrine text."[57] But on this occasion (so important to him in his ongoing apologia with the papacy) his authority is the "divine Jerome," who "here follows Origen as is his custom" to support his declaration that this text is not referring to the papacy in the singular but to all the apostles who receive a promise of security for all the church. M. Mattox's study of how the Reformers used certain key texts about the church, however, has also shown that Luther, when no one was particularly arguing with him, was more approving of the fathers than one might have thought, and actually used them far more extensively than his own dismissive words would lead one to believe. And what is more, Mattox surprisingly reveals that the chief ancient authority among those he used was none other than Origen of Alexandria![58] In his early career, before apologetics had become his daily bread, as it were, he even refers to Origen in a sermon of March 1518 and calls him "That wise and acute Magister."

Theodore Beza

Theodore Beza (1519–1605) was a French-speaking Reformer, a disciple of John Calvin, who succeeded Calvin as spiritual leader of the Republic of Geneva. He first studied with Melchior Wolmar at Orléans and Bourges, the latter of which had become the center of Reformation thought in France, but after Francis I legislated against ecclesiastical disturbances in 1534 Wolmar returned to Germany and Beza went back to Orléans to study law at the request of his father. These studies did not inspire him, though he made a deep study of the Latin classics at this time. After 1539, he practiced law in Paris and became known, after the publication of his work *Poemata Juvenilia* in 1548, as a very skilled writer of Latin verses. In that same year, however, he suffered a crisis of health that corresponded to a religious conversion, and from that time onward he came under the mentoring of John Calvin and thereafter began the series of his many works, both literary and political, of

Protestant apologia. He is, perhaps, the most renowned humanist among the Calvinist party and was especially renowned in his own lifetime for his biblical work, not least his completion of the edition of the Psalms in 1561 and his Greek (and Latin) edition of the New Testament issued in 1565 (which relies on the editions of Stephanus and Erasmus before him).

It was through his exegetical work that Beza met with Origen, courtesy of Erasmus, in the main. He never made any great studies of the fathers themselves, at least none of the Greek Fathers, though his language skills were up to that. In fact, he simply uses Origen as a symbol of "the father of mistakes" in biblical exegesis. He sees him as the source of those of his opponents who disagree with his own exegetical interpretations, whether these were Erasmus or other Catholics, Lutheran commentators, or sometimes other Reformers.

Origen is handled only through a series of contemporary debates related to the presence of Christ in the eucharistic sacrament. Remembering how Origen was thought to have argued the perfect spherical shape of the risen body, Beza criticizes Brenz, one of his immediate opponents in the eucharistic debates, with the words: "Even the Origenists did not speak as foolishly as Brenz does in this regard."[59] At other times he describes Origen using pejorative adjectives such as "ridiculus" and "ineptissimus,"[60] chiefly as an apologetic tool to dispense with engaging with the argument and as a way of blackening his contemporary opponents, whom he characterizes as fools for reading this kind of literature in the first place. It is largely this charged apologetic approach of Beza's that gives Origen the generally gloomy reputation he comes to bear among the Reformers and their successors up to modern times.[61] Philip Melancthon had tended to adopt the same approach, negating all Origen had to say, without giving any credit for his foundational views (on inspiration and canonicity to say the least). He and Beza seemed to regard Origen as part and parcel of the dire influence of Catholicism that the Protestant movement needed to cast off in order to establish its identity. Beza gained what firsthand knowledge he had of Origen's text from reading Erasmus's edition of Origen's *Commentaries on Romans*, and after that tended to identify Erasmus with Origen on every point on which he was in dispute with him or the Catholics. One of his Protestant scholarly readers, Sir Anthony Cooke (1505–1576), noticed this recurrent dismissal of Origen throughout Beza's works and took him to task for it as an unjust estimate, calling Origen, in the process, "The most celebrated writer among the ancients."[62]

Giordano Bruno

The scholarly Italian Dominican friar Giordano Bruno (1548–1600) was, like Pico della Mirandola before him, a curious intellect and a man of many talents, interested in hermeticism, mathematics, cosmology, philosophy, and poetry. He studied in his youth, and was impressed by, Origen's symbolic style of exegesis, paying special attention to the Latin version Erasmus had made of the *Two Homilies on the Song of Songs* and to the ancient Latin version Rufinus had made of the *Commentary on the Song of Songs*, which Erasmus had also included in that edition. Erculei, who has made a detailed study of the presence of Origenian thought throughout Bruno's work, recognizes that the influence was the result of a lifelong admiration leading to a "constant yet mostly implicit" presence of Origen's thought across his writings.[63]

In the opening letter of his treatise *Cabala*, Bruno takes a swipe at Luther without naming him, saying that he himself is no "friend of the letter" but that by preference he belongs "to the party of Origen" (allegorical interpreters). This was acknowledging the impact Luther's book *De servo arbitrio* had already had, where a simple style of biblical reading was pressed strongly and where Luther mocked Origen in the process of making that case. Bruno, who had pondered many scientific matters and realized the full impact the Copernican shift of cosmology would have on one's approach to biblical interpretation, knew that unless one was willing to admit the central importance of the allegorical tradition within Christian exegesis and theology, a woodenly literal reading "of the simple" would lead inevitably to a great crash between religion and science, the cosmological details of the biblical narrative being so naïvely fictive.[64] Bruno ultimately believed that the two systems had separate rules of meaning and application that ultimately meant science and religion should stay out of each other's narratives, a conclusion Origen would never accept since his doctrine of how the Logos underpinned all existence as its origin and goal (*arche* and *telos*) conjoined the personal with the cosmological abstract in a fundamental unity of the ontology of love.

Bruno's work *De gli eroici furori* is described by Erculei as "Bruno's personal version of the *Canticum Canticorum*."[65] He took Origen's concept that the infinity of God always exceeded the capacity of human thought and linguistic definition and applied it more generally to the inability of philosophy (or any of the church's theologians) to arrive at any singular and acceptable statement that encompassed the truth. In this case the search for God (the soul's restless quest in the Song of Songs) becomes, for Bruno, an "endless aspiring" like the furious hunting of Actaeon, which ends (tragically in this instance) in the glimpsing of the nude goddess Artemis (which he calls the mirror of the inaccessible Apollo). He surely took this larger concept of the transience of stages of apprehension and articulation from Origen, who specifically speaks in the *Commentary on the Song of Songs* about the transitioning of humanity (the soul) through many stages, the shadows of the law leading on to the brighter revelations of the Christian life, but which itself ultimately contains a long series of *epinoiai*, that is, revelatory "aspects" of the divine Logos, who comes to his disciples in sacraments and symbols similar to a vision in a mirror.[66]

Later, in his *Furori*, Bruno considers the various "great philosophers" of the past who have considered the pressing question of "the compatibility between infinite vicissitude and justice" and concludes that the church's theologians have completely missed the point through being led time after time to the attempt to instill into the masses a moral order by dint of threat of punishment. He says that there is "only one single theologian" who can stand with the great philosophers in their quest, and that is Origen of Alexandria.[67]

Sadly, Bruno lived in an age when the Roman Inquisition was highly active and obsessed with its perception of doctrinal deviations. Eventually, he was tried for his teachings and burned at the stake in Rome's Campo dei Fiori on February 17, 1600.[68] Elements of the teaching for which he was condemned included a favorable view on the notion of transmigration of souls[69] (for which Origen had himself been accused in antiquity even though he himself had explicitly denied the utility of the idea and any place for it in the Christian tradition), a rejection of the idea of an everlastingly long punishment for sins committed within our limited history, and a favorable view of the idea of *apokatastasis*.[70] Bruno found Origen a comforting support for his own views on these themes. His cosmological views now appear most interesting to modern sympathizers, among whom he is often acclaimed as an early martyr for the cause of science. He extended what were then the newly startling Copernican theories, with philosophical speculations of his own as to the possibility of innumerable worlds, with their own laws of existence. Origen too had once speculated about the possibility of the angelic order having a separate system of approaching God (atonement) to that of the material creaturehood, but left it all undeveloped, as one of several "possible seminar discussion themes" he raised with his advanced students. Bruno's undoubtedly was a free-ranging intellect, and it is this aspect of Origen's work, above all else, that he appreciated and found appealing in the ancient master, recognizing in him one of the antique theologians who truly valued and defended the principle of freedom. Erculei's study of the relations between Origen and Bruno elevates it as but one example of a wider intellectual dawning, calling it "a significant moment of the Origenian heritage at the beginning of modern philosophy."[71]

EARLY MODERN CONTROVERSIES AND SCHOLARLY REASSESSMENTS

The many events, movements, and personalities comprising what we now call "the Reformation" stirred up a great ferment in theological thinking in the West, for both the various reform groups and also the Catholic theologians. One of the results of the controversies was the rebirth of the genre of apologetics. The early church had many excellent apologists in its formative centuries: chiefly, theologians who reflected on the nature of religious freedom in the face of political oppression inflicted on them. The dawning of the era of religious tolerance, and then state sponsorship, that arrived after the fourth century saw the dwindling away of the need to advance apologetics in any serious way. There were many clashes after the fourth century, of course, and the advancement of the concept of heresy kept the adversarial style of theology very much alive in later centuries in contexts such as Augustine and the Donatists or Pelagians (always limited debates) or the Eastern writers in the long-drawn-out debates over Christology after Chalcedon or dealings with the "Saracens." But once the concept of heresy is robustly advanced in argument, apologetical reasoning is not often called for, the dialogic element now being very quickly dismissed and often clichés preferred to evidential-based scrutiny.

So it was that the extensive use of apologetics became a thing of the past until it was vigorously resurrected in the Western church in the second wave of the Reformation. The protagonists (having once realized that these variously proposed reforms had initiated secessions that appeared to be irresolvable), on both sides, Catholic and Protestant, turned to church history to demonstrate by proofs of precedent (a heritage of Roman law they shared) that each was right and the other side wrong. The Catholic side of this argument is manifested particularly by the examples of a line of notable scholars: Cardinal Baronius (the historian Cesare Baronio, 1538–1607), the Jesuit theologian Petavius (Denis Pétau, 1583–1652), Allatius (Leo Allatzes,1586–1669, the Greek-born librarian of the Vatican who worked extensively on ancient manuscripts with a view to reconciling the Catholic–Orthodox divide), and Huetius (Pierre Daniel Huet, 1630–1721, the bishop of Avranches), who beginning with fragments he had found in Sweden of Origen's Greek *Commentary on Matthew*, decided that he would begin a fresh series of translations of the Alexandrian, a task that, in turn, stimulated the two Benedictine scholars of the Abbey of St. Maur, Charles De La Rue (1684–1740) and his nephew Charles-Vincent de La Rue (1707–1762);[72] the first undertook to publish in Greek and Latin all the works of Origen, and the latter completed his uncle's monumental task. This edition was taken up by Abbé Jacques Paul Migne and became, in seven volumes of the *Patrologia Graeca* series, the very widely disseminated, indeed standard, text for Origen's work until the 20th century.[73] All the Greek texts were paralleled with Latin translations. A more scholarly edition (it tended to lodge itself only in a relatively smaller number of academic libraries—whereas that of Migne was to be found in most Catholic seminaries and scholarly presbyteries across the Catholic world) was published less than fifty years later.[74] The availability of the collected works caused a veritable modern explosion of interest in the ancient teacher, as we shall see.

Common to all of the Roman Catholic scholars was the apologetic intent of going back to the sources in order to show that the Protestant theologians, on matters such as papal authority, biblical inspiration, priestly orders, sacraments and ecclesiology, and core issues such as atonement theory, were innovating without due observance of the classical standards of received Christian doctrine.[75] The Protestant scholars, matching this intellectual assault, countered by arguing on two fronts: sometimes that the so-called "tradition" of the church had gone astray from its biblical purity at an early date, and so did not carry any weight of authority with it, or at other times that while it did carry weight, it could be shown that catholic tradition had misinterpreted the writings of the fathers, particularly in relation to things such as the authority of the pope or matters of sacramental theology. However, a very significant shift happened in theology at this time, around the seventeenth or eighteenth century, and that was the rise of the concept of patristic theology among Roman Catholic and Anglican theologians.

Continental Catholicism wished to use patristic evidence apologetically in a fight against Protestant principles such as *sola scriptura* (ironically, a principle Luther derived directly from Augustine, who certainly did not mean it to exclude ecclesiastical dogmatic tradition) and also to establish its own pedigree of authenticity by means of establishing the idea of "communion with the Petrine see" as the hallmark of Catholic authenticity. Anglican scholars of this time countered with a renewed interest in patristic studies.

Cranmer, Henry VIII's reformist archbishop of Canterbury, had been the architect of the new Anglican liturgy but was steeped in his study of the ancient Christian liturgies of the past, and while he might have surprised and alienated his Roman critics, many of the Eastern theologians would have found much there that was classically ancient. He also drafted the first two editions of the Book of Common Prayer. But the Anglicanism of King Edward VI's Book of Common Prayer was a matter of a much more radical reformist leaning, and it was not until the later Anglican divines that the concept was clarified of an Anglicanism that was both Reformed and patristically traditional.

John Jewel (or Jewell; 1522–1571) was one of the Anglican divines who set the terms of the engagement with patristics in the cause of arguing against Rome's monopoly on Christian authenticity from antiquity. His young pupil Richard Hooker (1554–1600) once called him "the worthiest divine that Christendom hath bred for some hundreds of years." Installed as Elizabeth I's bishop of Salisbury in January 1560, Jewel made a close study of patristic sources, including Origen of Alexandria, to prepare for the publication of his epochal *Apologia ecclesiae Anglicanae* (*An Apology on Behalf of the Anglican Church*). In this he consciously situated the Anglican church as a midway "golden mean" between the Puritans and "Romanists."[76] In a sermon delivered at St. Paul's Cross, the open-air pulpit at Old St. Paul's Cathedral in London, he delivered an open challenge to all comers to prove against himself the Roman case for doctrine either out of scripture or from the conciliar decisions or patristic theology of the first six hundred years. He would repeat the challenge a year later, when it was taken up by Doctor Henry Cole, the former dean of St. Paul's.

Cole had earlier embraced Anglicanism but reverted to Catholicism and was given many preferments under Queen Mary and was closely allied with Cardinal Pole. Under Elizabeth, he continued to defend the Catholic cause so volubly that in the summer of 1560 he was deprived of all his benefices, fined heavily, and committed to the Tower, after which he was confined in the Fleet prison for almost twenty years until his death. His exchange with Jewel launched what has since been known as the "Great Controversy," a series of sixty-four apologetic disputes that collectively set the tone and defined the character of the English church and its relation to Rome.

Origen's approach to the sacraments was one where he stressed that the spiritual sense was the core of the matter. This was so especially in relation to the eucharist, which should not be seen (as clearly his parishioners in Caesarea tended to see it; hence his argument against them in his homilies) as something higher and more sacred than the scriptures. As we have noted, Origen's context here was his complaint people in church approached the eucharist most reverently and quietly, holding their hands in such a way that not one particle of the eucharist might fall to the floor, even though a few moments before they had been chatting and behaving carelessly through the reading of the scriptures and his own expositional sermon on them. This occasional argument was elevated among the Reformation apologists as proof positive that Origen rejected the Catholic doctrine of the real presence. Jewell is a more moderate voice in this regard when he appeals to the fathers (Augustine and Origen as his primary choices) to set the proper compass points on sacramental theology: "'The faith of the sacraments,' saith St. Augustine, 'justifies, and not the sacrament.' And Origen also saith, 'He [Christ] is the priest as well as the propitiation, and the sacrifice; and that propitiation comes to everyone by way of faith.' And, therefore, agreeably hereunto, we say that the sacraments of Christ do not profit the living without faith."[77] Origen's theology of the priesthood, where he argued passionately (against Bishop Demetrios of Alexandria, who was accusing him of disloyalty to Pope Pontianus of Rome) that bishops who behave like tyrants do not merit obedience, for priestly authority within the church derives from the officeholder's personal sanctity not by virtue of their official rank, was also something that inspired Jewel, and many other Reformers who fought against the argument that catholic faith demanded communion with the Petrine see. He replies: "We have departed from that church . . . not out of contention, but out of obedience to God; and have sought the certain way of religion out of the sacred Scriptures, which we know cannot deceive us, and have returned to the primitive church of the ancient fathers and apostles, that is, to the beginning and first rise of the church, as to the proper fountain."[78]

Richard Hooker, who had been a pupil of Jewel's as a child, grew up to be a powerful successor, underlining his predecessor's definition of Anglicanism as a middle way between Rome and the radical reform. It was largely due to his work that England was steered away from much of Calvin's system. Hooker was critical of much in the Roman ecclesiology and was not greatly impressed by the reforms of the Council of Trent (1545–1563), but he retained a lifelong love of the Greek and Latin Fathers as well as the writings of Thomas Aquinas, and this broader perspective shaped his theology considerably, rebuffing the opinion of many of the radical Reformers that the writings of the patristic and scholastic theologians were pernicious rubbish. Hooker set himself to a close and interested study of the fathers, primarily to refute the Puritans' arguments against the Church of England (that they alone represented the pure doctrine of the early church), while also keeping Rome, which claimed to "own" the patristic heritage, at arm's length. Hooker brought a new and refined historical sense to his use of patristics, stressing the necessity to look to the *consensus patrum*, not simply use proof texts from individual writers. By this means, Hooker established Anglican traditions of the authoritative triad of scripture, tradition, and reason as foundations of a reformed catholic belief system.[79] It was an approach that would lead to an immense and learned focus on patristic writings within the Anglican Church (especially in its Oxford University schools) for centuries to come.

Hooker has no less than 774 references to the fathers of the first five centuries in his works,[80] mainly favoring the Latin writers (through which he absorbed Origen's preferred symbolic style of exegesis along with the rest of the Latin tradition via Jerome and Gregory the Great), but he is also very aware of the Greeks.[81] When discussing the need to take the consensus view "of the catholic fathers," he cites Origen, saying, "And Origen says the same thing . . . . Such arguments that Origen and other learned fathers thought to stand for good,"[82] clearly affording him authority both as a catholic and a learned mentality witnessing to the faith of the early church. In the *Ecclesiastical Polity*, he cites Origen as an authority that the church allowed only the canonical scriptures to be read in worship.[83] He also appeals to Origen's authority as a testimony to the importance of auricular confession and the spiritual discernment needed for choosing the confessor.[84]

But we can also see here both how piecemeal the Renaissance approach was, and how much it forced out-of-context gobbets into anachronistic arguments. Apart from featuring either behind the scenes or very much to the front of the argument, in terms of how he established the principles of symbolic exegesis of the scriptures, Origen featured in the arguments of this time as a patristic authority to the spiritual (rather than realist) theology of the eucharist,[85] as a voice that seemed to support the Reformers' doctrine of justification by faith alone (again only by wrenching his words out of context), and as a defender of the significance of the freely exercised human will (Origen would have spoken in terms of the soul's will) as a collaborative agent in God's grace, something that interested the writers who wished to scale back Augustine's theology of grace toward a position often caricatured as semi-Pelagianism by Roman theologians of the era, semi-Pelagianism being especially espoused, according to this view, by John Cassian of Marseilles (in fact, Cassian was intending to mount Origen's concept of grace in opposition to that of Augustine, which was gaining ground extensively at the time).

Much of this level of argumentation fed into Reformation apologetics, with both sides trying to find what Origen had to say about the core principle of "justification by faith alone." In fact, Origen said on separate occasions that it was both true and false, in that God did all things for the salvation of his creatures. And that God expected his creatures to do all things to collaborate with the workings of grace. The Reformation habit of partial and decontextualized citation of randomly cut-out proof texts from the early writers led to Luther, Melanchthon, Calvin, and Beza being shocked that Origen could have proved himself heretically "Pelagian" on this score, while the Catholic apologists Eck, Cochleus, and Pyghius delighted in lifting up the same texts (largely from Origen's *Commentary on Romans*) to show that the Protestant Reformers were innovating on this, their central doctrine, and had no precedent in the early church. The (poor) standard of the debate at this time is magisterially studied, in relation to the selective citation of Origen, by Thomas Scheck.[86] His book is fronted with lively cover art demonstrating the essential paradox of Origen's reception in the church: Origen stands, iconically, in a pulpit "teaching the saints"—all of them great masters of the patristic tradition who heavily leaned on his writings, who each have halos around their heads as they line up before him, though their *magister* is devoid of any halo, holding a scroll of his own writing that reads, "Above all else attend diligently to the reading of the scriptures." This is the work of a very distinguished (and beloved) modern iconographer.[87]

When the Reformers used Origen as a voice refuting the doctrine of the eucharistic "real presence," Catholic apologists such as Petavius were quick to point out that it was only a partial reading that allowed such a conclusion, since Origen's context as a priest in Caesarea showed that his liturgical custom was precisely that of affording the highest of reverence to the elements of bread and wine, a testimony per se to the very doctrine the Reformers were saying he denied.[88] In short, in all three fairly major Reformation controversies, therefore (justification by faith, the nature of the eucharist, and the doctrine of grace), the way Origen was used by both sides of the Reformation divide was lively but based on a very partial and anachronistic reading. It was Hooker, Baronius, Allatius, and Petavius, largely unaware of Origen as a factor of central focus, who set the terms for something different, in the sense that all four started a new movement of increased historical sensitivity in reading the ancient sources. Petavius was perhaps the first early modern writer to set out a system of historically rooted theological reflection, discussing (in a world that widely regarded Christian truths as eternal and unchanging from the beginning) the concepts of contextual development in a semantically sophisticated way.

This new openness to reading texts in the light of their original meanings and intellectual contexts would finally open up a reading of the great Alexandrian that was no longer conditioned by the many falsifications and clichés of the past that had so long dogged his name. It was to be fanned into flame, in the nineteenth century, by the new availability of much more extended editions of his work, in Greek and Latin versions, prepared by the scholars of the eighteenth century. An initial sign of this was the scholarly revision undertaken by C. H. E. Lommatzsch of the De La Rue version of Origen's extant works, which he issued in twenty-five volumes in Berlin between 1831 and 1848.[89] As we have already noticed, another more "critical" edition was also prepared in twelve volumes. It is known as the Berlin-Leipzig edition, sponsored first by the Prussian Royal Academy and continued by the Berlin-Brandenburg Academy.[90] In some of its instances, it remains the best edition for single works, though more recent French scholarship in the Sources Chrétiennes series has superseded it as a collective.[91]

Once Origen was available for scholars to read and access directly, it was only a matter of time before a revolution in his interpretation was destined to follow, and this took place at the end of the nineteenth century, heralded first by classical "Patrologies" or dictionaries of patristic authorities, chiefly meant for use in seminaries, which formerly had excluded Origen (on the basis that he could not be a Father of the Church if he had been condemned by an ecumenical council), now including him regularly and without fuss as one of the major thinkers and theologians (not simply exegetes) of the early church. The Roman Catholic Fathers of the Church series, based in Catholic University of America Press, for example, contains several important volumes of his works. He had very quietly returned, ushered gently back into the *aula* by learned and modest scholars of unimpeachable orthodoxy. The twentieth century, which saw Origen break through into numerous English translations (from the late nineteenth century onward in some places), fanned this interest into new flame once again.[92]

NOTES

1. Paschasius Radbertus, *De corpore et sanguine Domini cum appendice Epistola ad Fredugardum*, ed. B. Paulus, Corpus Christianorum Continuatio Mediaevalis 16 (Turnhout: Brepols, 1969); translated as *Radbertus, Paschasius: The Lord's Body and Blood*, ed. G. E. McCracken, Early Medieval Theology: The Library of Christian Classics (Philadelphia: Westminster Press, 1957).

2. *De Praedestinatione*, written 849–850. Both works are in *Patrologia Latina*, vol. 121, ed. J. P. Migne (Paris: Apud Garnieri Fratres, 1852), cols. 11–346 and 1153–56.

3. A long time later, in September 1050, Pope Leo IX condemned Ratramnus's treatise at the Synod of Vercelli. By then it was thought to be the work of John Scotus Eriugena.

4. Ridley, bishop of London, was a major influence in moving Cranmer, the archbishop of Canterbury, away from the doctrine of the real presence. He was a major shaper of the Anglican Book of Common Prayer and was burned by Queen Mary along with the reformist bishop of Worcester, Hugh Latimer, in 1555.

5. See Origen, *Homilies on Exodus* 13.3.66–84; *Homilies on Leviticus* 13.3. Also see F. Ledegang, "Eucharist," in McGuckin, *Westminster Handbook to Origen*, 96–99.

6. R. Heine, ed., *The Commentary of Origen on the Gospel of Matthew*, vol. 2 (Oxford: Oxford University Press, 2018), 694n159; Paschasius Radbertus, *Commentary on Matthew*, in *Patrologia Latina*, vol. 120, ed. J. P. Migne (Paris: Garnier, 1895), cols. 31–994; see also H. Vogt, "Origenes: Leben und Werke," in *Origenes als Exeget*, ed. W. Geerlings (Munich: Paderborn Schöningh, 1999), 9–22 (esp. 21).

7. Baugulf was abbot of the important monastery of Fulda by the Rhine.

8. M. Cappuyns, *Jean Scot Érigène, sa vie, son oeuvre, sa pensée* (Louvain: Mont César, 1933), 252–53.

9. The king is alleged to have asked Scotus, when sitting with him at a meal, what is the difference between an Irishman and a drunken fool? The joke works on the basis of "what separates a scottus from a sottus?" (*quid distas inter sottum et scottum?*), to which Scotus Eriugena answered, "Only a table" (*tabula tantum*). William of Malmesbury, *Gesta pontificum Anglorum*, book 5, cited in H. Waddell, *The Wandering Scholars* (Garden City, NY: Doubleday, 1955), 56.

10. The modality of asserting theological statements by negations and disallowances.

11. E. Artemi, "The Influence of Origen on John Scottus Eriugena concerning the Return of All Things to God," in *Origeniana Undecima*, ed. A. C. Jacobsen (Leuven: Peeters, 2016), 611.

12. Whom the Byzantines did not recognize as "emperor" but with whom they nonetheless wished to maintain good relations.

13. See J. Marenbon, *Early Medieval Philosophy* (London: Routledge, 1991), 53–70.

14. As in Eriugena, *Periphyseon* 5.925A.

15. The Greek term for "seeking out," signifying the manner in which Origen set out ideas he expected his advanced students to test out among each other in seminar discussion. Also known as the aporetic method (use of aporias as a teaching modality). Those who later did not recognize the antique learning method thought rather woodenly that every idea Origen proposed in class he was personally committed to.

16. Ramelli, "Origen in Western Theological and Philosophical Tradition," 463.

17. R. D. Crouse, "Origen in the Philosophical Tradition of the Latin West: St. Augustine and John Scottus Eriugena," in *Origeniana Quinta*, ed. R. J. Daly (Leuven: Peeters, 1992), 567.

18. R. D. Crouse, "Origen in the Philosophical Tradition," 567.

19. Proclus (412–485) was one of the last great successors (*diadochoi*) of Plato, via Plotinus.

20. Artemi, "Influence of Origen on John Scottus Eriugena"; Crouse, "Origen in the Philosophical Tradition," 567.

21. English translation in I. P. Sheldon-Williams, trans., *Eriugena: Periphyseon (The Division of Nature)*, rev. J. J. O'Meara, Cahiers d'études médiévales, Cahier special no.3 (Montreal: Dumbarton Oaks, 1987).

22. His extensive commentary is available in *Bernard of Clairvaux: On the Song of Songs*, 4 vols., Cistercian Fathers Series 4, 7, 31, and 40 (Spencer, MA: Cistercian Publications, 1971–1980).

23. See Leclerq, *Love of Learning*, 106n8.

24. See A. M. La Bonnardière, "Le Cantique des Cantiques dans l'oeuvre de saint Augustin," *Revue des Études Augustiniennes* 1 (1955): 225–37, esp. 225.

25. Proverbs, Ecclesiastes, and Song of Songs.

26. Augustine, *De Doctrina Christiana* 4.15.32.

27. Bernard of Clairvaux, *Sermons on the Song of Songs* 50.8.

28. Origen, *Commentary on the Song of Songs*, prologue, para. 3.

29. J. Leclercq, "S. Bernard et Origène d'après un ms. de Madrid," *Revue Bénédictine* 59 (1949): 194–95.

30. Jerome, *Epistles* 84.2: "laudavi interpretem non dogmatisten."

31. Abelard, *Theologia Christiana* 5.25, ed. T. M. Buytaert, Corpus Christianorum Continuatio Medievalis 12 (Turnhout: Brepols, 1969), 357.

32. Abelard, *Epistle* 8, ed. T. P. McLaughlin in *Medieval Studies* 18 (1956): 290.

33. Abelard, *Historia Calamitatum*, ed. D. N. Hasse (Berlin: De Gruyter, 2002), 42.

34. See M. W. Elliott, "Tracing the Romans Commentary of Origen in Abelard's," in *Origeniana Undecima*, ed. A. C. Jacobsen (Leuven: Peeters, 2016), 415–29; T. Georges, "Origen as Christian Philosopher in Peter Abelard," in Jacobsen, *Origeniana Undecima*, 431–40; E. M. Buytaert, "The Greek Fathers in Abelard's Theologies and Commentary on St. Paul," *Antonianum* 39 (1964): 429.

35. L. Bond, "Another Look at Abelard's Commentary on Romans 3.26," in *Medieval Readings of Romans*, ed. P. S. Hawkins and B. D. Schildgen, Romans through History and Culture (New York: T& T Clark International, 2008), 24; quoted in Elliot, "Tracing the Romans Commentary," 424.

36. See Elliott, "Tracing the Romans Commentary," 428.

37. Abelard, *Epistle* 5.

38. T. Georges, "Origen as Christian Philosopher in Peter Abelard," in Jacobsen, *Origeniana Undecima*, 435–39.

39. Gen. 26:12–33.

40. Abelard, *Epistle* 8, cited in Georges, "Origen as Christian Philosopher," 437.

41. Abelard, *Epistle* 8, cited in Georges, "Origen as Christian Philosopher," 437.

42. Jerome, *Epistle* 84.2: "I laud Origen the exegete, but not the dogmatician."

43. B. Pouderon, "La reception d'Origène à la Renaissance," in Jacobsen, *Origeniana Undecima*, 339–66, esp. 340.

44. He had been given this moniker, meaning "diamond bright" or "diamond hard," in antiquity.

45. *Origenis commentaria in sacram scripturam* (Rouen, 1608). Huet had discovered a fragment of a Greek manuscript of Origen at Stockholm in 1652 when he was in Sweden at the court of Queen Christina with the orientalist Samuel Bockhart. This set his interest alive in discovering all he could abut Origen.

46. He believed that Kabbalah and the writings of Hermes Trismegistus, which he advocated, were as old as the Old Testament and the Greek philosophers.

47. Lewis, *Philocalia of Origen*, vii: "In later times Picus of Mirandola ventured to maintain the cause of the great Father: the thesis was suppressed but the author remained uncensured: indeed a pious lady was said to have received a revelation not long before, which seemed to assure her of the forgiveness of Samson, Solomon and Origen. This hope, however, in the case of the last was admitted apparently by few; and Baronius expresses his surprise that any doubt of his condemnation could be raised after the sentence of Anastasius."

48. See A. Godin, *Erasme: Lecteur d'Origène* (Geneva: Librarie Droz, 1982).

49. English translation in Erasmus, *Enchiridion* (London: Methuen, 1905), available at https://oll.libertyfund.org/title/erasmus-the-manual-of-a-christian-knight.

50. Erasmus, *Enchiridion*, ch. 13.

51. See W. P. Stephens, *Zwingli le théologien* (Geneva: Labor et Fides, 1999), 43–47 and 85–111.

52. I. Backus, "Ulrich Zwingli, Martin Bucer and the Church Fathers," in *The Reception of the Church Fathers in the West*, vol. 2, *From the Carolingians to the Maurists* (Leiden: Brill, 1997), 627–60, esp. 637–38.

53. Augustine, *Commentary on Genesis* 8.7, 13.

54. M. Luther, *Du serf arbitre*, in *Oeuvres de M. Luther* (Geneva: Labor et Fides, 1958), 168.

55. *Luther Werke*, vol. 16 (Weimar, 1899), 113; see G. Pani, "In toto Origene non est verbum unum de Christo: Lutero e Origene," *Adamantius* 15 (2009): 135–49. It is an opinion that strikes the reader of Origen's primary texts as incredible, given how Christocentrically devoted Origen is. Of all Christian theologians, Origen ranks as one of the most high in terms of a personal and deeply fervent Christ-mysticism. It's spirit is palpable on almost on every page.

56. See J. Dechow, "Origen's Shadow over the Erasmus-Luther Debate," in *Origeniana Sexta*, ed. A. Le Boulluec and G. Dorival (Leuven: Peeters, 1995), 750–54.

57. Matt. 16:18: "You are Peter and on this rock I will build my church." *Luther Werke*, vol. 2 (Weimar, 1899), 188.

58. M. Mattox, "Sainte Sara, mère de l'Église: L'exégèse catholique de Genèse 18,1–15 par Martin Luther," *Positions luthériennes* 49, no. 4 (2001): 319–39.

59. Cited in B. Roussel, "Bèze et Origène," in *Origeniana Sexta*, ed. A Le Boulluec and G. Dorival (Leuven: Peeters, 1995), 759n3.

60. Laughable and most foolish.

61. In the latter part of the twentieth century and onward, there have been noticeable movements among Evangelical Christians to reclaim a fuller patristic heritage in doctrine and exegesis.

62. "I feel that your censure of Origen and Erasmus ought to have been much more moderate, since the one was the most celebrated writer among all the ancients and the other's work of translation (among those who have most recently accomplished this), has moved the cause of the Gospel greatly." Quoted in Roussel, "Bèze et Origène," 771n43.

63. E. Erculei, "Origen in the Philosophy of Giordano Bruno," in Jacobsen, *Origeniana Undecima*, 396.

64. As in the Psalms describing rain as "God's river in heaven brimming over" (Ps. 65:10) and many other instances of naïve cosmology.

65. Erculei, "Origen in the Philosophy of Giordano Bruno," 398.

66. Origen, *Commentary on the Song of Songs* 3.5.9–21; Erculei, "Origen in the Philosophy of Giordano Bruno," 399. On the *epinoiai*, see J. A. McGuckin, "The Changing Forms of Jesus according to Origen,' in *Origeniana Quarta*, ed. L. Lies (Innsbruck: Tyrolia-Verlag, 1987), 215–22.

67. G. Bruno, *De gli eroici furori*, in G. Bruno, *Dialoghi filosofici italiani*, ed. M. Ciliberto, 2nd ed. (Milan: Mondadori, 2001), 770.

68. The Municipality of Rome, as soon as it had freed itself from clerical control, set up a sympathetic memorial to Bruno in the Campo in 1889.

69. G. Bruno, *De triplici minimo et mensura* 1.43.

70. Part of his belief that there were so many (an infinity) of "vicissitudes" and alternative versions of truth that reaching the final and ultimate reality had to be an equally vast extension of possibilities.

71. Erculei, "Origen in the Philosophy of Giordano Bruno," 395.

72. In the Latin editions, they are written up as "Delarue."

73. J. P. Migne, *Origenis Opera Omnia: Opera et studio DD. Caroli et Caroli Vincentii Delarue*, Patrologiae Graecae Cursus Completus 11–17 (Paris: Petit Montrouge, 1857; repr., Turnhout: Brepols, 1977).

74. The *Griechischen christlicher Schriftsteller* (Berlin), which we shall notice in due course.

75. *Ressourcement* was the term that was used for a similar movement of reform in the latter part of the twentieth century when the Catholic Church turned once more to its past for matters of liturgical and theological renewal in the era of Vatican II. This too produced a massive and learned series of patristic texts (including the latest critical editions of Origen), published under the aegis of the Jesuit Order (*Sources Chrétiennes*).

76. See J. E. Booty, *John Jewel as Apologist of the Church of England* (London: SPCK, 1963); A. C. Southern, *English Recusant Prose 1559–1582* (London: Sands & Co., 1950), 60–66.

77. Jewel, *Apologia*, 2.17.

78. Jewel, *Apologia*, Conclusion 1.

79. See J. K. Luoma, "Who Owns the Fathers? Hooker and Cartwright on the Authority of the Primitive Church," *Sixteenth Century Journal* 8, no. 3 (1977): 45–59.

80. Luoma, "Who Owns the Fathers?," 57.

81. His favorites among the Greeks are Theodoret (22 instances), Chrysostom (22), and Gregory the Theologian (17), as well as the church historians Eusebius (23), Socrates (16), and Sozomen (14). Luoma, "Who Owns the Fathers?," 57n75.

82. Hooker, *Ecclesiastical Polity*, 2.6.4, citing Origen, *On Leviticus Homily 5*.

83. Hooker, *Ecclesiastical Polity*, 5.20.2, citing Origen, *Homily on Judges* 1.

84. Hooker, *Ecclesiastical Polity*, 6.4.7, citing Ps. Origen, *Homilia de Poenitentia Ninivitorum*.

85. See Lies, *Wort und Eucharistie bei Origenes*.

86. T. P. Scheck, *Origen and the History of Justification* (Notre Dame, IN: University of Notre Dame Press, 2008).

87. My wife, Eileen McGuckin (The Icon Studio, eileenmcguckin1003@gmail.com).

88. Origen, *Homilies on Leviticus* 13.5.52–65; *Homilies on the Psalms* 37.2.6.37–51; *Homilies on Jeremiah* 19.13.46–61; *Commentary on Ezekiel* 7.22; *Fragment on 1 Cor.* 34; *Commentary on Matthew* 10.25; *Homilies on Exodus* 13.3.68–72. Origen speaks about a group of Christians who have rejected baptism and the eucharist because they think their advanced spiritual state has transcended such material things, and he castigates this view as erroneous and pernicious in *On Prayer* (5.1). But he also stated in the *Series Commentary on Matthew* (85) that the words of Jesus about eating his body and drinking his blood are not references to the visible bread or drink but to the "word" of the Word of God that feeds and quenches the soul, and he exegetes the phrase "blood of the New Covenant" (1 Cor. 12:25) to signify the word by which we learn of Christ's Passion, and in his *Commentary on John* (1.30.208), he interprets the bread to mean the ethical teachings of Jesus and the wine to signify his mystical initiations. What the Reformation controversialists on both sides could not appreciate was the way Origen can teach several different points around the same instance, without meaning the one to contradict the other. See Ledegang, "Eucharist," 96–99.

89. C. H. E. Lommatzsch, *Origenis opera omnia quae graece vel latine tantum exstant et ejus nomine circumferuntur. Ed. C et C.V. Delarue. Denuos recensuit, emendavit et castigavit, C. H. E. Lommatzsch*, 25 vols. (Berlin: Haude und Spener, 1831–1848).

90. *Die griechischen christlichen Schriftsteller der ersten Jahrhunderte* (*GCS*), issued by seven different editors across two editions beginning in Leipzig (1899) and continuing to Berlin (1976). For details of editors and volume contents, see McGuckin, *Westminster Handbook to Origen*, 41–42.

91. For volume details of the thirty-seven Origen-related books to date, see McGuckin, *Westminster Handbook to Origen*, 42–43, reproduced as appendix 1 in this volume.

92. For a list of English editions of the works of Origen, see McGuckin, *Westminster Handbook to Origen*, 42–43. Since this was published, we also have now added three new and important critical editions/translations of Origen's major works: Ronald Heine, ed., *Origen: Commentary on the Gospel According to John, Books 1–10*, Fathers of the Church 80 (Washington, DC: Catholic University of America Press, 1989), and Ronald Heine, ed., *Origen: Commentary on the Gospel According to John, Books 13–32*, Fathers of the Church 85 (Washington, DC: Catholic University of America Press, 1993); John Behr, ed., *Origen on First Principles*, 2 vols. (Oxford: Oxford University Press, 2017); Ronald Heine, ed., *The Commentary of Origen on the Gospel of St. Matthew*, 2 vols. (Oxford: Oxford University Press, 2018).

Chapter 6

Modern Rediscoveries of Origen

What follows after the colon in this present sentence is a clause that should make a historian think twice before writing it: after the sixth century, it is *probably* not until the twentieth century that Origen began to be read once more holistically in terms of his overall output (instead of small and tendentiously selected gobbets) and with a clearer eye to the context of the school techniques of Late Antique philosophical circles (in other words, the original context in which Origen set out his teachings). This is not to say contemporary scholarship has the final grasp on everything Origen meant, for this would simply be hubris (and there have been many examples of recent books on Origen that have disagreed deeply among themselves, and several that seem to have no conception that he was a man of the church writing for philosophically educated believers). But I can make the confident statement that (1) because of the immense advances in the understanding of rhetorical technique in the twentieth century[1] and (2) the great advances in the understanding of the culture and philosophical schools of late antiquity and (3) the availability of so many first-class critical editions of the classics and the Christian literary corpus, there has never been a time since that of Origen himself when scholars were more enabled to make clear judgments about his meaning and intent. This profound richness has been the laborious work of scholars painstakingly gathering evidence, manuscripts, and printed editions, and now, in the twenty-first century, we stand on the shoulders of the great giants of the preceding three centuries of work.

In the twentieth century the story of the rediscovery of and growing admiration for Origen and his importance in the core Christian tradition begins with the Jesuit order. Eight Jesuit scholars stand out, and one Jesuit institution of higher learning. The scholars are the late Hans Urs von Balthasar,[2] Henri de Lubac,[3] Jean Daniélou,[4] Frédéric Bertrand,[5] Henri Crouzel,[6] and Lothar Lies,[7] and the still alive Robert Daly[8] and Brian Daley.[9] Three (Balthasar, de Lubac, and Daniélou) would be elevated as cardinals to signify the (eventual) approbation of their work by the Vatican. The Jesuit institution that had such an impact on Origenian studies (not to say the whole of modern European patristic study) was the printing house of the Sources Chrétiennes series, a Jesuit patronage and conception that has issued a massive number of critical texts of the fathers with original texts and facing French translations. The introductions and notes to these works are paradigms of learnedness. The Origen volumes in this series have been commissioned by the press from the leading Origen scholars of the day (see appendix 1).

It would be too much and too long a story to name the many other scholars who have played a great part in this rebirth of Origen scholarship since 1900. Their names are all found listed in the contents pages of *Origeniana Prima* through to *Origeniana Duodecima*, a research movement that developed as an idea to organize this scholarly movement (already recognized as a movement by the early decades of the twentieth century) into a series of productive international conferences. These were designed as meetings that would announce in advance a generic theme and ask for participants to write research papers within that protocol.

These conferences, bringing together scholars from all over the world, have met regularly (now convening every four years) and have produced a massive and impressive series of volumes of close and deep research on a very broad range of Origenian topics, all under the title *Origeniana*, issued (chiefly) by the academic press Peeters in Leuven, Belgium, whose own contribution to Origenian scholarship has been immensely impressive and generous. A brief description of these *Origeniana* volumes is given as appendix 2 to this book. They now number twelve volumes; the last, *Origeniana Duodecima*, being the record of the conference held in Jerusalem in 2017. The eleventh volume, *Origeniana Undecima*, published in 2016 and recording the researches of the 2013 Origen conference in Aarhus, was particularly concerned to map the influence and reception of Origen across Western Christian history (though within it there are studies of how he impacted the Late Antique and Byzantine East as well).

But apart from the foundational Jesuit "Origenians," other "big names" in Origen studies have also stood out in this time. Their books (and there were many more essays and research papers not recorded here) can be traced, in part, in the final select bibliography to this volume, and it might be useful (however limited an account) to note a few of them here in the sense of charting how this relatively modern revival of Origen studies took root and flowered. Notable among these were the Anglican theologians R. P. C. Hanson, C. Bammell, and M. Wiles; the French scholars Pierre Nautin, Marguerite Harl, and Gilles Dorival; the Italians L. Perrone and A. Monaci Castagno; and by no means least, the Americans Ronald Heine, Joseph Trigg, and Karen Torjesen. I would like here to make a short, more detailed, mention of only a very few of these to show some key recurring themes in modern scholarly analysis.

The select bibliography (and it is only a select few of the books written about Origen in recent times) will demonstrate how many have worked in this area over the last century, and to gain a sense of the much greater size of most of the significant articles that have appeared concerning Origenian thought, the immensely long contributors' lists for the *Origeniana Prima* through to *Origeniana Undecima* can be consulted. Henri Crouzel has also personally collated the *Bibliographie Critique D'Origène* and revised it several times up to his death.[10] My own little book, *The Westminster Handbook to Origen*,[11] was a gathering together of many of the world's English-speaking Origenian scholars, as A. Monaci Castagno had done with her Italian *Dizionario*,[12] and both works were meant to provide a new generation of students access to raw material so as to find the latest research about Origen on an A–Z variety of his key theological and exegetical themes. And this in order to replace reliance on so many heavily outdated textbooks that were still being used and still trotting out erroneous clichés about the ancient *magister*.

If we begin with the Jesuits of the early twentieth century, we see a turning of the strong educational focus of the order onto the origins of Christian tradition. This was a movement that engaged much Catholic intellectualism of this period and came to be called "ressourcement," or the going back to foundational sources. This happened for two reasons. First, it was believed that after a period of perceptible stagnation, the return to more robust antique traditions (a kind of code for leaving behind the shackles of medieval scholasticism that had so trammeled post-Reformation Catholicism) and more ancient forms of church expression in scripture, doctrine, and liturgical practice might prove to be a source of refreshment and renovation. Second, it was felt that a genuine ecumenical "rapprochement" might be the result of meeting other churches on the common ground of the scriptures and the early fathers, rather than on the basis of papal decrees, which had so often characterized earlier generations of Catholic apologetics.

The Jesuits took the lead in this in relation to the study of the Christian fathers, as the Dominicans and Benedictines did so in relation to scripture and liturgical study. All of this spiritual and intellectual ferment in continental Catholicism would come to a fruition in the later midcentury when the Second Vatican Council endorsed its approach. The stone that began the avalanche, as it were, was the Jesuit scholar (as he then was) Hans Urs von Balthasar. He composed an influential article signaling the importance of Origen and his unjustified neglect.[13] It was to be the beginning of a lifelong interest in Origen that impacted broad scope of this important theologian's systematics.

Jean Daniélou, later to be made a cardinal for his efforts, was a guiding spirit. Together with his mentor, Henri de Lubac, also to be made a cardinal, and their Jesuit colleague Claude Mondésert, at Lyon in 1942, they conceived the idea of presenting a whole series of patristic texts taken from all parts of the ancient church, East and West, that would offer the primary texts with facing modern French translations. It was their hope to get generations of future seminarians and scholars to start actually reading the primary sources instead of relying on textbook "summations" of what they meant (from a *weltanschauung* where such synopses were often painfully biased). The collection prided itself on being the latest critical editions and immediately superseded the Migne's *Patrologia Graeca* and *Patrologia Latina* and being much more accessible than the German *GCS* series of texts.[14] The Sources Chrétiennes soon grew in size to (almost) rival the capacity and range of Migne.

Daniélou and de Lubac were both immediately seized with enthusiasm for the writings of Origen when they came across him and realized that here was one of the leading intellects, and foundational systematicians, of the early church, whose voice had been stifled. So early on it was decided to bring out as complete an edition of the works of Origen as possible, and over a series of years, with several different but leading scholars, this was achieved. Daniélou also composed several studies devoted to Origen, a biography,[15] and an important study of Origen's exegetical technique.[16] In 1950 de Lubac composed an equally influential collection of Origen's key texts (as did Gregory Nazianzen and Basil the Great many centuries before in their *Philocalia Origenis*), which was also a focused study on Origen's exegetical methodology.[17] In the course of this study, de Lubac defended Origen's reputation, arguing that he was unjustifiably called a heretic and pointing out his immense contributions to the formation of catholic tradition as well as his lifelong dedication to the *regula fidei*. De Lubac also made specific defenses of things that Origen had been especially censured for in the West (his doctrine of *apokatastasis*, the sense that he undermined the literal reading of the Bible, and the notion that he did not see the cross as the once-for-all core of the atonement). In each case he demonstrated the falsity of the conclusions if one considered the totality of the writings (which his earlier critics had certainly not done or not been able to do).

De Lubac's magisterial four-volume study of the exegetical tradition of the Christian church, published between 1959 and 1965 in Paris, also cemented Origen's place as *magister ecclesiae* in a most definitive way.[18] One of de Lubac's most heartfelt efforts was the struggle he engaged in (with his Jesuit superiors' encouragement) to defend the reputation and orthodoxy of his recently deceased mentor, Fr. Teilhard de Chardin, whose life had been blighted by conservatives in the Ottaviani administration of the Vatican Holy Office who were bent on sniffing out imaginary heresies and had enforced a teaching and publishing silence on Teilhard de Chardin as an attempted *damnatio memoriae*. Soon this would also be a cloud that fell over de Lubac himself, hated as he was by many in the pre–Vatican II department of the *Propaganda Fidei* for his own role in spreading the so-called *nouvelle théologie*. Both he and Hans Urs von Balthasar would suffer long periods of this official Vatican disapproval for much the same reasons, and it was, perhaps, for both of them a sense of affinity with the Alexandrian *magister* that became a spur for the defense of Origen, whose reputation for unorthodoxy had similarly been assailed by loud voices that had never bothered to understand him.

Something that is often overlooked, and has never since either been translated or reprinted, but (at least to my mind) was an epochal study, was another Jesuit priest's little book that also added to the fire of the Origen revival that would grow from such flames to become the conflagration it has been in the late twentieth and early twenty-first centuries. This was Father Frédéric Bertrand's study *Mystique de Jésus chez Origène*.[19] In the slipstream of de Lubac, this book demonstrated the total falsity of Luther's oft-quoted remark that in all of Origen there was not a heartfelt word about Jesus. On the contrary, Bertrand showed the profoundly deep spirit of loving attention Origen gave, on almost every page of his writing, to what can only be called a Jesus-centered mysticism—at least if we understand "mysticism" in the robust sense of the early church, the way Paul applies his and the believer's sense of being "in Christ" (*en Christo*)[20] and the way the early fathers applied this in a most personal Christocentric way.

Indeed, Origen emerged from this as clearly the supreme Father of the Church who founded this Christocentric spirituality that so underpins most of patristic thought and devotion, and this revelation was something of a shock wave that lifted away ecclesiastical thinking of the time from the focus on medieval mysticism, which had placed such an emphasis on affectivity and had, rather inevitably, degenerated across the years into the more individualistically "emotional" type of spirituality that was predominant in Catholic circles of the late nineteenth and early twentieth centuries. Origen was like the tolling of a great bell that called for a new thinking through of how patristic theology was, at root and core, a fundamental lifestyle of spirituality, where mind and heart and soul were as one.

The focused interest of the Jesuits started to catch the attention of English-speaking Protestant scholars and turn them to look once more at Origen. Chief among them was the church of Ireland bishop (and university professor) Richard Hanson (1916–1988). Though in 1948 Hanson had contributed to *The Church of Rome: A Dissuasive*, he was nevertheless the first British contributor to the Jesuit Sources Chrétiennes program. He came into contact with Daniélou, whom he greatly respected as a patrologist, and began what became a long and very close friendship with the Jesuit Henri Crouzel, who was Daniélou's and De Lubac's junior colleague. It was Crouzel who would himself become an indefatigable publisher on all things Origenian, not least his popular biography *Origène*, written in 1985 and translated for the English market in 1989.

Crouzel, who was professor of early Christian studies at Toulouse, began his prolific publishing career with three important and detailed studies of Origen's theology and philosophy: *Théologie de l'Image de Dieu chez Origène* (1956), *Origène et la connaissance mystique* (1961), and *Origène et la philosophie* (1961). The first two monographs built on Bertrand and showed how much Origen's spiritual theology underpinned the foundations of the catholic tradition. The third signaled to those interested in the philosophy of late antiquity (an area that was also undergoing a great revival at this time) that here was a major thinker of the Second Sophistic era who needed attention. Robert Berchman would eventually rise to this challenge.[21]

It was Crouzel's biography, however, that really marked the moment when Origen was re-presented as a major figure much misunderstood to the wider world of students of antiquity, for it was an approachable book written by a scholar for generally interested readers. Hanson wrote a glowing review of it in *Zeitschrift fur Kirchengeschichte*: "Henri Crouzel must be acknowledged as the foremost scholar in the study of Origen alive today. 'Origen' is an important event for students of the history of doctrine in the early church . . . a fine book, written by an expert, and it will long remain a standard work which no scholar can afford to ignore."

Hanson himself also wrote studies of early Christian exegesis,[22] in which he was not particularly enamored of Origen's "Alexandrian" style (a typological way of understanding patristic exegesis that was prevalent at the time but has since come to be discredited as a useful matrix of understanding),[23] but Hanson was increasingly led by Crouzel to gain a deeper appreciation for Origen's dogmatics, and this shows in his last great work, *The Search for the Christian Doctrine of God*, where although he began his study with the Council of Nicaea, he gave a sympathetic and careful account of the importance of Origen behind the scenes of it all.

It would be the work of two American scholars, Karen Torjesen (b. 1945; now professor emerita at the School of Arts and Humanities at Claremont Graduate University) and Joseph W. Trigg (Episcopal priest-scholar, now retired from the Diocese of Washington), that typified the way that this new scholarship on Origen's original thought, now accurately analyzed and imaginatively presented, had arrived at a state that could confidently present itself to a new generation of students, rendering obsolete the old clichés about him that had inhabited the old patrologies.

Trigg's was a biography of Origen that firmly set him in the context of his own driving agenda—to read the Bible in the light of philosophy, but with philosophical concerns for systematic consistency ever faithful to the principles of divinely given revelation. His very readable study, *Origen: The Bible and Philosophy in the Third-Century Church*,[24] made even the scholars sit up and realize what an exciting and deep well of narrative there still was to produce about Origen. Maurice Wiles wrote the preface to the English edition of the book in 1985 and perspicaciously noted,

> It is hardly an exaggeration to say that his book does for Origen what Peter Brown did for Augustine. It weaves a study of the thought of Origen into the story of his biography and thereby quite literally brings it to life. In doing so he makes Origen more intelligible in terms of his own age, and at the same time more interesting to us and to our contemporary concerns . . . . But above all it fulfils the invaluable task of making Origen's thought much more accessible to that far wider range of people [than patristic specialists] concerned with the origins of Christian faith.

A few years later, Ronald Heine produced his own biography of Origen,[25] in which he showed in a masterly way that the phenomenal learning of the Alexandrian *magister* was not something accidental or peripheral but, on the contrary, a fundamental part of his life's mission to evangelize the educated (pagan) classes by demonstrating the church's claim to possess within itself the incarnation of divine Wisdom, that goal of all the ancient philosophical schools.[26] Accordingly, the church could not dare, without causing scandal or committing sacrilege, to present to the world an ignorant façade or the persona of an uneducated and narrow sect. It neglects its mission to disseminate wisdom at its peril. Heine showed Origen's exegetical and dogmatic work to be a core part of his priestly evangelism, and in so doing presented Origen as surely the patron saint of all Christian aspirations for learnedness. His role as the first founder of what could pass as a Christian university (at Caesarea Maritima, where for the first time he built his *schola* around a library with the bishop's blessing) was surely a symbol of the best of Christian missionary endeavors for the future.

Karen Torjesen's book on Origen's exegetical process was a cause célèbre when it appeared just before the quadrennial international gathering of patristics scholars at Oxford University in 1986. A slim volume from De Gruyter, of a size that belied the importance of its contents, Torjesen's book isolated the first English consideration of what *exactly* was Origen's hermeneutical method. Up until then, his method had been assumed, on a rather superficial level, to be different "senses" of the scripture corresponding to different spiritual levels of the hearers. What he himself described (as a loose analogy) about Jesus speaking sometimes to crowds in valleys, sometimes to disciples on the plains, sometimes to the elect on the mountains, was often used as a crude substitute for closer analysis and justified as what he "really meant" by an appeal to the rather wooden way that Gregory the Great had tried to copy him along this route,[27] without really understanding his more fundamental motivations about how theology was communicated within the church. Torjesen's book demonstrated clearly to all just how subtle Origen's method really was, and how much it corresponded to the sophisticated patterns of literary interpretation in his Late Antique environment. After her, it would no longer be possible to write the kind of essays Hanson and Wiles had both produced in *The Cambridge History of the Bible* when they discussed Origenian exegesis rather dismissively.

Ronald Heine was able to follow up on Torjesen's findings, with other examples of contemporary (non-Christian) interpreters of the Late Antique period who did similar things with Homer and the philosophical tradition, showing how this was a pattern also observed in some of the antique commentators on Aristotle.[28] At a stroke, it became startling clear how Origen's biblical project was both harmonized with the philosophical quest (the attentive exegesis of texts by the Commentators looking for the essential meaning in a prior fixed tradition) and thereby resonating with the *regula fidei* of the church. Although, ironically, Origen's ancient (and modern) critics had often accused him of departing from catholic tradition because of unwarranted philosophical "speculations," his opening chapters in the *Peri Archon* show just how clearly the elucidation of the core *regula fidei* of the catholic tradition was the fundamental motive of that whole treatise. Fr. John Behr's new critical edition of the *Peri Archon*[29] makes this clear once again after the many obfuscations caused by the Butterworth English edition of 1936.[30]

Elizabeth Dively Lauro built on Torjesen's scriptural work in her own elegant study setting out the principles involved in the way Origen consistently approaches the sacred scripture.[31] Peter Martens also produced, around this time, an excellent study of Origen's deep scriptural method and how it related to the traditions of the sophists.[32] As well as these, my own triad of studies attempted, similarly, to show how this complex "metaphysics of textual revelation" actually applied in Origen's close weave of theology, where philosophical commentary, spiritual encomium, and dogmatic insight were woven so closely and so brilliantly together that they could not be disentangled.[33] In the process, it became more clear, generally speaking, how Origen's life work reflected much of the sophistication of the scholars of the Great Library in Alexandria, who were actively pressing the boundaries of the relations between exegesis (of traditional texts) and the pursuit of the philosophical (sophistic) lifestyle.

These are only a few moments in the larger story of how much flowering there has been in the present generation of scholars concerning the life and works of the Alexandrian master. The whole story of that movement of rediscovery and reappreciation is far from being exhausted. It will surely go on for perhaps a generation to come. Nevertheless, it has already begun to require a wholesale rewriting of textbooks of church history and historical dogmatics in the years to come, and it will be in this secondary motion (a task I tried to presage in *The Westminster Handbook to Origen*, which I organized among a cluster of Origenian scholars some years ago)[34] that Origen's true reputation as a profound master of theology will be finally and unarguably established. This is the sage whom the martyr St. Pamphilus rightly called *magister ecclesiae* (a master among the church), and whom St. Gregory Nazianzen called the "whetstone of us all," and whom even his subsequent enemy, Jerome, once confessed to be "a man truly great even from his infancy."

NOTES

1. Schools of literary criticism, independent of theological or classics academies, gave the whole reading of history a new twist of perspective in the mid-twentieth century and in so doing provided a much more sure foundation for approaching Late Antique rhetoric.

2. Balthasar (1905–1988) began his ecclesiastical life as a Jesuit and was elevated as cardinal by John Paul II but died two days before his installation.

3. De Lubac (1896–1991) was offered the cardinal's hat in 1969 and again (receiving it the second time) in 1983.

4. Daniélou (1905–1974) was offered the cardinalate in 1969.

5. Bertrand has no apparent existence on the internet, not even in the listing of notable Jesuits—though he ought to have. His book on Origen's mystical thought gave the underpinning for the revival work of his more famous Jesuit contemporaries.

6. Crouzel (1918–2003) was professor of patrology at Toulouse University and one of the most dedicated Origenian scholars of the twentieth century.

7. Lies died in the Jesuit house at Innsbruck in 2008.

8. Emeritus professor of patristics at Boston College.

9. Emeritus professor of patristics at the University of Notre Dame.

10. H. Crouzel, *Bibliographie Critique D'Origène* (The Hague: Martin Nijhoff, 1959), with supplement 1 (The Hague: Martin Nijhoff, 1982) and supplement 2 (Turnhout: Brepols, 1996).

11. McGuckin, *Westminster Handbook to Origen*.

12. A. Monaci Castagno, ed., *Origene: Dizionario. La cultura, il pensiero, le opere* (Rome: Citta Nuova, 2000).

13. H. Urs von Balthasar, "Le Mysterion d'Origène," *Recherches de science religieuse* 26 (1936): 512–62; 27 (1937): 38–64.

14. *Griechische Christlicher Schriftsteller* (Berlin).

15. J. Daniélou, *Origène* (Paris: Table Ronde, 1948).

16. J. Daniélou, *Sacramentum Futuri: Études sur l'origine de la typologie biblique* (Paris: Beauchesne, 1950).

17. H. de Lubac, *Histoire et esprit: l'intelligence de l'Écriture d'après Origène* (Paris: Aubier, 1950); English ed., H. de Lubac, *History and Spirit: The Understanding of Scripture According to Origen*, trans. A. E. Nash and J. Merriell (San Francisco: Ignatius Press, 2007).

18. H. de Lubac, *Exégèse mediévale: Les quatre sens d'écriture*, 4 vols. (Paris: Aubier, 1959–1965).

19. F. Bertrand, *Mystique de Jésus chez Origène* (Paris: Aubier, 1951).

20. A core Pauline theology of mystical, redemptive union, which expresses his sense of how the resurrectional glory of the Lord passes on transfiguratively to his church, something Origen saw very clearly indeed. See Romans 3:24; 6:11; 6:23; 8:2; 8:31; 12:1, 5; 1 Cor. 1:2; 1:30; 15:22; 2 Cor. 2:14; 5:17, 19; Eph. 1:9, 11; 1:20; 2:10; 3:11; 4:32; Col. 2:6; 1 Tim. 1:14.

21. R. Berchman, *From Philo to Origen: Middle Platonism in Transition* (Chico, CA: Scholars Press, 1984).

22. See esp. R. P. C. Hanson, *Allegory and Event* (Richmond, VA: John Knox Press, 1959); repr., ed. and intro. J. Trigg (Louisville, KY: Westminster John Knox Press, 2002); and his entry "Biblical Exegesis in the Early Church," in *The Cambridge History of the Bible*, ed. P. R. Ackroyd and C. F. Evans (Cambridge: Cambridge University Press, 1970), 412–53.

23. The same can be said about Maurice F. Wiles's article in the same *Cambridge History of the Bible*: "Origen as Biblical Scholar," 454–88.

24. J. W. Trigg, *Origen: The Bible and Philosophy in the Third-Century Church* (Atlanta: John Knox Press, 1983; London: SCM Press, 1985).

25. R. E. Heine, *Origen: Scholarship in Service of the Church* (Oxford: Oxford University Press, 2010).

26. See also McGuckin, "Caesarea Maritima as Origen Knew It."

27. In the exegetical explanations of his *Pastoral Rule*.

28. R. Heine, "Origen's Commentary on John Compared with the Introductions to the Ancient Philosophical Commentaries on Aristotle," in *Origeniana Sexta*, ed. G. Dorival and A. Le Boulluec (Leuven: Peeters, 1995), 1–12.

29. J. Behr, ed., *Origen: On First Principles*, 2 vols. (Oxford: Oxford University Press, 2017).

30. Butterworth translated the Koetschau Berlin edition of the text and adopted Koetschau's unfounded belief that a Greek surviving fragment was always superior to a Latin (translated) one—as a result, he wove into the primary text of Origen everything that his Greek enemies "said that he had said," thus completely falsifying all the "controversial" aspects of the text and argument of the *Peri Archon*. Koetschau and Butterworth have, between the two of them, done sterling service on behalf of the medieval enemies of Origen and their ongoing slanders as to core aspects of his teaching. Butterworth's edition became the standard English teaching text for Origen for so many years and was reprinted many times even to the present without any warning given to students of the very peculiar editorial decisions behind the choices of text.

31. E. A. Dively Lauro, *The Soul and the Spirit of Scripture within Origen's Exegesis*, The Bible in Ancient Christianity (Atlanta: Society of Biblical Literature, 2010).

32. P. W. Martens, *Origen and Scripture: The Contours of the Exegetical Life* (Oxford: Oxford University Press, 2012).

33. McGuckin, "Structural Design and Apologetic Intent"; J. A. McGuckin, "Origen as Literary Critic in the Alexandrian Tradition," in *Origenianum Octavum*, ed. L. Perrone (Leuven: Peeters, 2003), 121–36; J. A. McGuckin, "Exegesis and Metaphysics in Origen's Biblical Philosophy," in *Festschrift for T. Stylianopoulos*, ed. E. Pentiuc (Brookline, MA: Hellenic College Press, 2015); repr. in J. A. McGuckin *Seeing the Glory*, Collected Studies 2 (Crestwood, NY: St. Vladimir's Seminary Press, 2017), 159–74.

34. McGuckin, *Westminster Handbook to Origen*.

Chapter 7

Epilogue

The final emergence into a truer appreciation of Origen's sanctity, and profundity, that I anticipate will only happen when his exegesis stops being caricatured, by those who have not understood it, as wildly unattached to the text, and when the false ascription of heretical metaphysics to him (by the misattributions of the sixth-century synodal anathemata) is more generally recognized as erroneous.[1] Whether a believer who died in the reputation of heroic sanctity can be posthumously condemned centuries after his death is one thing; whether it is legitimate for this to be done by sleight of hand under the impression it was an act of a great council is another; and whether it is at all acceptable that the evidence for the making of that negative judgment is proven to be entirely falsely attributed is yet another. Indeed, the whole business of Origen's censure is a historical miscarriage of justice (or at least a massive act of ecclesial ungenerosity) waiting to be righted.

I hope that this little volume (as did the larger set of studies contained in *Origeniana Undecima*)[2] will contribute to that cause: restoring honor to a theologian whose every word need not be engraved in stone for the benefit of the church, but whose discourse was a cause of inspiration to most of the intellectual great fathers of the early church, and whose accomplishments under the inspiration of the Holy Spirit set the groundwork for most of Christian exegetical preaching ever after him, and for many of the fundamental structures of the catholic *regula fidei* that he set out to explain to new generations.

Ilaria Ramelli put it very well when, considering Origen's overall impact on later ages, she summed up Origen's historical importance:

> The reception of Origen's ideas in philosophy and theology is staggering and focuses on protology, eschatology, anthropology, ethics and the importance of freewill, ontology (monism), apophaticism, Biblical allegoresis, and partially ecclesiology. I should also add the theological anti-subordinationism of the Son

(and the Spirit) and the description of the Trinity as one *ousia* in three *hypostases* with *hypostasis* meaning "individual substance" of one Person.[3]

As I write these closing remarks, a major international research project on the history of intellectual freedom is being undertaken from the base of Aarhus University.[4] The project is part of the ITN–Marie Curie "The History of Human Freedom and Dignity in Western Civilization" project. Origenian scholar Anders Christian Jacobsen is a leading figure in this collaboration across six universities as well as several printing houses and church institutions. A chief element in this research into the history of the reception of ideas is the very honorable place Origen, as religious philosopher, holds as one of history's great defenders of the principle of freedom. We can wait for the results of this collaboration, which will certainly support the view that Origen was truly one of the earliest philosophers of freedom considered as a basic structure of human ontology. The project will add to the swell of voices that must count him not only as simply a Christian theologian but as one of the most important philosophical voices of the age of late antiquity.

Origen himself, of course, would insist that a philosopher *has to be* a theologian, and vice versa. But in an age where what C. P. Snow once called the "Great Divorce"[5] has not ceased to exercise its thrall on institutions of higher learning, we seem to have dug ourselves even deeper into narrower and narrower tracks of culture—so much so that it is now perfectly possible (maybe even common) for an educated person to be described as "very learned but not very wise," "deeply informed but profoundly uncultured," or (even worse) "highly reverent, but rather stupid." Origen is the patron saint for an enduring hope that the life of the mind can be harmonized with the life of the heart and that of the soul, and that when this harmony is restored a person will reemerge as the very image of what they were meant to be (*Arche kai Telos*): an icon of the divine light on earth.

NOTES

1. I am not arguing here that the synodical anathemata themselves are erroneous: they correctly declare that the propositions they list are not part of the catholic and orthodox ecumenical tradition, and rightly censure them. I am simply saying that they erroneously attribute such ideas to Origen, as we have already noted. He himself is far from being an Origenist as they thought.

2. Jacobsen, *Origeniana Undecima*.

3. I. L. E. Ramelli, "The Reception of Origen's Ideas in Western Theological and Philosophical Traditions," in Jacobsen, *Origeniana Undecima*, 463.

4. The website gives fuller details: http://itn-humanfreedom.eu/.

5. Between scientific modes of analysis and those of the humanities.

Appendix 1

The Origen Volumes in the Sources Chrétiennes Series (SC)

Entretien d'Origène avec Héraclide. Edited by J. Scherer. SC 67. Paris: Editions du Cerf, 1960.

Homélies sur Josué. Edited by A. Jaubert. SC 71. Paris: Editions du Cerf, 1960.

Homélies sur S. Luc. Edited by H. Crouzel, F. Fournier, and P. Périchon. SC 87. Paris: Editions du Cerf, 1962.

Homélies sur le Cantique des Cantiques. Edited by O. Rousseau. SC 37. Paris: Editions du Cerf, 1966.

Commentaire sur S. Jean, 1. Books 1–5. Edited by C. Blanc. SC 120. Paris: Editions du Cerf, 1966.

Contre Celse, 1. Books 1–2. Edited by M. Borret. SC 132. Paris: Editions du Cerf, 1967.

Contre Celse, 2. Books 3–4. Edited by M. Borret. SC 136. Paris: Editions du Cerf, 1968.

Contre Celse, 3. Books 5–6. Edited by M. Borret. SC 147. Paris: Editions du Cerf, 1969.

Contre Celse, 4. Books 7–8. Edited by M. Borret. SC 150. Paris: Editions du Cerf, 1969.

Remerciement à Origène de Grégoire le Thaumaturge suivi de la lettre d'Origène à Grégoire. Edited by H. Crouzel. SC 148. Paris: Editions du Cerf, 1969.

Commentaire sur l'Évangile selon Matthieu, 1. Books 10–11. Edited by R. Girod. SC 162. Paris: Editions du Cerf, 1970.

Commentaire sur S. Jean, 2. Books 6–10. Edited by C. Blanc. SC 157. Paris: Editions du Cerf, 1970.

La chaine palestinienne sur la psaume 118 (Origène, Eusèbe, Didyme, Apollinaire, Athanase, Théodoret). Edited by M. Harl and G. Dorival. SC 189–90. Paris: Editions du Cerf, 1972.

Commentaire sur S. Jean, 3. Book 13. Edited by C. Blanc. SC 222. Paris: Editions du Cerf, 1975.

Homélies sur la Genèse. Edited by L. Doutreleau. SC 7. Paris: Editions du Cerf, 1976.
Contre Celse, 5 (Introduction générale–tables et index). Edited by M. Borret. SC 227. Paris: Editions du Cerf, 1976.
Philocalie 21–27 sur le libre arbitre. Edited by E. Junod. SC 226. Paris: Editions du Cerf, 1976.
Homélies sur Jéremie, 1. Homilies 1–11. Edited by P. Nautin. SC 232. Paris: Editions du Cerf, 1976.
Homélies sur Jéremie, 2. Homilies 12–20 and Latin Homilies. Edited by P. Nautin. SC 238. Paris: Editions du Cerf, 1977.
Traité des Principes, 1. Books 1–2. Edited by H. Crouzel and M. Simonetti. SC 252. Paris: Editions du Cerf, 1978.
Traité des Principes, 2. Books 1–2, Fragments. Edited by H. Crouzel and M. Simonetti. SC 253. Paris: Editions du Cerf, 1978.
Traité des Principes, 3. Books 3–4. Edited by H. Crouzel and M. Simonetti. SC 268. Paris: Editions du Cerf, 1980.
Traité des Principes, 4. Books 3–4, Fragments. Edited by H. Crouzel and M. Simonetti. SC 269. Paris: Editions du Cerf, 1980.
Homélies sur le Lévitique, 1. Homilies 1–7. Edited by M. Borret. SC 286. Paris: Editions du Cerf, 1981.
Homélies sur le Lévitique, 2. Homilies 8–16. Edited by M. Borret. SC 287. Paris: Editions du Cerf, 1981.
Commentaire sur S. Jean, 4. Books 19–20. Edited by C. Blanc. SC 290. Paris: Editions du Cerf, 1982.
Philocalie, 1–20, Sur les Écritures, et le lettre d'Africanus sur l'histoire de Suzanne. Edited by M. Harl and N. De Lange. SC 302. Paris: Editions du Cerf, 1983.
Traité des Principes, 5 (Compléments et index). Edited by H. Crouzel and M. Simonetti. SC 312. Paris: Editions du Cerf, 1984.
Homélies sur l'Exode. Edited by M. Borret. SC 321. Paris: Editions du Cerf, 1985.
Homélies sur Samuel. Edited by P. Nautin and M.-T. Nautin. SC 328. Paris: Editions du Cerf, 1986.
Homélies sur Ézéchiel. Edited by M. Borret. SC 352. Paris: Editions du Cerf, 1989.
Commentaire sur le Cantique des Cantiques. 2 vols. Edited by L. Brésard, H. Crouzel, and M. Borret. SC 375–76. Paris: Editions du Cerf, 1991–1992.
Commentaire sur S. Jean, 5. Books 28 and 32. Edited by C. Blanc. SC 385. Paris: Editions du Cerf, 1992.
Homélies sur les Juges. Edited by P. Messié, L. Neyrand, and M. Borret. SC 389. Paris: Editions du Cerf, 1993.
Homélies sur les Psaumes 36 à 38. Edited by H. Crouzel and L. Brésard. SC 411. Paris: Editions du Cerf, 1995.
Homélies sur les Nombres, 1. Homilies 1–9. Edited by L. Doutreleau. SC 415. Paris: Editions du Cerf, 1996.
Homélies sur les Nombres, 2. Homilies 11–19. Edited by L. Doutreleau. SC 442. Paris: Editions du Cerf, 1999.

Appendix 2
The Origeniana Series of Studies on Origen

Origeniana. Premier colloque international des études origéniennes, Montserrat, 18–21 septembre 1973. Edited by H. Crouzel, G. Lomiento, and J. Rius-Camps. Quaderni di Vetera Christianorum 12. Bari: Istituto di letteratura cristiana antica, Università di Bari, 1975.

Origeniana Secunda. Second colloque international des études origeniennes, Bari, 20–23 septembre 1977. Edited by H. Crouzel and A. Quacquarelli. Quaderni di Vetera Christanorum 15. Bari: Edizioni del Ateneo, 1980.

Origeniana Tertia. Third International Colloque for Origen Studies, University of Manchester, September 7–11, 1981. Edited by R. P. C. Hanson and H. J. Crouzel. Rome: Edizioni del Ateneo, 1985.

Origeniana Quarta. Die Referate des 4. Internationalen Origenes-kongresses, Innsbruck, 2–6 September 1984. Edited by L. Lies. Innsbrucker theologische Studien 19. Innsbruck: Tyrolia-Verlag, 1987.

Origeniana Quinta. Papers of the Fifth International Origen Congress, Boston College, 14–18 August, 1989. Edited by R. J. Daly. Bibliotheca Ephemeridum Theologicarum Lovaniensium 105. Leuven: Peeters, 1992.

Origeniana Sexta: Origène et la Bible. Actes du Colloquium Origenianum Sextum, Chantilly, 30 aoÛt–3 septembre 1993. Edited by G. Dorival and A. Le Boulluec. Bibliotheca Ephemeridum Theologicarum Lovaniensium 118. Leuven: Peeters, 1995.

Origeniana Septima. Origenes in den Auseinandersetzungen des 4. Jahrhunderts; Die Referate des 4. Internationalen Origenes-kongresses, Hofgeiser-Marburg, 1997. Edited by W. A. Bienert and U. Kühneweg. Bibliotheca Ephemeridum Theologicarum Lovaniensium 137. Leuven: Peeters, 1999.

Origeniana Octava: Origen and the Alexandrian Tradition. Acts of the Eighth International Origen Colloquium, Pisa, August 2001. Edited by L. Perrone. Bibliotheca Ephemeridum Theologicarum Lovaniensium 164. Leuven: Peeters, 2003.

Origeniana Nona: Origen and the Religious Practice of His Time. Papers of the Ninth International Origen Congress, Pécs, Hungary, 29 August–2 September 2005. Edited by G. Heidl and R. Somos. Bibliotheca Ephemeridum Theologicarum Lovaniensium 228. Leuven: Peeters, 2009.

Origeniana Decima: Origen as Writer. Acts of the Tenth International Origen Conference, University School of Philosophy and Education, Ignatianum, Kraków, Poland, 31st August–4 September 2009. Edited by S. Kaczymarek and H. Pietras. Bibliotheca Ephemeridum Theologicarum Lovaniensium 224. Leuven: Peeters, 2011.

Origeniana Undecima: Origen and Origenism in the History of Western Thought. Acts of the Eleventh International Origen Conference Held at Aarhus University, Denmark, in August 2013. Edited by A. C. Jacobsen. Bibliotheca Ephemeridum Theologicarum Lovaniensium 279. Leuven: Peeters, 2015.

Origeniana Duodecima: Origen's Legacy in the Holy Land—a Tale of Three Cities: Jerusalem, Caesarea and Bethlehem. Proceedings of the Twelfth International Origen Congress, Jerusalem, 25–29 June, 2017. Edited by B. Bitton-Ashkelony, O. Irshai, A. Kofski, H. Newman, and L. Perrone. Bibliotheca Ephemeridum Theologicarum Lovaniensium 302. Leuven: Peeters, 2019.

Select Bibliography

Albrecht, M. C. "Reincarnation and the Early Church." *Update: New Religious Movements* 7, no. 2 (1983): 34–39.

Andresen, C. *Logos und Nomos: Die Polemik der Kelsos wider das Christentum.* Berlin: De Gruyter, 1955.

Babcock, H. E. "Origen's anti-Gnostic Polemic and the Doctrine of Universalism." *Unitarian Universalist Christian* 38, nos. 3–4 (1983): 53–59.

Balas, D. "The Idea of Participation in the Structure of Origen's Thought." In *Origeniana*, vol. 1, edited by H. Crouzel, G. Lomiento, and J. Rius-Camps, 257–75. Bari, Italy: Istituto di letteratura cristiana antica, 1975.

Bammel, E. "Die Zitate aus den Apokryphen bei Origenes." In *Origeniana Quinta*, edited by R. J. Daly, 131–36. Leuven: Peeters, 1992.

Bammell, C. P. "Philocalia IX, Jerome Ep. 121 and Origen's Exposition of Romans VII." *Journal of Theological Studies* 32 (1981): 50–81.

———. "Adam in Origen." In *Orthodoxy: Essays in Honour of Henry Chadwick*, edited by R. Williams, 62–93. Cambridge: Cambridge University Press, 1989.

———. "Law and Temple in Origen." In *Templum Amicitiae*, edited by W. Horbury, 464–76. Sheffield, UK: Sheffield University Press, 1991.

———. "Augustine, Origen and the Exegesis of St. Paul." *Augustinianum* 32 (1992): 341–68.

———. "Origen's Pauline Prefaces and the Chronology of His Pauline Commentaries." In *Origeniana Sexta*, edited by G. Dorival and A. Le Boulluec, 495–513. Leuven: Peeters, 1995.

———. "Justification by Faith in Augustine and Origen." *Journal of Ecclesiastical History* 47 (1996): 223–35.

Banner, W. A. "Origen and the Tradition of Natural Law Concepts." *Dumbarton Oaks Papers* 8 (1954): 49–82.

Bardy, G. "La règle de foi d'Origène." *Recherches de science religieuse* 9 (1919): 162–96.

Bastit-Kalinowska, A. "Conception du commentaire et tradition éxégetique dans le *In Matthaeum* d'Origène et de Hilaire de Poitiers." In *Origeniana Sexta*, edited by G. Dorival and A. Le Boulluec, 675–92. Leuven: Peeters, 1995.

Beck, G. "Das Werk Christi bei Origenes." Diss., University of Bonn, 1966.

Behr, J. *The Way to Nicaea*. Crestwood, NY: St. Vladimir's Seminary Press, 2001.
———. *Origen: On First Principles*. Oxford: Oxford University Press, 2017.
Berchman, R. *From Philo to Origen: Middle Platonism in Transition*. Chico, CA: Scholars Press, 1984.
Berthold, G. "Origen and the Holy Spirit." In *Origeniana Quinta*, edited by R. J. Daly, 442–48. Leuven: Peeters, 1992.
Bertrand, F. *Mystique de Jésus chez Origène*. Paris: Aubier, 1951.
———. "Piété et sagesse dans le *Peri Euches*." In *Origeniana Quinta*, edited by R. J. Daly, 476–80. Leuven: Peeters, 1992.
Bettencourt, S. T. *Doctrina ascetica Origenis: seu quid docuerit de ratione animae humanae cum daemonibus*. Rome: Pontifical Institute S. Anselmi, 1945.
Bienert, W. A., and U. Kühneweg, eds. *Origeniana Septima: Origenes in den Auseinandersetzungen des 4. Jahrhunderts*. Leuven: Peeters, 1999.
Bianchi, H. *Arche e Telos: L'Antropologia di Origene e di Grigorio di Nissa*. Milan: Vita e Pensiero, 1981.
Bigg, C. *The Christian Platonists of Alexandria*. Oxford: Clarendon Press, 1886. Repr., 1981.
Blanc, C. "Le baptême d'après Origène." *Studia Patristica* 11 (1972): 113–24.
———. "L'angélologie d'Origène." *Studia Patristica* 14 (1976): 73–109.
Blosser, B. *Become Like the Angels: Origen's Doctrine of the Soul*. Washington, DC: Catholic University of America Press, 2012.
Blowers, P. M. "Origen, the Rabbis, and the Bible." In *Origen of Alexandria: His World and His Legacy*, edited by C. Kannengiesser and W. L. Petersen, 96–116. Notre Dame, IN: University of Notre Dame Press, 1988.
Borret, M. "Celsus: A Pagan Perspective on Scripture." In *The Bible in Greek Christian Antiquity*, edited by P. Blowers, 259–88. Notre Dame, IN: University of Notre Dame Press, 1997.
Bostock, G. "The Sources of Origen's Doctrine of Pre-Existence." In *Origeniana Quarta*, edited by L. Lies, 259–64. Innsbruck: Tyrolia-Verlag, 1987.
Bright, P. "The Origenian Understanding of Martyrdom and its Biblical Framework." In *Origen of Alexandria: His World and His Legacy*, edited by C. Kannengiesser and W. L. Petersen, 180–99. Notre Dame, IN: University of Notre Dame Press, 1988.
———. "The Epistle to the Hebrews in Origen's Christology." In: *Origeniana Sexta: Origen and the Bible*, edited by G. Dorival and A. Le Boulluec, 559–565. Leuven: Peeters, 1995.
———. "The Combat with the Demons in Antony and Origen." In: *Origeniana Septima*, edited by W. A. Bienert and V. Kühneweg, 339–45. Leuven: Peeters, 1999.
Burke, G. "Des Origenes Lehre vom Urstand des Menschen." *Zeitschrift fur Katholische Theologie* 72 (1950): 1–39.
Cadiou, R. *La Jeunesse d'Origène: Histoire de l'école d'Alexandrie au début du IIIe siècle*. Études de théologie historique. Paris: Editions du Cerf, 1935.
Capelle, B. "L'Entretien d'Origène avec Héraclide." *Journal of Ecclesiastical History* 2 (1951): 143–57.

Chadwick, H. "Origen, Celsus, and the Resurrection of the Body." *Harvard Theological Review* 14 (1948): 83–102.

———. *Christianity and the Classical Tradition.* Oxford: Oxford University Press, 1966. 2nd ed., 1984.

Chenevert, J. *L'Église dans le Commentaire d'Origen sur le Cantique des Cantiques.* Paris: Desclée de Brouwer, 1969.

Clark, E. A. *The Origenist Controversy: The Cultural Construction of an Early Christian Debate.* Princeton, NJ: Princeton University Press, 1992

Cocchini, F. *Il Paolo di Origene: Contributo alla storia della recezione delle epistole paoline nel III secolo.* Rome: Edizione Studium, 1992.

———. "Paolo in Origene nel periodo allesandrino." In *Origeniana Quinta*, edited by R. J. Daly, 167–73. Leuven: Peeters, 1992.

———. "Il progresso spirituale in Origene." In *Spiritual Progress*, edited by J. Driscoll and M. Sheridan, 29–45. Rome: Pontificio ateneo San Anselmo, 1994.

Coman, J. "La présence du Christ dans la nouvelle création." *Revue d'histoire et de philosophie religieuses* 48 (1968): 125–50.

Cornélis, H. "Les fondements cosmologiques de l'eschatologie d'Origène." *Revue de sciences philosophiques et théologiques* 43 (1959): 32–80, 201–47.

Crouzel, H. *Théologie de l'Image de Dieu chez Origène.* Paris: Aubier, 1956.

———. *Origène et la connaissance mystique.* Paris: Desclée de Brouwer, 1961.

———. *Origène et la philosophie.* Paris: Aubier, 1961.

———. "L'École d'Origène à Césarée." *Bulletin de littérature écclésiastique* 71 (1970): 15–27.

———. *Bibliographie critique d'Origène.* The Hague: M. Nijhoff, 1971. With *Supplement* to the same (valid up to 1980), ibid., 1982.

———. "La première et la seconde résurrection des hommes d'après Origène." *Didaskalia* 3 (1973): 3–19.

———. "Qu'a voulu faire Origène en composant le *Traité de Principes*?" *Bulletin de Litterature Ecclésiastique* 76 (1975): 161–86, 241–60.

———. "Geist (Heiliger Geist)." *Reallexicon fur Antike und Christentum* 9 (1976): 490–545.

———. "Thème du mariage mystique chez Origène et ses sources." *Studi Missionalia* 26 (1977): 37–57.

———. "Hades et la gehenne selon Origène." *Gregorianum* 59, no. 2 (1978): 291–331.

———. "La doctrine origénienne du corps ressuscité." *Bulletin de littérature écclesiastique* 81 (1980): 175–200.

———. "The Literature on Origen: 1970–1988." *Theological Studies* 49 (1988): 499–516.

———. *Origen.* Edinburgh: T&T Clark, 1989. French ed., *Origène*, 1985.

———. *Les fins dernières selon Origène.* Aldershot, UK: Variorum, 1990.

———. "La théologie mariale d'Origène." In *Origène: Homélies sur s. Luc.* Sources Chrétiennes 87. Paris: Editions du Cerf, 1998.

———. "Les condemnations subies par Origène et sa doctrine." In *Origeniana Septima*, edited by W. Bienert and W. A. Kühneweg, 311–15. Leuven: Peeters, 1999.

Crouzel, H., G. Lomiento, and J. Rius-Camps, eds. *Origeniana: Premier colloque international des études origéniennes*. Bari, Italy: Istituto di letteratura cristiana antica, 1975.

Crouzel, H., and A. Quacquarelli, eds. *Origeniana Secunda*. Rome: Edizioni del'Ateneo, 1980.

Daly, R. J. "Sacrificial Soteriology in Origen's Homilies on Leviticus." *Studia Patristica* 18, no. 2 (1982): 872–78.

———, ed. *Origeniana Quinta*. Leuven: Peeters, 1992.

Daley, B. *The Hope of the Early Church: A Handbook of Patristic Eschatology*. Grand Rapids, MI: Baker Academic, 1991.

———. "What Did Origenism Mean in the 6th Century?" In *Origeniana Sexta*, edited by G. Dorival and A. Le Boulluec, 627–38. Leuven: Peeters, 1995.

———. "Origen's *De Principiis*: A Guide to the Principles of Christian Scriptural Interpretation." In *Nova et Vetera: Patristic Studies in Honor of Patrick Halton*, edited by J. Petruccione, 3–21. Washington, DC: Catholic University of America Press, 1998.

Daniélou, J. *Platonisme et theologie mystique: essai sur la doctrine spirituelle de saint Gregoire de Nysse*. Paris: Aubier, 1944.

———. *Les Anges et leurs mission d'après les Pères de l'Église*. Collection Irenikon, n.s., 5. Paris: Editions du Cerf, 1952. English trans. in *The Angels and Their Mission: According to the Fathers of the Church*, trans. D. Heimann (Westminster, MD: Christian Classics, 1976).

———. *Origen*. London: Sheed and Ward, 1955.

———. *From Shadows to Reality*. London: Burnes and Oates, 1960.

Dassmann, E. "Zum Paulusverständnis in der östlichen Kirche." *Jahrbuch fur Antike und Christentum* 29 (1986): 27–39.

Dawson, D. *Allegorical Readers and Cultural Revision in Ancient Alexandria*. Berkeley: University of California Press, 1992.

———. *Christian Figural Reading and the Fashioning of Identity*. Berkeley: University of California Press, 2002.

De Berardino, A., ed. *Encyclopedia of the Early Church*. 2 vols. Oxford: Lutterworth Press, 1992. Expanded into 3 vols., Downers Grove, IL: IVP Academic, 2014.

———. "The *Regula Fidei* and the Narrative Character of Early Christian Faith." *Pro Ecclesia* 6 (1997): 199–228.

De Boysson, A. "Avons nous un commentaire d'Origène sur l'Apocalypse?" *Revue biblique internationale*, n.s., 10 (1913): 555–67.

Dechow, J. "The Heresy Charges against Origen." In *Origeniana Quarta*, edited by L. Lies 112–22. Innsbrucker Theologischen Studien 19. Innsbruck: Tyrolia-Verlag, 1986.

———. *Dogma and Mysticism in Early Christianity: Epiphanius of Cyprus and the Legacy of Origen*. North American Patristics Society Monograph Series 13. Macon, GA: Mercer University Press, 1988.

De Faye, E. *Origène*. Paris: Geuthner, 1928.
De Lange, N. R. M. *Origen and the Jews*: *Studies in Jewish–Christian Relations in 3rd Century Palestine*. Cambridge: Cambridge University Press, 1976.
De Lubac, H. *Histoire et Esprit: L'Intelligence de l'Écriture d'après Origène*. Paris: Editions du Cerf, 1950.
———. *Medieval Exegesis: The Four Senses of Scripture*. Translated by M. Sebanc and E. M. Macierowski. 2 vols. Grand Rapids, MI: Eerdmans, 1998, 2000.
De Margerie, B. *Introduction à l'histoire de l'exégèse*. Vol. 1, *Les Pères grecs et orientaux*. Paris: Editions du Cerf, 1980.
Diekamp, F. *Die origenistischen Streitigkeiten im sechsten Jahrhundert und dasfunfte allgemeine Concil*. Munster: Aschendorff. 1899. Repr., Norderstedt, Germany: Hansebooks, 2017.
Dillon, J. "Plotinus, Philo, and Origen on the Grades of Virtue." In *Platonismus und Christentum*, edited by H. D. Blume and F. Mann, 92–105. Jahrbuch for Antike und Christentum 10. Munster: Aschendorffsche Verlagsbuchhandlung, 1983.
Dively Lauro, E. A. "Reconsidering Origen's Two Higher Senses of Scriptural Meaning: Identifying the Psychic and Pneumatic Senses." *Studia Patristica* 34 (2001): 306–17.
———. *The Soul and the Spirit of Scripture within Origen's Exegesis*. The Bible in Ancient Christianity. Atlanta, GA: Society of Biblical Literature, 2010.
Dorival, G. "L'apport des chaines exégétiques grecques à une réédition des Hexaples d'Origène." *Revue d'histoire des textes* 4 (1974): 39–74.
———. "Origène a-t-il enseigné la transmigration des âmes dans les corps d'animaux? (A propos de *P.Arch* 1.8.4)." In *Origeniana Secunda*, edited by H. Crouzel and A. Quacquarelli, 11–32. Rome: Edizioni del'Ateneo, 1980.
———. "Versions anciennes de la Bible." In *Dictionnaire encyclopédique de la Bible*, 1304–11. Brepols, Belgium: Turnhout, 1987.
———. "L'apport d'Origène pour la connaissance de la philosophie grecque." In *Origeniana Quinta*, edited by R. J. Daly, 198–216. Leuven: Peeters, 1992.
G. Dorival, and A. Le Boulluec, eds. *Origeniana Sexta: Origène et la Bible*. Leuven: Peeters, 1995.
Drewery, B. *Origen and the Doctrine of Grace*. London: Epworth Press, 1960.
Dupuis J. *L'esprit de l'homme: Étude sur l'anthropologie religieuse d'Origène*. Bruges: Desclée de Brouwer, 1967.
Edwards, M. "Did Origen Apply the Word Homoousion to the Son?" *Journal of Theological Studies 49*, no. 2 (Oct. 1998): 658–70.
———. *Origen Against Plato*. Aldershot, UK: Ashgate, 2002.
Eno, R. B. "Origen and the Church of Rome." *American Ecclesiastical Review* 167 (1973): 41–50.
Ferguson, E. "Origen and the Election of Bishops." *Church History* 43 (1974): 26–33.
Ferwerda, R. "Two Souls: Origen's and Augustine's Attitude toward the Two Souls Doctrine. Its Place in Greek and Christian Philosophy." *Vigiliae Christianae* 37 (1983): 360–78.
Florovsky, G. "Origen, Eusebius, and the Iconoclastic Controversy." *Church History* 19 (1950): 77–96.

Frede, M. "Origen's Treatise against Celsus." In *Apologetics in the Roman Empire*, edited by M. Edwards, 131–55. Oxford: Oxford University Press, 1999.

Garijo, M. M. "Vocabulario origeniano sobre el Espírito Divino." *Scriptorium Victoriense* 11 (1964): 320–58.

Ginzburg, C. "Idols and Likenesses: Origen, Homilies on Exodus 8.3. and Its Reception." In *Sight and Insight: Essays in Honour of E. H.Gombrich at 85*, edited by J. Onians, 55–72. London: Phaidon, 1992.

Godin, A. *Erasme: Lecteur d'Origène*. Geneva: Librarie Droz, 1982.

Gould, G. "The Influence of Origen on 4th Century Monasticism: Some Further Remarks." In *Origeniana Sexta*, edited by G. Dorival and A. Le Boulluec, 591–98. Leuven: Peeters, 1995.

Grant, R. M. "Eusebius and His Lives of Origen." In *Forma Futuri: Studi in Onore del Cardinale M. Pellegrino*, 635–49. Turin: Bottega d'Erasmo, 1975.

Greer, R. A. *Origen: Selected Texts*. Classics of Western Spirituality. New York: Paulist Press, 1979.

Guillaumont, A. *Les "Kephalaia Gnostika" d'Evagre le Pontique et l'histoire de l'origénisme chez les Grecs et chez les Syriens*. Patristica Sorbonensia 5. Paris: Editions du Seuil, 1962.

Guinot, J. N. "La fortune des Hexaples d'Origène en IVè et Vè siècles en milieu antiochien." In *Origeniana Sexta*, edited by G. Dorival and A. Le Boulluec, 215–25. Leuven: Peeters, 1995.

Hallstrom, G. *Fides Simpliciorum according to Origen of Alexandria*. Helsinki: Societas Scientiarum Fennica, 1984.

Halperin, D. J. "Origen, Ezekiel's Merkabah, and the Ascension of Moses." *Church History* 50 (1981): 261–75.

Halton, T. "The New Origen: *Peri Pascha*." *Greek Orthodox Theological Review* 28 (1983): 73–80.

Hammerstaedt, J. "Der trinitarische Gebrauch des Hypostasenbegriffs bei Origenes." *Jahrbuch fur Antike und Christentum* 34 (1991): 12–20.

Hanson, R. P. C. *Origen's Doctrine of Tradition*. Cambridge: Cambridge University Press, 1954.

———. *Allegory and Event*. Richmond, VA: John Knox Press, 1959. Repr., with introduction, ed. J. Trigg (Louisville, KY: Westminster John Knox Press, 2002).

———. *The Search for the Christian Doctrine of God: The Arian Controversy 318–381*. Edinburgh: T&T Clark, 1988.

Harl, M. *Origène et la fonction révélatrice du verbe incarné*. Paris: Editions du Seuil, 1958.

———. "Recherches sur l'origénisme d'Origène: la satiété (*koros*) de la contemplation comme motif de la chute des âmes." *Studia Patristica* 8 (1966): 374–405.

———. "Structure et cohérence du *Peri Archon*." In *Origeniana*, vol. 1, edited by H. Crouzel, G. Lomiento, and J. Rius-Camps, 11–32. Bari, Italy: Istituto di letteratura cristiana antica, 1975.

———. "La préexistence des ames dans l'oeuvre d'Origène." In *Origeniana Quarta*, edited by L. Lies, 238–58. Innsbrucker Theologischen Studien 19. Innsbruck: Tyrolia-Verlag, 1987.

Hartmann, P. "Origène et la théologie du martyre d'après le *Protreptikos* de 235." *Ephemerides Theologicae Lovanienses* 34 (1958): 773–824.

Haykin, M. A. G. "The Spirit of God: The Exegesis in 1. Cor. 2. 10–12 by Origen and Athanasius." *Scottish Journal of Theology* 35, no. 6 (1982): 513–28.

Heine, R. E. "Origen's Commentary on John Compared with the Introductions to the Ancient Philosophical Commentaries on Aristotle." In *Origeniana Sexta*, edited by G. Dorival and A. Le Boulluec, 1–12. Leuven: Peeters, 1995.

———. "Reading the Bible with Origen." In *The Bible in Greek Christian Antiquity*, edited by P. Blowers, 131–48. Notre Dame, IN: University of Notre Dame Press, 1997.

———. *The Commentaries of Origen and Jerome on St Paul's Epistle to the Ephesians*. Oxford: Oxford University Press, 2002.

———. *Origen: Scholarship in Service of the Church*. Oxford: Oxford University Press, 2010.

———. *The Commentary of Origen on the Gospel of Matthew*. 2 vols. Oxford: Oxford University Press, 2018.

Heither, T. *Translatio Religionis: Die Paulusdeutung des Origenes in seinem Kommentar zum Römerbrief*. Cologne: Bonner Beiträge zur Kirchengeschichte, 1990.

———. "Glaube in der Theologie des Origenes." *Erkenntnis und Glaube* 67 (1991): 255–65.

Hennessey, L. R. "Origen of Alexandria: The Fate of the Soul and the Body after Death." *Theologischen Studien und Kritiken* 8 (1991): 163–78.

Hermas, T. *Origène: Théologie Sacrificielle du Sacerdoce des Chrétiens*. Théologie Historique 102. Paris: Beauchesne, 1996.

Hoffmann, R. J. *Celsus: On the True Doctrine*. Oxford: Oxford University Press, 1987.

Holdcroft, T. "The Parable of the Pounds and Origen's Doctrine of Grace." *Journal of Theological Studies* 24 (1973): 503–4.

Hombergen, D. *The Second Origenist Controversy: A New Perspective on Cyril of Scythopolis' Monastic Biographies as Historical Sources for Sixth-Century Origenism*. Rome: Pontificio Ateneo S. Anselmo, 2001.

Horn, H. J. "Ignis Aeternus: une interprétation morale du feu éternel chez Origène." *Revue des études grecques* 82 (1969): 76–88.

Jackson, B. D. "Sources of Origen's Doctrine of Freedom." *Church History* 35 (1966): 13–23.

Jacobsen, A. C., ed. *Origeniana Undecima: Origen and Origenism in the History of Western Thought*. Leuven: Peeters, 2016.

Jaeger, W. *Early Christianity and Greek Paideia*. Cambridge: Cambridge University Press, 1961.

Junod, E. "Que savons-nous des 'Scholies' d'Origène." In *Origeniana Sexta*, edited by G. Dorival and A. Le Boulluec, 133–49. Leuven: Peeters, 1995.

———. "Controverses autour de l'héritage origénien aux deux extrémités du 4ième siècle: Pamphile et Rufin." In *Origeniana Septima*, edited by W. Bienert and W. A. Kühneweg, 215–23. Leuven: Peeters, 1999.

Kannengiesser, C. "Origen—systematician in the De Principiis." In *Origeniana Quinta*, edited by R. J. Daly, 395–405. Leuven: Peeters, 1992.

Kannengiesser, C., and W. L. Petersen, eds. *Origen of Alexandria: His World and His Legacy.* Notre Dame, IN: University of Notre Dame Press, 1988.

Keith, G. "Patristic Views on Hell. Part 1." *Evangelical Quarterly* 71, no. 3 (1999): 217–32.

Kelly, D. M. "Origen: Heretic or Victim? The Apokatastasis Revisited." *Patristic and Byzantine Review* 18–19 (2000–2001): 273–86.

Knauber, A. "Das Anliegen der Schule des Origenes zu Casarea." *Munchener Theologische Zeitschrift* 19 (1968): 182–203.

Koch, H. *Pronoia und Paideusis: Studien uber Origenes und sein Verhaltnis zum Platonismus.* Berlin: De Gruyter, 1932.

Layton, R. A. "Origen as Reader of Paul: A Study of the Commentary on Ephesians." Ph.D. diss., University of Virginia, 1996.

Le Boulluec, A. "De la croissance selon les Stoïciens à la résurrection selon Origène." *Revue des études grecques* 8 (1975): 143–55.

———. *La notion d'hérésie dans la littérature grecque: IIe–IIIe siècles.* Études Augustiniennes. Paris: Editions du Cerf, 1985.

———. "Vingt ans de recherches sur le Contre Celse: État des lieux." In *Discorsi di verità: Paganesimo, giudaismo, e cristianesimo a confronto nel Contro Celso di Origene*, edited by L. Perrone, 9–28. Rome: Institutum Patristicum Augustinianum, 1998.

Lécuyer, J. "Sacerdoce des fidèles et sacerdoce ministériel chez Origène." *Vetera Christianorum* (Bari, Italy) 7 (1970): 254–59.

Ledegang, F. "Anthropomorphites and Origenists in Egypt at the End of the 4th Century." In *Origeniana Septima*, edited by W. Bienert and W. A. Kühneweg, 375–79. Leuven: Peeters, 1999.

———. *Mysterium Ecclesiae: Images of the Church and Its Members in Origen.* Leuven: Peeters, 2001.

Letelier, J. "Le Logos chez Origène." *Revue des sciences philosophiques et théologiques* 75 (1991): 587–612.

Lienhard, J. T. "Origen as Homilist." In *Preaching in the Patristic Age: Studies in Honor of Walter J. Burghardt, S.J.*, edited by D. Hunter, 36–52. New York: Paulist Press, 1989.

———. "Origen and the Crisis of the Old Testament in the Early Church." *Pro Ecclesia* 9, no. 3 (2000): 355–66.

Lies, L. *Wort und Eucharistie bei Origenes: Zur Spiritualisierungstendenz des Eucharistieverständnisses.* Innsbruck: Tyrolia, 1978.

———, ed. *Origeniana Quarta.* Innsbrucker Theologischen Studien 19. Innsbruck: Tyrolia-Verlag, 1986.

———. *Origenes Peri Archon: Eine undogmatisches Dogmatik: Einfuhrung und Erlauterung.* Darmstadt, Germany: Wissenschaftliche Buchgesellschaft, 1992.

———. "Origenes und Reinkarnation." *Zeitschrift fur katholische Theologie* 121 (1999): 139–58, 249–68.

Lyman, R. *Christology and Cosmology: Models of Divine Activity in Origen, Eusebius, and Athanasius*. Oxford: Oxford University Press, 1993.

———. "Origen as Ascetic Theologian: Orthodoxy and Authority in the 4th Century Church." In *Origeniana Septima*, edited by W. Bienert and W. A. Kühneweg, 187–94. Leuven: Peeters, 1999.

Martens, P. W. *Origen and Scripture: The Contours of the Exegetical Life*. Oxford: Oxford University Press, 2012.

Mazzucco, C. "Il culto liturgico nel pensiero di Origene." In *Dizionario di Spiritualita Biblico-Patristica*, edited by S. Panimolle, 12:203–220. Rome: Borla, 1996.

McGuckin, J. A. "Origen's Doctrine of the Priesthood." *Clergy Review* 70, no. 8 (August 1985): 277–86; no. 9 (September 1985): 318–25.

———. "The Changing Forms of Jesus according to Origen." In *Origeniana Quarta*, edited by L. Lies, 215–22. Innsbrucker Theologischen Studien 19. Innsbruck: Tyrolia-Verlag, 1986.

———. "Origen on the Glory of God." *Studia Patristica* 21 (1989): 316–24.

———. "Caesarea Maritima as Origen Knew It." In *Origeniana Quinta*, edited by R. J. Daly, 3–14. Leuven: Peeters, 1992.

———. "Martyr Devotion in the Alexandrian School (Origen to Athanasius)." In *Martyrs & Martyrologies*, edited by D. Wood, 35–45. Studies in Church History 30. Oxford: Blackwell, 1993.

———. "Structural Design and Apologetic Intent in Origen's Commentary on John." In *Origeniana Sexta*, edited by G. Dorival and A. Le Boulluec, 441–57. Leuven: Peeters, 1995.

———. "Origen on the Jews." In *Christianity & Judaism*, edited by D. Wood, 1–13. Studies in Church History 29. Oxford: Blackwell, 1997.

———. "Il Lungo Cammino Verso Calcedonia" [The Long Road to Chalcedon: The Unfolding Nexus of Christological Definition from Origen to Dioscorus]. In *Il Concilio di Calcedonia 1550 Anni Dopo*, edited by A. Ducay, 13–41. Rome: Libreria Editrice Vaticana, 2002.

———. "Origen as Literary Critic in the Alexandrian Tradition." In *Origenianum Octavum*, edited by L. Perrone, 121–36. Leuven: Peeters, 2003.

———. *The Westminster Handbook to Origen*. Louisville, KY: Westminster John Knox Press, 2004.

———. "Exegesis and Metaphysics in Origen's Biblical Philosophy." In *Festschrift for T. Stylianopoulosi*, edited by E. Pentiuc. Brookline, MA: Hellenic College Press, 2015. Repr. in J. A. McGuckin, *Seeing the Glory*, Collected Studies 2 (Crestwood, NY: St. Vladimir's Seminary Press, 2017), 159–74.

———. "Origen of Alexandria and Conscience." *Wheel* 21–22 (Spring/Summer 2020): 19–21.

———. "Origen's Eschatology." In *The Oxford Handbook to Origen*, edited by R. Heine and K. J. Torjesen, chap. 23. Oxford: Oxford University Press, 2021.

———. "The Kenosis of the Lord According to Origen of Alexandria." In *A Festschrift for F. Bruce*, edited by P. Nimmo. Grand Rapids, MI: Eerdmans, forthcoming.

———. "Origen as Apologist." In *The Wiley Dictionary of Christian Apologists and Their Critics*, edited by D. Geivett and R. Stewart. Oxford: Wiley, forthcoming.

Ménard, J. E. "Transfiguration et polymorphie chez Origène." In *Epektasis: Mélanges patristiques offerts à J Daniélou*, edited by C. Kannengiesser and J. Fontaine. Paris: Beauchesne, 1972.

Monaci Castagno, A. "L'idea della preesistenza delle anime e l'exegesi di Rom. 9.9–21." In *Origeniana Secunda*, edited by H. Crouzel and A. Quacquarelli, 69–78. *Quaderni di Vetera Christanorum* 15. Rome: Edizioni dell'Ateneo, 1980.

———. "Il diavolo e i suoi angeli. Testi e tradizioni (secoli I–III)." *Biblioteca Patristica* (Florence) 28 (1996): 353–466.

———, ed. *Origene: Dizionario. La cultura, il pensiero, le opere*. Rome: Citta Nuova, 2000.

Muller, G. "Origenes und die Apokatastasis." *Theologische Zeitschrift* 14 (1958): 174–90.

Munnich, O. "Les Hexaples d'Origène à la lumière de la tradition manuscrite de la Bible grecque." In *Origeniana Sexta*, edited by G. Dorival and A. Le Boulluec, 167–85. Leuven: Peeters, 1995.

Nardoni, E. "Origen's Concept of Biblical Inspiration." *Second Century* 4, no. 1 (1984): 9–23.

Nautin, P. "Origène predicateur." In *Origène: Homélies sur Jérémie*, edited by P. Nautin. Sources Chrétiennes 232. Paris: Editions du Cerf, 1976.

———. *Origène: Sa Vie et on Oeuvre*. Paris: Beauchesne, 1977.

Nemeshegyi, P. *La paternité de Dieu chez Origène*. Bibliotheque de Théologie Paris: Editions du Cerf, 1960.

Norris, F. W. "Universal Salvation in Origen and Maximus." In *Universalism and the Doctrine of Hell*, edited by N. M. de S. Cameron, 35–72. Grand Rapids, MI: Baker, 1992.

Norris, R.A. "Heresy and Orthodoxy in the Later Second Century." *Union Seminary Quarterly Review* 52, nos. 1–2 (1998): 43–59.

Orbe, A. *La Epinoia*. Rome: Pontificia Universitas Gregoriana, 1955.

Osborne, C. "Neoplatonism and the Love of God in Origen." In *Origeniana Quinta*, edited by R. J. Daly, 270–83. Leuven: Peeters, 1992.

Outler, A. C. "Origen and the Rule of Faith." *Second Century* 4 (1984): 133–41.

Pazzini, D. "Cristo Logos e Cristo Dynamis." In *Origeniana Quinta*, edited by R. J. Daly, 424–29. Leuven: Peeters, 1992.

Perrone, L. "I paradigmi biblici della preghiera nel Peri Euches di Origene." *Augustinianum* 33 (1993): 339–68.

Philippou, A. J. "Origen and the Early Jewish–Christian Debate." *Greek Orthodox Theological Review* 15, no. 1 (1970): 140–52.

Pierre, M. J. "L'ame dans l'anthropologie d'Origène." *Proche-Orient Chrétien* 34, nos. 1–2 (1984): 21–65.

Pizziolato, L. F., and M. Rizzi, eds. *Origene: Maestro di vita spirituale*. Studia Patristica Mediolanensia 22. Milan: Vita e pensiero, 2001.

Poffet, J. M. *La méthode exégétique d'Héracléon et d'Origène commentateurs de Jn 4: Jésus, la Samaritaine et les Samaritains.* Fribourg: Editions Universitaires, 1985.

Prinzivalli, E. "The Controversy about Origen before Epiphanius." In *Origeniana Septima*, edited by W. Bienert and W. A. Kühneweg, 195–213. Leuven: Peeters, 1999.

Puech, H. C. "Les nouveaux écrits d'Origène et de Didyme découverts à Toura." *Revue d'histore et de philosophie religieuse* 31 (1951): 293–329.

Quispel, G. "Origen and the Valentinian Gnosis." *Vigiliae Christianae* 28, no. 1 (1974): 29–42.

Rabinowitz, C. E. "Personal and Cosmic Salvation in Origen." *Vigiliae Christianae* 38, no. 4 (1984): 319–29.

Rahner, K. "La doctrine d'Origène sur la pénitence." *Recherches de science religieuse* 37 (1950): 47–97, 252–86, 422–56.

———. "The Spiritual Senses in Origen." In *Theological Investigations*, vol. 16, *Experience of the Spirit*, 82–103. New York: Crossroad, 1979.

Ramelli, I. *The Christian Doctrine of the Apokatastasis: A Critical Assessment from the New Testament to Eriugena.* Vigiliae Christianae Supplementa 12. Leiden: Brill, 2013.

———. *A Larger Hope? Universal Salvation from Christian Beginnings to Julian of Norwich.* Eugene, OR: Cascade Books, 2019.

Reardon, P. H. "Providence in Origen's *Contra Celsum*." *Ekklesiastikos Pharos* (Alexandria) 55 (1973): 501–16.

Rist, J. M. *Eros and Psyche: Studies in Plato, Plotinus and Origen.* Toronto: University of Toronto Press, 1964.

Rius-Camps, J. *El Dinamismo trinitario en la divinización de los seres racionales según Orígenes.* Rome: Pontificium Institutum Orientalium Studiorum, 1970.

———. "La suerte final de la naturaleza corpórea según el *Peri Archon* de Orígenes." *Studia Patristica* 14 (1976): 167–79.

———. "Subordinacianismo en Orígenes?" In *Origeniana Quarta*, edited by L. Lies, 154–86. Innsbruck: Tyrolia-Verlag, 1987.

Rizzi, M. "Problematiche politiche nel dibattito tra Celso e Origene." In *Discorsi di Verita: Paganesimo, giudaismo, e cristianesimo a confronto nel Contro Celso di Origene*, edited by L. Perrone, 171–206. Rome: Institutum Patristicum Augustinianum, 1998.

Roselli, A. "Ho Technites Theos: La practica terapeutica come paradigma dell'operare di Dio in Philoc.27, e *PArch* 3.1." In *Il cuore indurito del Faraone: Origene e il problema del libero arbitrio*, edited by L Perrone, 65–83. Genoa: Marietti, 1992.

Roukema, R. *The Diversity of Laws in Origen's Commentary on Romans.* Amsterdam: Free University Press, 1988.

———. "Origenes' visie op de rechtvaardiging volgens zijn Commentaar op Romeinen." *Gereformeerd theologisch tidjschrift* 89 (1989): 94–105.

———. "Die Liebe kommt nie zu Fall. (1 Cor 13.8a) als Argument des Origenes gegen einen neuen Abfall der Seelen von Gott." In *Origeniana Septima*, edited by W. Bienert and U. Kühneweg, 15–23. Leuven: Peeters, 1999.

Rowe, J. N. *Origen's Doctrine of Subordination.* Bern: Peter Lang. 1987.
Rubensen, S. "Origen in the Egyptian Monastic Tradition of the 4th Century." In *Origeniana Septima*, edited by W. Bienert and U. Kühneweg, 319–37. Leuven: Peeters, 1999.
Runia, D. T. *Philo and the Church Fathers.* Leiden: Brill, 1995.
Schadel, E. "Zum Trinitätskonzept des Origenes." In *Origeniana Quarta*, edited by L. Lies, 203–14. Innsbruck: Tyrolia-Verlag, 1987.
Schaeffer, T. *Das Priester-Bild im Leben und Werk des Origenes.* Cologne: Peter Lang, 1977.
Scheck, T. P. "Justification by Faith Alone in Origen's Commentary on Romans and Its Reception during the Reformation Era." In *Origeniana Octava*, edited by L. Perrone, 1277–88. Leuven: Peeters, 2003.
Scott, A. B. *Origen and the Life of the Stars: A History of an Idea.* Oxford: Oxford University Press, 1991.
———. "Opposition and Concession: Origen's Relationship to Valentinianism." In *Origeniana Quinta*, edited by R. J. Daly, 79–84. Leuven: Peeters, 1992.
Sfameni Gasparro, G. "Doppia creazione e peccato di Adamo nel Peri Archon: Fondamenti biblici e presupposti platonici dell'esegesi origeniana." In *Origeniana Secunda*, edited by H. Crouzel and A. Quacquarelli, 57–67. Quaderni di Vetera Christanorum 15. Rome: Edizioni dell'Ateneo, 1980.
———. *Origene e la Tradizione Origeniana in Occidente: letture storio-religiose.* Biblioteca di scienze religiose 142. Rome: Libreria Ateneo salesiano, 1988.
Sgherri, G. *Chiesa e Sinagoga nelle opere di Origene.* Milan: Vita e Pensiero, 1982.
———. "Pasqua." In *Origene: Dizionario: la cultura, il pensiero, le opere*, edited by A. Monaci-Castagno, 341–44. Rome: Citta Nuova, 2000.
Sheerin, D. "The Role of Prayer in Origen's Homilies." In *Origen of Alexandria: His World and His Legacy*, edited by C. Kannengiesser and W. L. Petersen, 200–214. Notre Dame, IN: University of Notre Dame Press, 1988.
Shin, D. "Some Light from Origen: Scripture as Sacrament." *Worship* 73, no. 5 (1999): 399–425.
Simonetti, M. "Due note sull'angelologia origeniana." *Rivista di cutura classica e medievale* 4 (1962): 169–208.
———. "La morte di Gesu in Origene." In *Studi sulla cristologia del II e III secolo*, 145–82. Rome: Institutum Patristicum Augustinianum, 1993.
Smith, A. J. "The Commentary of Pelagius on Romans, Compared with That of Origen-Rufinus." *Journal of Theological Studies* 20 (1919): 127–77.
Spada, C. A. "Origene e gli apocrifi del Nuovo Testamento." In: *Origeniana Quarta*, edited by L. Lies, 44–53. Innsbruck: Tyrolia-Verlag, 1987.
Strutwolf, H. *Gnosis als System: Zur Rezeption der valentinianischen Gnosis bei Origenes.* Göttingen: Vandenhoeck & Ruprecht, 1993.
Tollinton, R. B. *Selections from the Commentaries and Homilies of Origen.* London: SPCK Press, 1929.
Torjesen, K. J. "Body, Soul, and Spirit, in Origen's Theory of Exegesis." *Anglican Theological Review* 67 (1985): 17–30.

———. *Hermeneutical Procedure and Theological Method in Origen's Exegesis.* Berlin: De Gruyter, 1986.

———. "Influence of Rhetoric on Origen's OT Homilies." In *Origeniana Sexta*, edited by G. Dorival and A. Le Boulluec, 13–25. Leuven: Peeters, 1995.

Trigg, J. W. "The Charismatic Intellectual: Origen's Understanding of Religious Leadership." *Church History* 50 (1981): 5–19.

———. *Origen: The Bible and Philosophy in the Third Century Church.* London: SCM Press, 1983.

———. *Message of the Fathers of the Early Church: Biblical Interpretation.* Wilmington, DE: Michael Glazier, 1988.

———. "Origen, Man of the Church." In *Origeniana Quinta*, edited by R. J. Daly, 51–56. Leuven: Peeters, 1992.

Tsirpanlis, C. N. "Origen on Free Will, Grace, Predestination, Apocatastasis, and Their Ecclesiological Implications." *Patristic and Byzantine Review* 9 (1990): 95–121.

Tzamalikos, P. *The Concept of Time in Origen.* Bern: Peter Lang, 1993.

———. *Origen: Philosophy of History and Eschatology.* Supplements to Vigiliae Christianae 85. Leiden: Brill, 2007.

Urbach, E. E., "Rabbinic Exegesis and Origen's Commentary on the Song of Songs, and Jewish–Christian Polemics." *Tarbiz* 30 (1960): 148–70.

Vagaggini, C. *Maria nelle opere di Origene.* Rome: Pontifical Institutum Orientalium Studiorum, 1942.

Van den Eynde, D. *Les normes de l'enseignement chrétien dans la littérature patristique des trois premiers siècles.* Paris: Gabalda et Fils, 1933.

Van Den Hoek, A. "Clement and Origen as Sources on Noncanonical Scriptural Traditions during the Late Second and Earlier Third Centuries." In *Origeniana Sexta*, edited by G. Dorival and A. Le Boulluec, 93–113. Leuven: Peeters, 1995.

———. "The Catechetical School of Early Christian Alexandria and Its Philonic Heritage." *Harvard Theological Review* 90 (1997): 59–87.

———. "Philo and Origen: A Descriptive Catalogue of Their Relationship." *Studia Philonica Annual* 12 (2000): 44–121.

———. "Assessing Philo's Influence in Christian Alexandria: The Case of Origen." In *Shem in the Tents of Japheth: Essays on the Encounter of Judaism and Hellenism*, edited by J. L. Kugel, 223–39. Supplements to the *Journal for the Study of Judaism* 74. Leiden: Brill, 2002.

Van Winden, J. C. M. "Origen's Definition of Eucharistia in De Oratione 14.2." *Vigiliae Christianae* 28, no. 2 (1974): 139–40.

Vilela, A. *La condition collégiale des prêtres au IIIe siècle.* Paris: Beauchesne, 1971.

Vogt, H. J. *Das Kirchenverständnis des Origenes.* Bonner Beiträge zur Kirchengeschichte 4. Cologne: Böhlau, 1974.

———. "Wie Origenes in seinem Matthäuskommentar Fragen offen lässt?" In *Origeniana Secunda*, edited by H. Crouzel and A. Quacquarelli, 191–98. Rome: Edizioni del'Ateneo, 1980.

Völker, W. "Paulus bei Origenes." *Theologische Studien und Kritiken* 102 (1930): 258–79.

———. *Das vollkommenheitsideal des Origenes.* Tübingen: Paul Siebeck, 1931.

———. *Gregor von Nyssa als Mystiker.* Wiesbaden: Franz Steiner Verlag, 1955.

Waldram, J. "Illuminatio verbi divini. Confessio fidei. Gratia baptismi. Wort, Glaube und Sakrament in Katechumenat und Taufliturgie bei Origenes." In *Fides sacramenti, Sacramentum fidei: Studies in Honour of Pieter Smulders*, edited by H. J. Auf der Maur, 41–95. Assen, the Netherlands: Van Gorcum, 1981.

Widdicombe, P. *The Fatherhood of God from Origen to Athanasius.* Oxford: Oxford University Press, 1994.

———. "Knowing God: Origen and the Example of the Beloved Disciple." *Studia Patristica* 31 (1997): 554–58.

Wiles, M. F. "Origen as Biblical Scholar." In *The Cambridge History of the Bible*, vol. 1, 454–89. Cambridge: Cambridge University Press, 1963.

———. *The Divine Apostle: The Interpretation of St. Paul's Epistles in the Early Church.* Cambridge: Cambridge University Press, 1967.

Wilken, R. L. "Alexandria: A School for Training in Virtue." In *Schools of Thought in the Christian Tradition*, edited by P. Henry, 15–30. Philadelphia: Fortress Press, 1984.

Williams, R. "Does It Make Sense to Speak of Pre-Nicene Orthodoxy?" In *The Making of Orthodoxy: Essays in Honour of Henry Chadwick*, edited by R. Williams, 1–23. Cambridge: Cambridge University Press, 1989.

———. "Damnosa haereditas: Pamphilus' Apology and the Reputation of Origen." In *Logos: Festschrift fur Louise Abramowski*, edited by H. C. Brennecke, E. L. Grasmuck, and C. Markschies. Berlin: De Gruyter, 1993.

Wolinski, J. "Le recours aux *epinoiai* du Christ dans le *Commentaire sur Jean* d'Origène." In *Origeniana Sexta*, edited by G. Dorival and A. Le Boulluec, 465–92. Leuven: Peeters, 1995.

Ziebritzki, H. *Heiliger Geist und Welstseele: Das Problem der dritten Hypostase bei Origenes, Plotin und ihren Vorläufern.* Tübingen: Mohr-Siebeck, 1994.

Index

Abelard, Peter, 111–14, 129–30
Acacius of Caesarea, 55–56
Alexandria, 3, 6–18, 20–21, 29, 32–34, 36, 44–47, 49, 51–53, 56–59, 62, 68, 72–75, 79, 82–86, 88, 92, 94, 97, 140, 142, 145, 151, 154, 156, 161, 165–66
Ambrose, of Milan, 32, 71, 94–95, 99, 108, 116
Alfred the Great, 108
Ambrose, of Nicomedia, 8, 13, 45
Aquinas, Thomas, 113, 125
arianism, viii, 34–35, 38, 48–53, 55–56, 58–60, 62, 67, 70, 73–74, 82, 93
Athanasius, of Alexandria, ii, viii, 18, 34, 52–56, 58–59, 72–74, 76, 92–93, 159–61, 166
Augustine, of Hippo, 3, 94–98, 103, 109–13, 116–17, 122–24, 126, 129, 141, 153, 157

Balthasar, Hans Urs von, 135, 137, 139, 143
Baronius, Caesar, 122, 127, 130
Barsanuphius, of Gaza, 87, 92, 101
Basil, of Caesarea, viii, 32, 35, 54–56, 60–62, 65–67, 75, 92, 138
Behr, John, 133, 142, 144, 154
Berchman, Robert, 140

Bernard, of Clairvaux, 111–13, 129
Beza, Theodore, 118–19
bible: always symbolic, 23; levels of meaning within, 26–29; logocentricity of, 27; nothing unworthy of God, 28; plan of salvation, 26–27

Caesarea, Cappadocia, 35, 60, 61, 66, 75
Caesarea, Palestina, viii, 3–5, 10, 12–17, 34–36, 44–48, 51–53, 55–59, 60, 72, 77, 95, 106, 124, 126, 141, 152, 161
Cappadocians (fathers), 60–71
Cassiodorus, 98–100, 104
Codex (Sinaiticus), 5
Codex (Vaticanus), 5
Cole, Fr. Henry, 124
Cranmer, Thomas, 123, 128
Crouzel, Henri, 79–80, 100, 135, 137, 139–40, 143, 149–51, 153, 155–56

Daniélou, Jean, 66, 76, 135, 137–39, 143, 156, 162
Demetrios (of Alexandria), 7–11, 36, 44, 58, 73, 79, 124
Dionysius (of Alexandria), 32, 45, 73–74, 92

Dionysius (Ps. Areopagite), 73, 86, 93, 101, 108–9
Dively-Lauro, Elizabeth, 142, 144, 157

Edwards, Mark, 16, 59, 69, 74, 77, 157
Epiphanius (of Salamis), 16, 54, 79–80, 83, 85, 101, 156, 163
Erasmus, 48, 81, 115, 116–20, 130
Eriugena, John Scotus, 73, 96, 108–10, 128–29, 163
Eusebius (of Caesarea), 5–7, 11, 15–18, 34, 44–45, 47–48, 51–55, 59, 71, 77, 132, 157–58, 160
Eusebius (of Nicomedia), 59
Evagrius (of Pontus), 11, 60, 66–72, 74, 76–77, 79, 82–88, 93–94, 96, 101–2

Gottschalk, 105
Gregory (of Nazianzus), viii, 4, 21, 32, 35, 37, 44, 54–56, 60–67, 75–76, 92–94, 96, 99, 102, 108–9, 132, 138, 143, 168–69
Gregory (of Nyssa), viii, 32, 54, 56, 60, 64–67, 75–76, 92, 96, 108–9, 111, 165
Gregory I, Pope, 29, 32, 62, 113, 125, 142
Gregory Thaumaturgos, 17, 37, 46, 54, 60, 72

Hanson, Richard, 74, 136, 140, 142, 144, 151, 158
Heine, Ronald, 107, 128, 133, 136, 141–42, 144, 159, 161
Heraclas (of Alexandria), 8, 33, 44–45, 58, 73
hexapla, 12, 47
Hincmar (of Rheims), 105
Hippolytus (of Rome), 9, 13, 34, 36
Holy Spirit, 6, 9, 19, 21, 24, 28, 30, 33–34, 36, 45, 50, 53, 55, 58–60, 81, 112, 114, 147–48, 154, 158–59, 163
Homoousion, 34, 52, 54–55, 58–59, 62, 81
Hooker, Richard, 123, 125, 127, 132

icon, viii
incorporeality of God, 23, 34–35, 109

Jerome, viii, 3, 6, 15–18, 25, 32, 45, 51, 55, 57, 61, 70–75, 77, 79–83, 85, 95–101, 103–4, 111, 114–18, 125, 129–30, 143, 153, 159
Jesuits, modern Origenian, 135–36, 137–40
Jewel, John, 123–25, 132
John (of Jerusalem), 70, 77, 80–83, 95
Julia, Empress, 9
Justinian, viii, 59, 79, 86–88

Logos, divine, 4, 23–28, 30–31, 34, 38, 50, 55–56, 59, 63, 74, 76, 90–91, 114
Luther, Martin, 117–18, 120, 123, 126
Marcellus (of Ancyra), 16
Maximus (the confessor), viii, 32, 58–59, 62, 73, 76, 92–94, 102, 108, 110, 162
McGuckin, John Anthony, 15–18, 39, 71–72, 76, 100–121, 128, 131–33, 144–45, 161Melania (the younger), 67, 70, 73, 77, 82–84, 95
Methodius (of Olympus), 51, 100

Nicaea, council of, 34, 48, 52, 56–57, 59–60, 140, 154. *See also* Homoousion

Origen (of Alexandria): apokatastasis doctrine, 11, 17, 38, 51, 62–66, 68, 73, 76, 91, 97–98, 101, 111–12, 121, 138, 160, 162–63; aporetic methodology, 25, 49–50, 57, 62–64, 106, 129; censure of his writings, 3, 11–12, 32, 33, 51, 88–92, 100n4, 102n24, 112, 144n30, 147; critical editions of, 149–50; Demetrios, clash with, 7–11; educational mission, 46–47; eucharistic theology, 35–36, 39, 105–7, 119, 124, 126–28, 160, 165; exegesis, focus on, 9, 141–42; first disciples, 44–45;

gnostics, relation to, 8, 10, 20–21;
humanity, divine ascent of 22–23;
incorporeality of God, 23, 34, 109;
life and times, 3–18; Logos theology,
4, 20, 22–26, 30, 34, 36, 38, 56,
58–59, 63, 74, 76, 93, 98, 110,
114, 120; modern conferences on,
151–52; persecutions, involved in
7, 10, 13, 14; Platonists, relation to,
8–9, 13, 21–23, 31, 57–58, 69, 110;
priesthood, theology of, 9–10, 36,
39; punishments, divine, 11; sanctity,
reputation of, 3–6, 15, 147; school
in Caesarea, 4, 5, 12, 45–47; Song
of Songs, 13, 30–32, 66, 93, 96,
111–12, 114–15, 120; soteriology,
21; synodical consultancies, 12–14,
46; theological architecture, 43–44,
110, 147–48; trinity, divine, 19, 74
origenism, 35, 53, 68, 72, 74, 79, 80,
83, 88, 92–93, 100, 102–3, 152,
156, 158–59

Pamphilus, vii, 5, 16, 47–51, 54, 57, 74,
81, 98–99, 101, 103, 115, 143, 166
Paschasius Radbertus, 105–7, 128
pelagianism, 97–98, 103, 122, 126
Perrone, Lorenzo, 14, 136, 145,
151–52, 160–64
Petavius, 122, 126–27

philokalia, 35, 54, 62, 75
Photios, 16, 48–49, 56, 72–73, 105
Pierios (of Alexandria), 56–58
Pontianus, Pope, 10, 13, 124

Ratramnus of Corbie, 105–8
reformation-era writers, 35–36,
52, 105–33
renaissance-era writers, 114–16
Rufinus (of Aquileia), 15, 17, 48, 59,
67, 70, 72–74, 77, 79–83, 95–96,
98–99, 101, 114–15, 120, 164

Stephen Bar Sudhaile, 86–88, 101

Tall Brothers, 84–85
Theognostos (of Alexandria),
56–57, 59, 73–74
Theophilus (of Alexandria), 3, 79–80,
83–85, 101
Torjesen, Karen, 38, 136, 140–
42, 161, 164
Trigg, Joseph, 18, 43, 71, 103, 136, 140,
144, 158, 165

Vigilius, Pope, 99–100, 103

Wiles, Maurice, 102, 136, 141–42, 166

Zwingli, Huldrych, 117

About the Author

The Very Revd. Professor John Anthony McGuckin, of Irish extraction, is an archpriest of the Orthodox Church in the Patriarchate of Romania's Archdiocese in Western Europe and the rector of St. Gregory's Chapel in St. Anne's on Sea in northwest England. In 1997 he came to the United States from England, where he had been reader in patristic and Byzantine theology at the University of Leeds, to serve as professor of church history at Union Theological Seminary in New York. Over two decades, he was the Nielsen Professor of Early and Byzantine Church History at Union and professor of Byzantine Christianity at Columbia University; he is now emeritus. He is currently professor in the Theological Faculty of Oxford University, where he assists with examining and mentoring duties for higher degrees in the domain of early Christianity. He is also a senior professorial research fellow at Emory University's School of Law. He founded and directed the New York Sophia Institute in 2008 as an advanced research forum for Eastern Orthodox thought and culture, one intended to bring together some of the brightest intellectual lights in contemporary English-speaking Orthodoxy for collaborative studies on church and society. The institute has issued eight volumes of critical studies on the Orthodox tradition under its own imprint, Theotokos Press, by young and established Orthodox scholars, both male and female, including important studies of the role of women in contemporary Orthodoxy and on the Eastern Christian world's attitudes to significant concerns, such as the theology of liberation, biblical interpretation, art and music, and monastic experience.

He is born of two families, the McGuckins and the McMahons, who both worked in the ship industries of northern England at Wallsend. His grandfather Patrick and father, Francis, were both involved in rope making for the then great British shipping fleets in days when great woven ropes of natural fiber were still in vogue. The first member of his family to attend university, his academic career began when he studied philosophy at Heythrop College, London, from 1970 to 1972. From there, he went on to read for a divinity degree at the University of London, graduating with first-class honors in 1975, while studying for holy orders, then among the RC Passionist monastic order in 1969. His tutors in early Christianity at Heythrop were the Jesuit early church scholars Maurice Bévenot, Robert Butterworth, and Joseph Laishley. For his doctoral researches at Durham University (1980), where his *Doktorvater* was Orthodox Protopresbyter George Dion Dragas, he studied the politics and theology of the early Constantinian era, with a thesis on the thought of Lucius Caecilius Lactantius, the emperor Constantine's pacifist Christian tutor and political advisor. While he was a student at Durham, he composed his first book, an English edition of the *Theological Chapters of St. Symeon the New Theologian*, the medieval Byzantine poet and mystic. He became an Orthodox Christian in 1989 and was ordained to the Diaconate in Baia Mare (Romania) in 1996 and to the priesthood with a pastoral care for Romanians in England, also in 1996. Since his first book on St. Symeon, he has published over thirty-three books on religious and historical themes and two volumes of poetry, becoming internationally recognised as a leading interpreter of the early Christian and Eastern Orthodox traditions. His works have been translated into many languages, including Romanian, Spanish, Russian, Dutch, Korean, and Chinese. He has taught in numerous universities, both in America and in Europe, as visiting distinguished professor or as visiting scholar, including Kiev, Sibiu, Bucharest, Oslo, Iasi, Cambridge, Belfast, Oxford, Yale, Sydney, and Moscow. He was elected a fellow of the British Royal Society of Arts in 1986 and a fellow of the Royal Historical Society in 1996. He was selected as the prestigious Luce Fellow in Early Christianity in 2006. For his contributions to academic theology, he was awarded the Order of St. Stephen the Great, the Cross of Moldavia and Bukovina, by the Romanian Patriarch Daniil in 2008. In 2013, He was awarded the right to wear the second jeweled cross at St. Vladimir's by Metropolitan Tikhon of the Orthodox Church in America, the highest honor bestowed on married clergy by the Orthodox churches, on the occasion of his award of an honorary doctorate in divinity from St. Vladimir's Seminary. In November 2014, he was awarded an honorary doctorate in letters by the Andrei Saguna Theological Faculty of Lucian Blaga University of Sibiu.

Among his publications are *The Transfiguration of Christ in Scripture and Tradition* (1986), *St. Cyril of Alexandria: The Christological Controversy* (1994), *At the Lighting of the Lamps: Hymns from the Ancient Church* (1995; repr., 1997), *St. Gregory of Nazianzus: An Intellectual Biography* (2000; nominated for the 2002 Pollock Biography Prize), *Standing in God's Holy Fire: The Spiritual Tradition of Byzantium* (2001), *The Book of Mystical Chapters* (2002), *The Westminster Handbook to Origen* (2004), and *The Westminster Handbook to Patristic Theology* (2004). His large-scale study of Eastern Christianity, *The Orthodox Church: An Introduction to Its History, Theology, and Spiritual Culture*, appeared in the summer of 2007. A subsequent project was the making of the largest-ever English-language *Encyclopedia of Eastern Orthodoxy*, which he edited and which appeared in 2010. His most recent books are *Prayer Book of the Early Church* (2012), *The Ascent of Law: Patristic and Byzantine Reformulations of Antique Civilization* (2012), *The Path of Christianity: The First Thousand Years* (2016), and *Eastern Orthodoxy: A New History* (2019). In addition to his scholarly books, he has published more than 150 research articles in scholarly journals, ranging in subject matter from New Testament exegesis to art history and Russian mysticism to human rights theory. His collected works were brought out in 2019 in three volumes. The central focus of his research has revolved around the thought of the fourth-to fifth-century Christian fathers and the Byzantine mystical writers.

Professor McGuckin has appeared many times on American, British, and Italian television programs, as well as on radio in Europe, America, and Canada, commenting on religious issues. In 2011, his film *Mysteries of the Jesus Prayer*, coauthored with Emmy Award–winning director Norris Chumley, was released in cinemas, on cable TV, and on DVD (it is also largely available on YouTube). In 1994, his first collection of poetry, *Byzantium and Other Poems*, was published; a second retrospective collection appeared in 2010 (*Selected Poems*). While teaching higher graduate courses in New York, Fr. John also served as the rector of the Eastern Orthodox Chaplaincy of St. Gregory the Theologian, looking after English-speaking Orthodox students in upper Manhattan. Now he is the rector of the small Orthodox chapel in St. Anne's.

He is married to Eileen McGuckin, a professional master iconographer in the Byzantine and Slavic styles, with a very pronounced clarity of line and colour in her work. She maintains a busy studio (http://www.sgtt.org/NewIconStudio/), fulfilling commissions for individuals as well as churches. Their family consists of three married children and seven grandchildren, the makings of a small Irish clan.

Milton Keynes UK
Ingram Content Group UK Ltd.
UKHW041836221123
433062UK00007B/49